Early Modern Literature in History

General Editor: **Cedric C. Brown**
Professor of English and Head of Department, University of Reading

Within the period 1520–1740 this series discusses many kinds of writing, both within and outside the established canon. The volumes may employ different theoretical perspectives, but they share an historical awareness and an interest in seeing their texts in lively negotiation with their own and successive cultures.

Titles include:

Anna R. Beer
SIR WALTER RALEGH AND HIS READERS IN THE SEVENTEENTH CENTURY
Speaking to the People

Cedric C. Brown and Arthur F. Marotti (*editors*)
TEXTS AND CULTURAL CHANGE IN EARLY MODERN ENGLAND

Martin Butler (*editor*)
RE-PRESENTING BEN JONSON
Text, History, Performance

Jocelyn Catty
WRITING RAPE, WRITING WOMEN IN EARLY MODERN ENGLAND
Unbridled Speech

Danielle Clarke and Elizabeth Clarke (*editors*)
'THIS DOUBLE VOICE'
Gendered Writing in Early Modern England

James Daybell (*editor*)
EARLY MODERN WOMEN'S LETTER-WRITING, 1450–1700

John Dolan
POETIC OCCASION FROM MILTON TO WORDSWORTH

Henk Dragstra, Sheila Ottway and Helen Wilcox (*editors*)
BETRAYING OUR SELVES
Forms of Self-Representation in Early Modern English Texts

Sarah M. Dunnigan
EROS AND POETRY AT THE COURTS OF MARY QUEEN OF SCOTS AND JAMES VI

Elizabeth Heale
AUTOBIOGRAPHY AND AUTHORSHIP IN RENAISSANCE VERSE
Chronicles of the Self

Pauline Kiernan
STAGING SHAKESPEARE AT THE NEW GLOBE

Ronald Knowles (*editor*)
SHAKESPEARE AND CARNIVAL
After Bakhtin

James Loxley
ROYALISM AND POETRY IN THE ENGLISH CIVIL WARS
The Drawn Sword

Anthony Miller
ROMAN TRIUMPHS AND EARLY MODERN ENGLISH CULTURE

Arthur F. Marotti (*editor*)
CATHOLICISM AND ANTI-CATHOLICISM IN EARLY MODERN
ENGLISH TEXTS

Sasha Roberts
READING SHAKESPEARE'S POEMS IN EARLY MODERN ENGLAND

Mark Thornton Burnett
CONSTRUCTING 'MONSTERS' IN SHAKESPEAREAN DRAMA AND EARLY
MODERN CULTURE

MASTERS AND SERVANTS IN ENGLISH RENAISSANCE DRAMA AND CULTURE
Authority and Obedience

The series Early Modern Literature in History is published in association with
the Renaissance Texts Research Centre at the University of Reading.

Early Modern Literature in History
Series Standing Order ISBN 0–333–71472–5
(*outside North America only*)

You can receive future titles in this series as they are published by placing a standing order.
Please contact your bookseller or, in case of difficulty, write to us at the address below with
your name and address, the title of the series and the ISBN quoted above.

Customer Services Department, Macmillan Distribution Ltd, Houndmills, Basingstoke,
Hampshire RG21 6XS, England

Autobiography and Authorship in Renaissance Verse

Chronicles of the Self

Elizabeth Heale

First published 2003 by
PALGRAVE MACMILLAN
Houndmills, Basingstoke, Hampshire RG21 6XS and
175 Fifth Avenue, New York, N.Y. 10010
Companies and representatives throughout the world

PALGRAVE MACMILLAN is the global academic imprint of the Palgrave
Macmillan division of St. Martin's Press, LLC and of Palgrave Macmillan Ltd.
Macmillan® is a registered trademark in the United States, United Kingdom
and other countries. Palgrave is a registered trademark in the European
Union and other countries.

ISBN 0–333–77397–7

This book is printed on paper suitable for recycling and made from fully
managed and sustained forest sources.

A catalogue record for this book is available from the British Library.

Library of Congress Cataloging-in-Publication Data
Heale, Elizabeth, 1946–
　　Autobiography and authorship in Renaissance verse: chronicles of the
　　self/Elizabeth Heale.
　　　　p. cm. – (Early modern literature in history)
　　Includes bibliographical references and index.
　　ISBN 0–333–77397–7
　　　1. English poetry – Early modern, 1500–1700 – History and criticism.
2. Self in literature. 3. Autobiography in literature. 4. Renaissance – England.
5. Poets in literature. I. Title. II. Early modern literature in history (Palgrave
Macmillan (Firm))
PR535.S44 H43 2003
821'.309353—dc21　　　　　　　　　　　　　　　　　　2002032698

10　9　8　7　6　5　4　3　2　1
12　11　10　09　08　07　06　05　04　03

Printed and bound in Great Britain by
Antony Rowe Ltd, Chippenham and Eastbourne

To
Graeme, Beatrice and Tilda

What are Communication's

Mistakes in the magic medium doing
To us? It matters only in
So far as we want to be telling

Each other alive about each other
Alive.

W.S. Graham, 'What is the Language Using Us for?'

Contents

Acknowledgements

In the course of writing this book I have incurred many debts which cannot adequately be acknowledged. I am particularly grateful to my colleagues in the Department of English at the University of Reading, who have provided me with heady intellectual stimulation, selfless practical support, and a great deal of friendship. I must acknowledge special debts to the lively members of the Theory Discussion Group, and to those colleagues who took over my teaching and administration during two terms of AHRB funded research leave. Were it not for the AHRB research leave award, this book could not have been completed. Versions of Chapters 3 and 4 benefited from discriminating comments when they were presented as papers at a Tudor Symposium and to a research seminar of the Early Modern Research Centre at Reading University. I am particularly grateful to Professor Cedric Brown for encouragement, and for suggestions which, I believe, have substantially improved the final version of my text.

The support and encouragement of a number of friends has been crucial to me during the writing of this book, especially that of Dr Tom Woodman, Dr Janette Dillon, Carole Robb, and my sister, Judith Heale. They know how vast are my debts of gratitude. Dr Janette Dillon and Paola Baseotto kindly read drafts of some of the material, and my husband, Graeme Watson read everything. If this book is not a better one it is because my abilities do not always match theirs.

My greatest debts are to members of my family who have borne the brunt of my inability to separate work from home.

ELIZABETH HEALE

Introduction

The sub-title of this book, *Chronicles of the Self*, is adapted from a line in *'Gascoignes voyage into* Holland, An.1572, *written to the ryghte honourable the Lorde Grey of* Wilton'. The poet offers, for the entertainment of his patron, an account of his own shipwreck at sea:

> But since I know the pith of my pastaunce [pastime]
> Shall most consist in telling of a truth,
> Vouchsafe my Lord (*en bon gré*) for to take
> This trustie tale the storie of my youth,
> This Chronicle which of my selfe I make,
> To shew my Lord what healplesse happe ensewth,
> When heddy youth will gad without a guide,
> And raunge untied in leas of libertie,
> Or when bare neede a starting hole hath spide
> To peepe abroade from mother Miserie. (ll. 10–19)[1]

Gascoigne identifies himself as a client poet. His role is to entertain (provide 'pastaunce'), but a good entertainment should have 'pith', the drawing out of a moral or 'truth', to give the entertainment some point. The 'truth' he will tell, however, does not depend on the accuracy of his account of the events of the shipwreck or their impact on Gascoigne himself, but on the moral truisms the episode can be made to teach. Autobiography is being deployed to reinforce the well-recognized 'truths' of the culture rather than as a tool for the discovery of new, and previously hidden, truths within.

'*Gascoignes voyage*' is in some respects typical of the verse I study in this book. The poem is autobiographical in so far as it identifies Gascoigne as both the writer and the protagonist of its narrative. Gascoigne would

1

not, of course, have described the poem as 'autobiographical'. As has often been pointed out, the term is a nineteenth-century coinage produced at the heyday of that search for a unique individuality that Charles Taylor has described as one of 'the recurring themes of modern culture', and whose inaugurating moment he locates at the end of the sixteenth century and particularly in the writings of Montaigne:

> Montaigne...inaugurates a new kind of reflection which is intensely individual, a self-explanation, the aim of which is to reach self-knowledge by coming to see through the screens of self-delusion which passion or spiritual pride have erected. ... Montaigne is at the point of origin of...that...self-discovery [whose]...aim is to identify the individual in his or her unpredictable difference.[2]

'*Gascoignes voyage*' is not such a text of 'self-explanation' or 'self-discovery' whose primary addressee, Taylor implies, would be the writer himself.[3] On the contrary, it constructs Gascoigne the writer-hero of its narratives to please and influence the two audiences for whom it was designed: his patron, Lord Grey, and the readership of Gascoigne's miscellany, *A Hundreth Sundrie Flowres*, in which the poem was printed sometime between the spring and autumn of 1573, just weeks after the voyage took place.[4] The contradictory and inconsistent writer-hero Gascoigne produced by the poem is a result of the competing purposes of the poem and the diverse audiences it seeks to address.

Gascoigne figures within the poem as a client-poet addressing a patron, and, in the course of the narrative, as a brave and virtuous soldier shipwrecked through the drunken incompetence or treachery of the Dutch, on whose behalf the English soldiers are going to fight against the tyranny of Roman Catholic Spain. The protagonist and the tale are fraught with contradictions and inconsistencies. On the one hand, Gascoigne claims the tale will show what ensews 'when heddy youth will gad without a guide...in leas of libertie', and on the other hand, it will show what disasters happen when 'bare need' attempts by its own enterprise to get on in the world ('to peepe abroade from mother Miserie'). Gascoigne as 'heddy youth' (the historical Gascoigne was 38 years old in 1573) implies some guilty prodigality, while Gascoigne as a victim of 'bare neede' who seeks to better his fortunes, implies laudable enterprise.

The poem's contradictions have much to do with its multiple purposes and multiple addressees. In the first instance the poem is addressed to a patron, Lord Grey, a committed Protestant with a long interest in military enterprises against England's Roman Catholic enemies.[5] Gascoigne hedges his bets in his bid for patronage by figuring himself variously as a reformed prodigal in need of a steadying influence, as a poor and unfortunate soldier in need, as a pious man who takes to his knees in prayer in a moment of crisis, as an experienced campaigner, and as a potential agent, who hints in the final lines of his poem, at his usefulness as a source of news from Holland.[6] The poem, however, implicitly addresses not only an aristocratic patron, but also a print readership. The hero-poet appears for such an audience as a patriotic Englishman for whom all Dutchmen are drunkards and thieves, as a lad about town who discovers Dutch nuns are whores, and as a jester who regales us luridly with an account of his own sea-sickness.

There is little evidence in this 'chronicle … of my selfe' of an effort at self-exploration or a quest for self-knowledge. The presentation of the autobiographical author is flagrantly opportunist and self-promotional. He situates himself on the margins of established society, aspiring to the patron's grace that will translate him from his present plight as the victim, deserved and undeserved, of misfortune, or sharing with his print readership, the rude fellowship of those who feel themselves in the murky hinterland of social success.

At the same time as the first person subject is defined in terms of his lack of social and economic success, however, he is placed centre stage as not only the teller and hero of his own story, but also as its named author, Gascoigne, who skilfully shapes for our pleasure sympathetic and assuaging versions of himself. The perspectives he voices are neither those of the court nor of the educational establishment, but at an angle to both, based on the authority of his own experience, and asserting his distinctive voice and perspectives by right of his power, however contingent and imperfect, over the pen. In these respects, '*Gascoignes voyage*' is typical of the texts I discuss in this book. Claiming authority over their own discourse, and invoking their own experience, the first person subjects of these texts assert the validity of their own perspectives, however socially marginal or excluded from the established hierarchies of power they represent themselves as being. In so doing, I suggest, these texts inaugurate a new kind of writing in the early Elizabethan period, that shapes what can be said, and by whom, for the writers who follow. Through their possession of the pen, these autobiographical authors literally make themselves.

Twentieth-century theorists have, of course, taught us to regard the self-originating claims of subjects, authors, and selves, however persuasive, as textual effects. Subjectivity itself, the possibility of speaking with the authority of the first person, is produced from within discourse itself. The linguist Emile Benveniste, for example, describes the first person position not as the source of language and meaning, but as a particular instance of language and discourse:

> Language is...the possibility of subjectivity because it always con-
> tains the linguistic forms appropriate to the expression of subjectiv-
> ity, and discourse provokes the emergence of subjectivity because it
> consists of discrete instances. In some way language puts forth
> 'empty' forms which each speaker, in the exercise of discourse, appro-
> priates to himself and which he relates to his 'person', at the same
> time defining himself as *I* and a partner as *you*.[7]

The 'I' acquires definition only within discourse and in relation to what it is not, the 'you' in terms of which it comes into being. 'The condition of the subject' according to Jacques Lacan's description of the psychic formation of the self, 'depends on what is being unfolded in the Other'.[8] Kaja Silverman argues that Benveniste's description helps us to under- stand not only the contingent, unstable nature of subjectivity, but also the possibility of its historical and cultural specificity:

> Benveniste's discontinuous subject may depend for its emergence
> upon already defined discursive positions, but it has the capacity to
> occupy multiple and even contradictory sites. This descriptive model
> thus enables us to understand the subject in more culturally and his-
> torically specific ways...in terms of a range of discursive positions
> available at a given time, which reflect all sorts of economic, political,
> sexual, artistic, and other determinants.[9]

At the same time, if subjectivity is structured by the discourses in which it is articulated, then each new act of writing restructures the field of discourse and alters, even marginally, what can be said. The concepts of subject, self, and author may be textual effects, but some texts are more concerned with these effects than others. In his famous essay 'What is an author?', Michel Foucault describes the ascription of author- ship as a new way of reading and categorizing literary texts, an innova- tion that he dates to the seventeenth and eighteenth centuries:

> The author's name manifests the appearance of a certain discursive
> set and indicates the status of this discourse within a society and a
> culture. It has no legal status, nor is it located in the fiction of the
> work; ... in a civilization like our own there are a certain number of
> discourses that are endowed with the 'author-function', while others
> are deprived of it.[10]

For Foucault, the phenomenon of denoting a piece of writing as 'authorial' is not 'located in the fiction of the work' but is a question of genre and the conventions attached to that genre by society. Foucault is surely right in rejecting the idea of an author as the extra-textual source of a work, a being that precedes the text and ultimately controls its meanings. Nevertheless, the texts studied in this book suggest that by the mid-sixteenth century, kinds of writing in which the subject could be figured as both authorial and self-expressive, however tentative and unstable its fictions, had become a commonly acknowledged discursive possibility.

Autobiographical writing and a sophisticated sense of the self as subject of discourse existed, of course, long before the sixteenth century. Medievalists have rightly objected to the notorious claim of Jacob Burckhardt, echoed by some more recent writers, that in the Middle Ages 'man was conscious of himself only as a member of a race, people, party, family or corporation'. It was not until the Renaissance that 'man became a spiritual *individual*, and recognized himself as such'.[11] An example of an autobiographical poem, written in the early fifteenth century, which shares many of the characteristics of the sixteenth-century texts I study, is Thomas Hoccleve's 'Complaint'. Hoccleve was a professional scrivener, a public servant employed as a clerk of the Privy Seal, who wrote verse to further his career through patronage.[12] Like Gascoigne, he represents himself as socially and economically insecure and vulnerable to misfortune and misrepresentation. There are, nevertheless, significant differences between the Hoccleve who writes his own story in 'Complaint' and the first person writing of the self that I find in the sixteenth-century texts studied in this book. A brief comparison of the use of the trope of the mirror as a reflection of inner and outer selves in Hoccleve's text and in the 'autobiographical' manuscript written by Thomas Whythorne in *c*.1576 (discussed in Chapter 2) may help to focus attention on some significant differences.

Thomas Hoccleve's 'Complaint' is the first of a series of five texts, probably written in the period 1419–21, forming a group called the *Series*, whose primary addressee was Humphrey, Duke of Gloucester.[13] The 'Complaint' identifies its first person subject as the writer of his own story, naming him as Hoccleve in the second poem of the *Series*, the 'Dialogue'. Hoccleve laments the repercussions of a mental breakdown from which he has recovered. Not everyone believes in his recovery, however, and the speaker describes his social ostracism and sense of isolation from former friends and associates. Like many of the sixteenth-century writers I study, he longs to be accepted and achieve social success but identifies himself as marginal and unfortunate.

In this distress of mind, the speaker looks at his own image in the mirror in an attempt to compose his features in an expression that will be acceptable to others:

> I streighte vnto my mirour / and my glas
> To looke how þat me / of my cheere thoghte,
> If any othir were it / than it oghte
> For fayn wolde I / if it had nat been right,
> Amendid it / to my konnynge and might.
>
> Many a saut made I / to this mirour
> Thynkynge / 'If þat I looke / in this maneere
> Among folk / as I now do / noon errour
> Of suspect look / may in my face appeere. (ll. 157–65)[14]

In spite of these attempts to achieve a decorously sensible expression, and to appear to others as he feels himself to be, Hoccleve continues to feel isolated and alienated. Only at the conclusion of the poem does the speaker find comfort, not in the restored and accepting companionship of his fellows, but in an old book in which he reads of the consolations given by a personified Reason to another melancholy man:

> Wo / heuynesse / and tribulacioun
> Commune arn to men alle / and profitable ...
> And to whom Goddes strook / is acceptable
> Purueied ioie is / for God wowndith tho
> Þat he ordeyned hath / to blisse go. ('Complaint' ll. 351–2, 355–7)

The old book augments the authority of a personified Reason who purveys the unquestionable teachings of God, and thus provides for the troubled Hoccleve an identity, as a man afflicted with woe for the good of his soul, that renders other social and worldly identities irrelevant.

Hoccleve's 'Complaint' constructs a vivid sense of a self-conscious individual, aware, like the subjects of many of the texts I study, of the potential mismatch between others' judgement of him and his own sense of himself. Lee Patterson's suggestion that 'the dialectic between an inward subjectivity and an external world that alienates it from itself' is fundamental to the medieval idea of selfhood, could well be extended to the texts studied in this book, and confirms a significant continuity between the production of versions of the self in the medieval and early modern periods.[15]

J.A. Burrow has suggested Hoccleve's 'Complaint' and the rest of the *Series*, were written to help rehabilitate the poet after his illness.[16] By representing himself as a submissive and pious sufferer from ills not of his own making, the client Hoccleve may hope to persuade his patron, Duke Humphrey, to take pity on his plight. There is much in common between Hoccleve's socially vulnerable and self-promotional version of himself in 'Complaint', and the authorial selves that figure in many of the Elizabethan poems I study. Hoccleve, however, claims to find final closure and identity in the authorizing discourses of God conveyed through the authoritative words of Reason. The secular Elizabethan texts I study find no such resolution to the competing discourses and identities that shape their first-person speakers. Their subjects are characterized by contingency and instability and by a lack of trust, implicit or explicit, in the capacity of language to offer a firm and final grounding in truth.

The Hoccleve of the 'Complaint' peers at the imperfect reflection of his features in the steely surface of his mirror, but finds his true self beyond worldly sight and judgement in an inherited book containing an authoritative discourse. In spite of having suffered for a number of years from a 'wylde infirmitee... which me out of myself / caste and threew' (ll. 40, 42), Hoccleve's inner judgement of himself, having read the book, is presented as reliable because it is firmly grounded in patient submission to an indisputable source of authority. The mirror focuses our attention on the difference between the vanity of the visible things of this world and the truths of the next.

Hoccleve's image of himself in the mirror may be compared to Thomas Whythorne's meditation on his mirror image in his autobiographical manuscript. Where for Hoccleve the disjunction between what he seemed to himself and what others saw in him, is a sign of the imperfection of the world and the vanity of seeking satisfaction in it, the disjunction is for Whythorne a mark of the inadequacy of the mirror as a satisfactory record of the self in the world:

> þe glas sheweth but þe dispozision of þe fas for þe tým prezent, and not az it waz in tým past. also it sheweth þe fas þe kontrary way, þat iz to say, þat which seemeth to be þe riht sýd of þe fas iz þe left sýd in deed. and so lýkwýz þat which seemeth to be þe left sýd iz þe riht.[17]

Achieving the desired outer image was a matter of the greatest importance to Whythorne. In a perfect outer image the subject could admire what he had made himself to be, seen from the same perspective by all.

For these reasons, Whythorne prefers paintings to mirrors and he records having three portraits of himself painted. Whythorne's manuscript is addressed to a friend, but seems to have been written as a kind of verbal self portrait. By gathering his struggles and achievements into a single narrative, the writer's life could be weighed against the supposed criteria for successful completion of the three stages of man set out in the title of his manuscript: 'A book of songs and sonetts, with longe discoorses sett with them, of the chylds lyfe, togyther with A yoong mans lyfe, and entring into the old mans lyf'. The manuscript attempts to produce, as a mirror cannot, a perfected image of Whythorne for himself, in which the inner man is seen to be as well-framed as the outer man. The manuscript is fraught, however, with unresolved struggles and remains unfinished, as the life was unfinished in 1576. For Whythorne, a working musician from relatively humble origins who insists on his status as an accomplished gentleman, success lies in producing himself, visibly, in the world, in conformity to idealized social and cultural models none of which proves quite compatible with the others.

Where in Hoccleve's text the subjectivity of the speaker is finally grounded, in spite of social ostracism, in the authorizing discourse of Reason and submission to a godly dispensation at odds with that of the world, in Whythorne's text the authorial subject is constructed out of competing fragments and models. While the first person of '*Gascoignes voyage*' manipulated contradictory self-representations with apparent indifference to consistency or plausibility, the subject of Whythorne's manuscript searches for consistency and coherence, registering anxiety and dissatisfaction whenever signs of inconsistency and contradiction appear. One such moment of uncertainty is the mirror image whose impermanence and reversed perspectives challenge the fragile construct of the subjective authorial self. In the absence of a single, dominant, validating paradigm for the self, the Renaissance author produces proliferating roles and paradigms, amongst which the possibility of a single true identity becomes, increasingly and self-evidently, an illusion.[18]

Whythorne's manuscript has been hailed as 'the first autobiography in the English language'.[19] Significantly the prose narrative that constitutes this autobiography exists, at least in part, to provide context and explanation for Whythorne's own amorous and epigrammatic verses. In this respect, Whythorne's manuscript is very similar to, and may well have been influenced by, Gascoigne's 'The Adventures of Master F.J.' which was printed in *A Hundreth Sundrie Flowres* in 1573, and which also provides a proliferating prose narrative at least ostensibly to contextualize and explain a manuscript of amorous verse.[20] This study focuses on autobiographical writing in verse for a number of reasons. Verse, which until the advent of print, often circulated unattributed, and was open to appropriation, copying, and alteration by anyone, shows particularly clearly a shift in the 1560s and 1570s to a more privatized form of presentation, with collections attributed to a named poet and contributing to his authorial self-presentation. Poetry lent itself particularly readily to appropriation by authorial voices because of its extensive use of the first person subject position either for the effects of amorous self-expression, or, in epigrammatic verse and first-person complaint, as a voice that confirms through experience, cultural truisms and traditional wise saws. With its well-established generic models for voices and narratives, verse provided readily available paradigms for the development of authorial personae. In addition, the self-evident artfulness of verse, its foregrounded artifice, may well have suited not only the promotional self-display of many of the writers I study, but have offered genres in which autobiographical and authorial selves could appear as safely figurative and rhetorical.

The first three chapters of this study concentrate on the ways in which verse offered prestigious and in many cases marketable forms in which writers, seeking to advance their fortunes in the world and to please potential patrons, could present plausible versions of themselves as gentlemen, or exceptionally, in the case of Isabella Whitney, as a gentlewoman, of accomplishments and wit, afflicted by misfortunes not of their own making, and fit objects for generous patronage and support. In Chapter 1, I look at the ways in which the amorous and epigrammatic verse gathered and printed in *Tottel's Miscellany* (first published in 1557) offered useful models for those who wished to catch the eye of courtly patrons, and present themselves as adept in courtly skills, or well-stocked with moral aphorisms on the vicissitudes of life and the ills that beset the virtuous. A spate of single-authored miscellanies appropriated the elite verse of *Tottel's Miscellany* for such self-promotional purposes. Chapter 2 looks in detail at Thomas Whythorne's remarkable manuscript that seems to have begun, in part, as his own, private, single-author miscellany.

Short verses allowed writers the flexibility to present themselves in a variety of first-person voices, as amorists and moralists. In Chapter 3, I examine a genre of longer autobiographical poems that became very popular in the early Elizabethan period. These poems figure their author-heroes as men of experience and effort, attempting to get on in the world through their own travails or travels. In each case the established paradigms of virtue that shape the author-hero – man of education and enterprise, brave soldier, or epic adventurer – are threatened and undermined by narratives of injustice, misfortune or, in some cases, foreign outlandishness. These career narratives contain some of the most fascinating and least studied writing of this period.

Edmund Spenser repeatedly figured versions of himself in his own verse. In *Colin Clovts Come Home Againe*, discussed among the narratives of career and travel in Chapter 3, and *Amoretti and Epithalamion*, discussed in Chapter 4, Spenser represents the poet as a man who, through his personal experience, his vision and his eloquence, is able to instruct and transform his own society. Writing from the political margins in Ireland, and from a social background very similar to those of writers studied in Chapters 1 and 3, Edmund Spenser established a precarious position for himself within an expatriate social elite. In *Amoretti and Epithalamion*, he presents himself and his marriage in Ireland, on the margins of the English political body, as a model to his readers of what virtuous Protestant English civility should be, dependent on the self-rule of each of its citizens. However, in ways that this study suggests is characteristic of all amorous writing in this period, the language of passion proves unsettling to claims of self-rule.

Spenser's civil citizen must learn to master that which is disorderly both in himself and in society. In Chapter 5, I examine the language of the disordered and passionate self in the narratives of two writers, George Gascoigne's 'The Adventures of Master F.J.' which weaves a narrative around amorous lyric poems, and Sir Philip Sidney's *Astrophil and Stella*. In both texts, we find that the language of the heart, that which lies intimately within, is found to be not only destructive of the ordered self, but exposes the fiction of a single, authorial, controlling presence. In exploring the language of passionate self-expression, both texts call into question the possibility of ever finding the 'I' who speaks.

The radical instability of the 'Will' of *Shakespeare's Sonnets* forms the subject of Chapter 6. The lover-poet of the sonnets, like most of the Elizabethan writers of versions of the self that I study, identifies himself as belonging on the margins of courtly society, clearly differentiated by his demotic status from the splendid and aristocratic young man who is the object of his admiration. However, through the course of the sequence, the language of passion, through which the poet-lover articulates his subjectivity, exposes all distinctions of class, individuality, and even of gender as unstable. The poet-lover is given his authorial name only at the moment in which all individual Wills are confounded in the undifferentiating discourse of desire.

1
'To mak my self to be known of many': miscellanies and the well-formed gentleman[1]

The autobiographical potential of first-person verse is exploited in a flurry of single-author verse miscellanies that appeared in print in the 1560s and 1570s.[2] These early Elizabethan miscellanies are mixed collections of verse, attributed mainly or entirely to a single named author, and including 'songs and sonnets' (any short poem, often stanzaic, on the subject of love), verse letters, epigrams, and longer complaints in poulters measure or fourteeners. In the first section of this chapter, I shall argue that a latent 'autobiographical assumption' in such verse is carefully developed to present the named authors in various self-promotional guises.[3] However the appropriation of such verse for autobiographical effects could prove double-edged, leading on occasion to unwanted readerly identifications of the author with the passionate lover in ways that threatened the careful framing of the authorial self. In the second section of the chapter, I shall discuss how, in the miscellanies of George Gascoigne and George Turbervile, amorous verse sequences expose anxieties about a dangerous, feminized, instability in language that calls into question the inscription of the well-framed, masculine authorial self. In the final section of the chapter, I consider the very different representations of gender in the work of the only female miscellanist, Isabella Whitney.

The single-author miscellanists were almost exclusively gentlemen, or men who aspired to gentry status, for whom writing and printing verse should be understood, at least partly, in terms of social definition and career advancement.[4] Through their printed miscellanies they could display themselves to potential patrons, as courtly, verbally adept, morally reliable, men well equipped for employment as secretaries, clerks in official service, private tutors, or as witty producers of aristocratic entertainments. As Daniel Javitch has commented, early Elizabethan verse was composed and circulated by 'writers seeking administrative jobs ... to exhibit their humanist learning and oratorical proficiency in the hope that such talents would be put to pragmatic use.'[5]

With the notable exception of the collections of Isabella Whitney, most single-author miscellanies of the early Elizabethan period seem to be primarily concerned with constructing distinctly masculine identities for their authors, and in articulating a decidedly male point of view. Although sometimes dedicated to female patrons, and modelled, via *Tottel's Miscellany*, on courtly manuscript verse that was used by women as well as by men, women function in most of the single-author miscellanies as objects of fear and suspicion, as that against which authorial masculine virtue is defined.[6] Two potentially conflicting masculine identities are particularly evident in the miscellanies. On the one hand, there is the humanist subject of an educational system that, in the words of Mary Thomas Crane in her detailed investigation of the system and its effects on mid-century verse, used 'aphoristic fragments to constitute and control a middle-class subject able to move upward within the changing hierarchies of the early modern state.'[7] The primary aim of this educational project was the formation of a male subject who could take his part in public affairs as a servant of the state or a counsellor of great men.[8] The 'aphoristic fragments' on which this system was based were approved sayings, proverbs, commonplaces, or *sententiae*, 'fragments of authoritative texts' (p. 6), largely classical and biblical but augmented by vernacular proverbs.[9] Educated through the careful gathering and often memorization of such fragments of the approved wisdom of the past, the humanist subject was 'framed' for 'eloquence in talke and vertue in deedes'.[10] Gascoigne displays his mastery of this well-stored and copious humanist eloquence when he claims to have composed, *ex tempore*, on a horseback journey, elegant and sententious verses 'uppon five sundry theames' delivered him by five gentleman.[11]

Potentially in conflict with the well-stored, aphoristic wisdom of the humanist subject, were the skills and implied behaviours of the courtier, the gestures of social ease and wit that were designed to differentiate the 'natural' gifts of the born gentleman from the dusty labours of the scholar.[12] The verse contained in the single-author collections is presented as socially embedded, implying a privileged world of elegant pastime whose most elegant manifestation is the courtship of women.[13] Whythorne defined courtship as 'in company with women, to talk with þem, to toy with þem, to 3ẏb and to 3est with þem, to discoors with þem, and to be mery with þem.'[14] As producers of such courtly verse, with its implied participation in elite social occasions, the authors of the miscellanies are figured as cultivated gentlemen. Whether asked to hold their own in the coterie of a patron's chamber, to offer wittily couched counsel, or to pen a fashionable sonnet for a less adept social superior, the writers of these miscellanies display themselves, in their courtly as in their aphoristic verse, as worthy of employment and advancement. In turn the printers of these pamphlets offer a highly saleable commodity to aspiring young men eager to learn the skills and behaviours of a cultivated elite.

The humanist moral self, considered as 'gathered', controlled, and prudent, was commonly defined explicitly in opposition to all that was considered feminine or effeminate. Ascham, for example, warned that

> if ye suffer the eye of a yong Ientleman, once to be entangled with vaine sightes, and the eare to be corrupted with fond or filthie taulke, the mynde shall quicklie fall seick, and sone vomet and cast vp, all the holesome doctrine, that he receiued in childhoode, though he were neuer so well brought vp before.[15]

The well-ordered male is ruled by his reason, keeping the disorderly feminine world of his own passions, senses and fantasies under strict control and thus able to take his place in a hierarchical world in which rational males 'naturally' assumed authority over women, the unstable embodiments of such unreasonable disorder. The world of the court and courting, however, offered a dangerous threat to such a gathered masculine self. The court was itself often perceived as an effeminate place, a perception exacerbated in the second half of the sixteenth century by the rule of female monarchs. Spenser, no admirer of courts, associated them with corrupt pride in his description of the court of the maiden queen Lucifera in *The Faerie Queene*. The courtiers are undifferentiated by gender, but all behave effeminately:

> Her Lordes and Ladies all this while device
> Themselves to setten forth to straungers sight:
> Some frounce their curled heare in courtly guise;
> Some pranke their ruffes; and others trimly dight
> Their gay attire; each others greater pride does spight. (1. iv.14)

The negotiation of a courtly manner that avoided the dangers of a degenerate effeminacy was among the trickiest of the many careful manoeuvres required of the miscellanist hoping for advancement through his verse.

The gentleman's miscellany: Tottel and his imitators

The mid-century single-author miscellanies are crucially shaped by the printing of *Tottel's Miscellany* in 1557.[16] It went through three separate printings in 1557, the first year of its appearance, and at least nine editions before the end of the century.[17] Tottel's project was to make public the private poems of courtly and gentlemanly amateurs previously circulating in manuscripts owned by, in Tottel's ironic phrase, 'the ungentle horders up of such treasure' (I. 2). As we hold Tottel's small quarto in our hands, our sense is not of private matters drawn forth on to the public stage, but of privileged access into a cultivated private world. The volume gives us the illusion that it has merely extended the process of manuscript copying to reach a wider network of coterie readers, some of whom seem to have treated it as they would a manuscript miscellany, answering, adapting and freely imitating individual items.[18] Those who bought *Tottel's Miscellany* were given access to the social and political verse of 'the noble Earle of Surrey and the depewitted sir Thomas Wyat the elder' and their like (I. 2). Part of Tottel's purpose in printing such poetry, he tells his readers, is to encourage them to imitate their betters, both their courtly verse and their courtly refinement. Thus 'the unlearned [might]…learne to be more skilfull, and to purge that swinelike grosseness, that maketh the swete maierdome not to smell to their delight' (I. 2). As Wendy Wall has suggested, *Tottel's Miscellany* and its imitators 'marketed exclusivity…[they] functioned as conduct books…because they demonstrated to more common audiences the poetic practices entertained by graceful courtly readers and writers'.[19]

The poems in Tottel are by many hands and are the products of diverse occasions over many years, but their collection within one volume had the effect of 'marketing' a composite courtly behaviour, comprising both the graceful passion of the lover and the 'deep-wittedness' of the sage counsellor. Early readers of Tottel seem not to have been particularly attentive to the different identities of contributors. The book's title page announced that it contained *Songes and Sonettes, written by the ryght honorable Lorde Henry Haward late Earle of Surrey, and other* and it seems that for many readers, all the poems were, in effect, Surrey's, and read as the varied performances of the ideal nobleman/courtier represented by Surrey.[20]

Tottel's lyrics typically develop topics of intimacy, retirement and privacy. A number of Surrey's own poems dramatize a first-person voice of private integrity and introspection set in opposition to, or alienated from, the world at large.[21] Crane suggests the amorous lyrics of the

Henrician court give 'expression to a privatized individual feeling self...
rediscovered...as a means of countering the centralized and increasingly impersonal power of the Tudor monarchy'.[22] The second part of
Crane's statement reminds us that such 'expression' is produced by
social and cultural constraints. The first person speakers of Tottel's verse
are typically figured as men of integrity and faith confronted by deceptions and betrayals, whether those of fortune and political ambition,
or those of faithless mistresses. Many poems in the *Miscellany* develop
the themes of the dangers of courtly service and the virtues of retirement, or the 'meane' (i.e. middling) estate.[23] A central rhetorical trope of
poems of good counsel, such as those on the mean estate, is the mutual
authorization of ancient wisdom and personal experience.[24] The verse
of Wyatt and Surrey sometimes refers to aspects of the author's life to
reinforce truisms. Wyatt's epistle, 'Of the Courtiers life written to Iohn
Poins' (I. no. 125), for example, personalizes its conventional topic (skilfully translated from the Italian of Luigi Alamanni) of the corruption of
courtly ambition and the pleasures of retirement, by adding strategic
allusions to Wyatt's own personal circumstances in 1536.[25] The explicit
use of autobiographical details acts as a rhetorical device to authorize
the moral generalizations of the poems.

Many of the ironies and political manoeuvrings inherent in a poem
about virtuous retirement by a courtier as ambitious as Wyatt, are easily
lost when the poem is removed from the milieu in which it was written.
In Tottel, Wyatt's artful epistles tend to become elegant expressions of
the themes signalled in Tottel's added titles: 'Of the Courtiers life' or 'Of
the meane and sure estate'. The titles announce the topic, or, particularly in the case of the amatory verse, the supposed occasion: 'The lover
sheweth how he is forsaken of such as he sometime enjoyed', 'The lover
hopeth of better chance'. Paradoxically the effect of such titles is both to
represent the poems as the spontaneous and intimate expression of
individuals participating in an exemplary amorous narrative in a privileged social world, and at the same time to erase all sense of idiosyncracy
and possible irony. Surrey, Wyatt and the anonymous 'lovers' and gentlemen poets of Tottel are presented to us as exemplary and plaintive
models of a socially elite behaviour and sensibility.

In emphasizing the sentimental or moral 'contents' of the poems,
Tottel's titles tend to erase their artfulness and focus our attention on the
feelings of the speaker, the 'expression of a privatized, individual, feeling
self', in Crane's terms.[26] This effect of an exemplary first-person voice
that seems to speak of personal experience but can be appropriated by
any number of individual speakers is evident in the easy slippage in

Tottel's titles between references to individual poets as 'he' or 'his', and the conventional 'lover' referred to in many titles. Thus a sonnet by Surrey entitled 'Description and praise of his loue Geraldine' is preceded by one entitled 'Complaint of the louer disdained' and followed a few poems further on by 'Prisoned in windsor, he recounteth his pleasure there passed', a poem that explicitly alludes to Surrey's personal circumstances (I. nos 7, 8 and 15). It is uncertain whether the 'he' of the Geraldine sonnet should refer to Surrey or to the conventional 'lover' who figured in the previous poem. The distinction between an historical Surrey and a conventional lover may not be important for Tottel, who is more concerned with the exemplary function of his courtly poems, but evidence that a slippage did in fact take place, encouraging in readers an 'autobiographical assumption' is well illustrated by the after-life of Surrey's Geraldine sonnet.

The addressee of the Geraldine sonnet, 'From Tuscan cam my ladies worthi race', has been identified as Lady Elizabeth Fitzgerald, a girl who may have been only nine years old when the poem was written.[27] Nothing more is known of any relationship between Surrey and this young girl and the poem is almost certainly a playful courtly compliment. The embryonic tendency in the *Miscellany* to elaborate this single sonnet as a moment of lyric expression in a romantic narrative may explain the appearance, in the second edition of *Tottel's Miscellany* only, of a form of her name 'Garrat' in a second sonnet, 'The golden gift'.[28] Much later in the century, such hints were spectacularly developed by Thomas Nashe in his novel *The Unfortunate Traveller, or The Life of Jack Wilton* (1594), which depicts a ludicrously fictive Earl of Surrey travelling to Florence to defend the honour of Geraldine's beauty against all comers. The lovesick Surrey is described penning spontaneous 'extemporal ditties' to Geraldine (of Nashe's composition).[29] The story was taken up more soberly by Michael Drayton in *Englands Heroicall Epistles* (1597–9), two of which relate to a supposed affair between Surrey and Geraldine. Surrey is imagined writing to Geraldine from Florence, once again composing verse from an over-flowing heart and carving his lines (of Drayton's composition this time) on the trunk of a tree.[30] In his notes to the poems, Drayton claims that a number of Surrey's poems from *Tottel's Miscellany* refer to his love for Geraldine. Even Wyatt's 'Tagus, farewell' is tentatively purloined as evidence of the sentimental patriotism of his semi-fictional Earl.[31]

In marketing exclusivity to a new audience of aspiring gentlemen and courtiers, Tottel sold a very specific notion of what it was like to be cultivated and 'gentle'. The accomplished courtier was a man who might participate in a courtly amour and could turn an elegant verse in praise of his mistress, but who also participated in the gentlemanly exchange of aphoristic verse and could show his personal mastery of the copia of classical and Christian moral teaching. In the series of mid-century single-authored miscellanies, a middling class of aspiring clients, gentle by birth, and well, or adequately, educated, but in need of appropriate employment, attempted to make themselves 'to be known of many in þe shortest týrm þat miht bee' through the medium of print and in imitation of Tottel's prestigious example.[32]

Newe Sonets and Pretie Pamphlets by Thomas Howell, Gentleman, is in many ways typical of the early Elizabethan single-author miscellanies. It survives in an undated revised edition 'newly augmented , corrected and imprinted', licensed to Thomas Colwell in 1567–8.[33] Another miscellany by Howell appeared a year later, *The Arbor of Amitie: Pleasant Poems and pretie Poesies*, printed by Henry Denham in 1568.[34] Howell presents himself as a writer and editor who has 'gathered together' 'my triflyng toyes, and far vnconning writes' (pp. 111 and 114). Both collections include Howell's own occasional poesies, epigrams, and ditties, as well as answers and epistles from others, thus giving the impression of a private manuscript collection, containing miscellaneous verses written for a variety of social occasions, now printed at the 'earnest request ... (after many denials) of a friend' (p. 111).[35]

Many individual items in *Newe Sonets* derive from *Tottel's Miscellany*, and the volume carefully follows its predecessor's mixing of love poems and poems of moral reflection. Howell advertises his gentlemanly status not only on the title page, but also through various signals about his background and his participation in the manuscript exchange of poems by cultivated men. Howell's own name figures prominently in the volume particularly in a number of poems exchanged with his friend John Keeper. At the end of *Newe Sonnets*, for example, there is a poem on '*The Unsertaintie of seruice by John Keeper to his friend Howell*' that warns of the perils of service at court (pp. 153–8). This is answered by Howell '*to his freinde Keper*' on the virtues of service to God (pp. 158–9). In turn, Keeper answers Howell's poem (p. 159). Howell is here displayed as a participant in cultivated exchange between friends. In another exchange, printed in the 1568 *Arbor*, John Keeper bids farewell to Howell who is reluctantly departing, as Keeper notes, 'To set thy selfe in sounder sort'. Howell's name is worked into a line: 'And stil I *Ho* to see him *well*' (pp. 94–5). Like Tottel, Howell provides titles indicating the subjects and supposed occasions of his poems, for example, '*The description of his loathsom life, to his friende*', or '*The Louer almost in desperation, moueth his estate*' (pp. 122 and 123). As in *Tottel's Miscellany*, the identity of an apparently conventional 'lover' continually elides, through the uncertain reference of 'he' and 'I', into the voice of the authorial poet, in this case the Howell who figures so conspicuously in his own volume.

The potential for autobiographical reading is reinforced by the first poem in *Newe Sonets*, entitled *'He declareth his greate mishappes, and lamentable sorowes of harte'* (pp. 117–19). This poem owes much in form and diction to a number of medium length poulter's measure complaints in *Tottel's Miscellany*.[36] Howell's complaint, however, is not against love but against ill-fortune which has deprived the speaker of the means to sustain the privileges of his upbringing:

> Would God when I began, to enter first in life,
> That present death had pearst my hart, and rid me cleane this strife.
> So should my Parents not, haue been at such great cost,
> To bringe me vp on whom by fate, their great good gifts are lost:
> Ne yet haue left to me, no whit such wealth at all,
> Whereby from wealth to miserie, might chaunce a soden fall.
>
> (pp. 117–18)

In some respects this is very conventional – the turns of fortune's wheel figured repeatedly in medieval literature as in *Tottel's Miscellany* – but the specificity of the poem's narrative of economic disappointment, and the speaker's complaint that the mean estate is hard to bear by someone used to something better, signals a different and idiosyncratic voice with a social perspective quite unlike those that Tottel presents to us in the *Miscellany*, in which the mean estate is repeatedly praised as a bucolic ideal. Howell's poem serves, at the head of *New Sonets*, to give its author-protagonist a precise social identity. Above all, he laments the loss of the personal liberty of a gentleman, a detail that lends sharpness to the advice in John Keeper's later poem on *'The Unsertaintie of seruice'*, in which Keeper warns:

> Now master calls, now mistris speakes, now vp and downe goe now,
> now tarie here, now goe thou theare, at all commaundes be thou.
> Yet when thy maister likes thee well, thy mistres may thee hate:
> and thus betwene Caribdis rockes, thou sailst in doubtfull state.
>
> (pp. 154–5)

The historical Thomas Howell seems in fact to have been a 'lady's manservant'.[37] His second volume, *The Arbor* (1568) addresses Lady Anne Talbot in whose 'daylie presence' Howell now is (p. 6). A later volume, *H. His Deuises* (1581) identifies the poet as the Countess of Pembroke's 'humble and faythfull Servant' and indicates that the poems were written in her household (pp. 165–6). If the first volume, *Newe Sonets*, was a gambit of self-promotion, advertising Howell as the gentleman he claimed to be, in manners and accomplishments as well as in birth, then it seems to have been successful, perhaps playing a part in his eventual employment by the literary Countess of Pembroke. Nevertheless, while the volume may have served Howell's career, it also constructs out of the discourses of elite verse, a distinctly different kind of subject, particularly evident in '*He declareth his greate mishappes*' (pp. 117–19), in which a narrative of economic and social disappointment and frustration is paradoxically a means of authorial self-assertion and a claim of self-definition. Out of the prestigious materials of *Tottel's Miscellany*, Howell, like other early Elizabethan verse writers, constructs a new kind of first-person subject who displays a self-promotional version of himself through implied narratives of social, economic, and cultural displacement and uncertainty.

Howell's volume uses typical strategies to negotiate a tension that is apparent in all the male-authored early Elizabethan collections: on the one hand the writer is displayed as a man of moral weight and virtue, able to receive and give good counsel and turn a pithy distich, on the other, courtly behaviour entails the courting of women who were habitually represented in Protestant humanist discourse as irrational, unfixed, a danger to male virtue, and deceitful.[38] As the inflammatory objects of masculine fancy and passion, they are represented as that which most threatens the gathered and well-framed male self. Writers like Howell, eager to display their credentials as gentlemen of courtly skills, yet equally eager to present themselves as men well-grounded in Protestant humanist precepts, faced a dilemma. Howell negotiates the difficulty, as many of the other mid-century writers do, by signalling that he does not personally take seriously his 'trifling toyes' (p. 111), and by interlacing occasional poems in the voice of a lover, with poems of warning against love and the untrustworthy nature of women. '*The britlenesse of thinges mortall, and the trustinesse of Vertue*' addressed to 'you faire Dames', for example, seems less a warning to women, than a reinforcement of misogynist disgust with women's bodies:

> To vertue therefore do your selues applie
> Cale *Cressids* lyfe vnto your youthly minde, ...
>
> Hir comly corpes that *Troylus* did delight
> All puft with plages full lothsomly there lay:
> Hir Azurde vaines, her Cristall skinne so whight,
> With Purple spots, was falne in great decay. (p. 122)[39]

The threat of contaminating a carefully framed masculine identity by songs and sonnets and the behaviours of courting, is even more apparent in Barnabe Googe's *Eglogs, Epitaphes and Sonettes* of 1563, the first of the volumes of miscellaneous verse printed in imitation of *Tottel's Miscellany*. The volume begins with a flurry of gentlemanly disclaimers and gestures designed to represent Googe's verses as peripheral to his preoccupation with more important concerns. Googe claims that his privately circulating poems, 'these trifles', were committed 'unpolished' to a printer by a well-meaning friend during Googe's absence abroad. Discovering what had happened, Googe tells us that 'without great hinderance of the poor printer' he could not halt the printing and so he compliantly gives it his blessing by writing a preface.[40] L. Blundeston, the well-meaning friend, in another preface, closely echoes Tottel who had offered a wider public 'those workes which the ungentle horders up of such treasure have hitherto envied thee'. Blundeston promises the appreciative reader of Googe's verse 'to make thee partaker of the like or far greater jewels' of gentleman poets who 'niggardly keep them to their own use and private commodity' (p. 40).

It is the third 'Sonnets' section of Googe's volume that owes the greatest debt to *Tottel's Miscellany*. The first two sections, of eclogues and epitaphs, demonstrate Googe's classical learning, his knowledge of ancient and modern languages, and his awareness of classical models. That Googe felt he needed to include a 'Sonnets' section at all tells us much about the influence of *Tottel's Miscellany*. Googe's humanist self-presentation, and no doubt his need to placate his powerful kinsman Sir William Cecil, later Lord Burleigh, are clearly at odds with the ethics of love poetry, yet the example of Tottel's courtier-poets makes some exercises in this *kind de rigueur* for one who wished to recommend himself to courtly as well as scholarly employers.[41] Googe tries to solve the problem by hedging his love poems about with all sorts of warnings. The 'Sonnets' section begins rather inauspiciously for courtly readers, with a poem addressed to Master Alexander Nowell, commending him for 'leaving things which are but fond and vain' and turning instead to study 'In sacred schools thy lucky years to train' (p. 84). This is followed by a flurry of short epistles exchanged with L. Blundeston and Alexander Nowell on such themes as the dangers of 'affections', beauty's bait, and self-betraying fancy:

> O fancy, flaming fiend
> Of hell. For thou in outward shape
> and colour of a friend,

> Dost by thy snares and slimèd hooks
> entrap the wounded hearts. (p. 88)

The incompatablity of poems of courtship with Googe's self-presentation as good student of moral virtue, produces some strikingly contradictory poems. 'To Mistress A.' (p. 91), for example, which is indebted to Wyatt's 'My lute awake', shifts direction halfway through, turning from a love complaint into a misogynist rant. Elsewhere, poems of courtship are menacingly surrounded by poems of moral warning. In 'To Mistress D.' the lover's letter comes to his mistress from a 'Dungeon deep... Whereas thy faithful servant lives' to wail his lack of 'his own dear mistress' sight' (pp. 94–5), but it is surrounded by epigrammatic warnings against love such as that 'Out of an old Poet': 'Fie, fie, I loath to speak: wilt thou, my lust, I Compel me now to do so foul an act?' (p. 95). The sense of dislocation, or of calculated performance, would have been intensified for those familiar with the poet, as the 'Dungeon' was apparently the name of Googe's house in Kent, thus giving particular autobiographical resonance to 'To Mistress D.'. *Eglogs, Epitaphes and Sonettes* carefully constructs Googe as not only a well-taught humanist student, but also, through the sonnets section, as a gentleman, able to turn his hand to a courting lyric, whether in his own voice or not, while demonstrating his morally-sound awareness of the dangers of fancy and its bait, female beauty. Googe concludes his collection with an allegorical dream poem, 'Cupido Conquered', in which, in a dream, the poet sees the forces of Cupid, idleness, gluttony, fancy and incontinence, routed by the soldiers of Diana who, through their actions, 'declare [their] manhood valiantly' (p. 121, l. 659). The poet is charged by the Muses to write down this allegorical dream, an undertaking presented as no less a proof of valiant manhood than that shown by Diana's troops, since no poet escapes 'evil tongues' (p. 110, l. 201). This anxiety to distance the author's manliness from a contaminating amorous discourse that the miscellany nevertheless feels compelled to include, suggests not only the fear of censure from powerful figures such as Lord Burleigh himself, but also the extreme fragility of the masculine identity constructed in the verse.

Googe's fears of censure were no doubt well founded. A not untypical Reformed view of secular and especially amorous verse is that of Thomas Becon who wrote to Wyatt's brother-in-law, Lord Cobham in 1542 that he wished 'all minstrels in the world... would once leave their lascivious, wanton, and unclean ballads, and sing such godly and virtuous songs as David teacheth them'.[42] Such attitudes are clearly in evidence in the 1560s and 1570s. Gascoigne rearranged his *A Hundreth Sundrie*

Flowres of 1573 into well-segregated sections of Flowers, Herbs, and Weeds when he republished versions of them in 1575 as *The Posies*, apparently in response to censure and to appease the 'reverend Divines' who had 'thought requysite that all ydle Bookes or wanton Pamphlettes shoulde bee forbidden'. In the preface 'To al yong Gentlemen' he explains that his division of his poems into sections puts the onus of choice onto the reader: 'If you will rather beblister your handes with a Nettle, than comfort your senses by smelling to the pleasant Marjoram, then wanton is your pastime and small will be your profite.'[43] Division of secular verse into weeds, herbs and fruits proved useful in this period to poets seeking to defend their verse from moral censure. Dividing his *The Rocke of Regard* of 1576 into four sections with such labels as 'The Arbour of Vertue' and 'The Ortchard of Repentaunce', George Whetstone made sure there could be no ambiguity about his personal attitude to the amorous poems in the 'The Garden of Unthriftiness' section by concluding it with an 'Epilogus' in which all the foregoing poems are explained as warning examples:

> For wantons heede here wrayed is the thrall,
> Of loving wormes, how both they frees and frie,
> How sweetest thoughtes are sawst with bitter gall.
> How care them cloyes that live in jelousie. ...[44]

Only such a miscellany as John Hall's *The Couurte of Vertue* (1565) might expect to evade censure altogether. Its full title: *The Couurte of Vertue Contaynynge Many holy or spretuall songes Sonettes psalms ballettes shorte sentences as well of holy scriptures as others & c* parodies an earlier, largely lost, miscellany of verse, *The Court of Venus*, as well as Tottel's *Songes and Sonnettes*.[45] In his Prologue to the volume, Hall tells us that the lady Vertue warns him of the dangers of 'trim songes of loue' that bring 'Mens souls in wretched vylaynie'.[46] Instead Hall is charged 'To make a boke of songes holy, | Godly and wyse, blaming foly.[47] Sober his songs may have been but there is little evidence that the *Court of Vertue* enjoyed anything like the success of *The Court of Venus* or *Tottel's Miscellany*.

Eager to please potential employers by displaying themselves as sober, well-formed gentlemen, the mid-century poets were also keen to demonstrate their courtly credentials as men able to turn a neat sonnet or balet, and to figure themselves as experienced participators in elegant pastimes. In the climate of moral censure in the early decades of Elizabeth's reign, reconciling the two self-representations required considerable care and ingenuity. Allusions to censure and criticism in prefaces and poems suggest that the advantages of appearing as a courtly writer in print may have been at least partly qualified by the risk of moral disapproval on the part of the public, and even worse, on the part of potential patrons. The degree to which single-author miscellanies flag their anxiety about moral censure indicates not only the potential damage of such censure, but also pervasive fears about the dangers to the well-framed masculine self of the writing of such amorous verse. While seeking to control the production of an approved and socially useful identity 'to be known of others' through their published volumes, the authors of those volumes often seem surprisingly vulnerable to their own productions, subject to that unstable medium language in what was esteemed its most skittish and trifling form, poesy and fancy.

Amorous narrative sequences

In 'Cupido Conquered' Googe's anxieties about the threats that amorous passion poses to virtue are developed as a narrative of the routing of Cupid's degenerate troops by the manly forces of Diana. Another narrative of the opposition between virtue and desire, popular in these mid-century volumes, is that of the reformed prodigal that Richard Helgerson argues, in his important study of the poetry of this period, served as a useful strategy for those seeking to negotiate Burleigh's known moralistic attitudes in their search for his patronage.[48] Yet another, which we have already touched on in the verse of Howell, is the Cressida story of female deceit and betrayal of the faithful male lover. In this section, I shall discuss ways in which incipient narratives, developed from the implied occasions of amorous verses, and from the dire warnings of moral and aphoristic verse, could be appropriated for autobiographical narratives.[49] The language of courtship, however, with its connotations of the feminine and deception was deeply threatening to a discourse of male authorial control. In amorous verse sequences by two of the early Elizabethan miscellanists, George Gascoigne and George Turbervile, the self-promotional masculine authorial subject finds himself implicated in tales that call attention to the unreliability of writing and the emasculating deceptions of discourse.

George Gascoigne's *A Hundreth Sundrie Flowers* (1573) illustrates spectacularly the contradictory programmes of the single-authored miscellanies. As Wendy Wall and Arthur Marotti have pointed out, it mimics a manuscript album.[50] Gascoigne's name appears not as the author, but as one of a number of contributors to what purports to be a surreptitiously printed collection of largely anonymous verse. A letter from 'The Printer to the Reader' at the head of the volume refers to a preface by H.W. This preface is found at the beginning of the third item contained in the volume, 'The Adventures of Master F.J.', but seems to refer not simply to that item but to the whole volume. H.W. weaves an elaborate fiction of a manuscript compiled by G.T. 'wherin he had collected divers discourses and verses, invented uppon sundrie occasions, by sundrie gentlemen' (pp. 141–2). Against G.T.'s express instructions, H.W. has copied the manuscript and taken it to the printer, and is now having it printed under the title '*A hundreth sundrie Flowers*', only pausing to 'cover all our names' to protect the contributors' privacy. He justifies his act by imagining the amusement and profit the book will give its readers who will 'sit and smile at the fond devises of such as have enchayned them selves in the golden fetters of fantasie, and having bewrayed them selves to the whole world, do yet conjecture that they walke unseene in a net' (p. 142). H.W. then copies a letter from G.T. reinforcing the moral framing of the amorous narratives the manuscript contains, and lamenting that 'amongst so many toward wittes no one hath bene hitherto encouraged to followe the trace of that worthy and famous Knight *Sir Geffrey Chaucer*, and after many pretie devises spent in youth, for the obtayning a worthles victorie [ie love poems], might consume and consummate his age in discribing the right pathway to perfect felicitie' (p. 143).[51] G.T. begs H.W. not to make the manuscript poems and discourses 'common' (p. 144), that is, he must keep them to himself. Their wit, he remarks in a second letter, should be understood in the context of the occasions which 'moved [the poets] to write' and he has therefore added head notes giving the circumstances in which they were written, rehearsed to him by the authors themselves (p. 145).

Gascoigne later explained in one of the prefaces to *The Posies* of 1575, that he wrote and published the earlier volume while abroad 'busied in martiall affayres … to notifie unto the worlde before my returne, that I coulde as well persusade with Penne, as pearce with launce or weapon: So that yet some noble minde might be incoraged both to exercise me in time of peace, and to emploie mee in time of service in warre' (p. 362). If this is to be believed, and the prefaces to the 1575 edition are a gallimaufry of contradiction and inconsistency, then Gascoigne seems to have designed the 1573 volume to promote his own name and talents while pretending that the volume as a whole was a surreptitious printing of a manuscript collection of gentlemen's verse, including his own. Gascoigne's name appears in *A Hundreth*, somewhat as the Earl of Surrey's did in Tottel, as the most prominent named contributor in a collection of coterie verse that has somehow got into the hands of a printer who brings the lives and writings of an elite before the eyes of the vulgar. The first two items in *A Hundreth*, translations of Ariosto's *Supposes*, and of Euripides' *Iocasta*, are credited to 'George Gascoygne of Grayes Inne Esquire' (p. 5). He thus first appears in a carefully modulated guise, translating both a courtly Italian text and a classical Greek tragedy.[52] Gascoigne is also named as the last and most prolific of the 'sundrie gentlemen' whose 'devises' or verses form the bulk of the volume. The editor, presumably G.T., tells us in a head note that he '*will now deliver unto you so many more of Master Gascoignes Poems as have come to my hands, who hath never beene dayntie of his doings, and therfore I conceale not his name*' (p. 263). Gascoigne thus appears as participating in the coterie circulation of gentlemen's verse, but as frank and free with his writings, unlike the 'ungentle horders up' of the treasure of *Tottel's Miscellany*.

The poems explicitly attributed to Gascoigne are carefully selected to display him as adept at courtly skills but distanced from amorous delinquency. A series of complaints in the voice of Gascoigne as a suffering lover are followed by a 'Recantation'. We are then given some virtuoso performances in which five poems on five Latin sayings or proverbs, given to Gascoigne by five Inns of Court friends, and '*devised ... [by him] admounting to the number of* .CCLVIII. *verses, riding by the way, writing none of them untill he came at the end of his Journey*' (p. 282). Gascoigne here presents himself as a humanist scholar and virtuoso, with a well-stored head, copious invention, and a well-trained memory. At the same time the presentation of these poems as 'exercises' displays Gascoigne as an outspoken critic of corruption in church and state while protecting him behind the claim to be simply writing amplifications of set classical themes for friends. These humanist performances are followed by poems of piety, by two letters of wise counsel to friends, Douglasse Dive and Bartholmew Withipoll, and, finally, by some examples of patronage poems: a masque for Lord Montague and two poems to Lord Grey, '*Gascoignes wodmanship*' and '*Gascoignes voyage*', one wittily obsequious, the other bluffly martial.[53] The Gascoigne who emerges from these carefully acknowledged verses, purportedly written in his own voice, is a sober, brilliant, pious man, frank about youthful foolishnesses from which he has learned wisdom and experience, and able to display all these gifts with eloquence, tact and wit; a worthy object of patronage and a suitable candidate for employment.

On closer inspection this splendid mirage proves illusory, depending as it does on rhetorical performances whose ostentatious artfulness undermines the very possibility of sincerity and integrity. This is evident, for example, in a series of love poems ending in recantation: '*Gascoigns*

Anatomie', *'araignement'*, *'passion'*, *'libell of Divorce'*, and *'Recantation'*.[54] It is the last of these that presents the preceding poems as part of a coherent autobiographical narrative sequence:

> I graunt my workes were these, first one *Anatomie*,
> Wherein I paynted every pang of loves perplexity:
> Nexte that I was araignde, with *George* holde up thy hande,
> Wherein I yeelded Beauties thrall, at hir commaunde to stande:
> Myne eyes so blynded were, (good people marke my tale)
> That once I soong, I *Bathe in Blisse*, amidde my wearie *Bale*:
> And many a frantike verse, then from my penne did passe,
> In waves of wicked heresie so deepe I drowned was,
> All whiche I nowe recante, and here before you burne
> Those trifling bookes, from whose leud lore my tippet here I turne.
> [I turn away from their vicious teaching] (p. 274)

The patently absurd claim that the reformed poet here and now burns before us the poems we have just read in print calls into question the seriousness of the whole poem, including its rhetoric of moral disgust. Gascoigne tells us that the lesson he has learned from his experience is a thorough suspicion of women: 'Their smyling is deceipt, their faire wordes traynes of treason, I Their witte always so full of wyles, it skorneth rules of reason' (p. 273). The excess of the attack, unjustified in terms of the narrative this recantation concludes, draws our attention to the formulaic nature of the recantation and its moralism. In the prefatory epistles to 'yong Gentlemen' that prefaces the 1575 edition, Gascoigne shares the joke that some readers '(having no skill at all) ... understande neyther the meaning of the Authour, nor the sense of the figurative speeches' and cites as an example 'the areignment and divorce of a Lover (being written in jeast) have bene mistaken in sad earnest' (pp. 365–6). If it is all jesting performance, we cannot be sure there is any 'sad earnest', whether the rhetorical style is amorous, aphoristic or pious.

Among the poems *'Gascoignes Recantation'* lists as part of Gascoigne's personal narrative of passionate error is the 'soong, I *Bathe in Blisse*, amidde my wearie *Bale'*. That song is in fact printed in *A Hundreth*, but not as part of Gascoigne's purportedly autobiographical sequence. Instead it appears as *'A straunge passion of another Author'* (p. 243) among the anonymous 'Devises of Sundrie Gentlemen'. When the 'Anatomye' sequence was reprinted in *Posies*, as the narrative of 'a lover' rather than of 'Gascoigne', 'I Bathe in Blisse' was inserted into it.[55] Its displacement in the 1573 volume may be an accident, but it exposes the instability of the verse Gascoigne is using to present himself to the public as, at least ostensibly, a stable, trustworthy, and frank individual. The words he speaks, the verse he writes, can be appropriated and assigned at will, its speaking voice a rhetorical effect, a mirage of presence. The Gascoigne so elaborately presented through this volume, who seems to speak to us so intimately in his own name and through his own 'private' verse, evaporates among the playful prefaces and rhetorical effects, the hints of presence and coy ironies that make of his self-presentation a conjurer's show.

The poet-lover of *A Hundreth* may be not only a manipulator of illusions, but also their victim. The narratives of courting with which his volume abounds, repeatedly construct the male poet-lover as contaminated by the glamorous vanity of the world he seeks to exploit and judge. While *A Hundreth* acknowledges Petrarch's sequence as a source, like other mid-century collections, its amorous narratives, as we have already seen in the case of Howell, owe more to the paradigm of the faithless Crisyede. The most elaborate of the narratives it contains is 'The Adventures of Master F.J.', which has all the tabloid ingredients of sex, secrecy, and high society. It is also a warning tale, like most of those Gascoigne tells, of female faithlessness and betrayal. The narrative offers its readers secrets, perhaps real secrets; Gascoigne tells us invitingly, in the 1575 rewriting, that in 1573 'The Adventures' were read as a *roman à cléf*: 'some busie conjectures have presumed to thinke that the same was indeed written to the scandalizing of some worthie personages, whom they woulde seeme therby to know' (pp. 362–3). It seems to offer its readers a glimpse of a glamorously exclusive social world, but the figure that suffers most is the poet-lover who creates it and initiates the action, Master F.J.

As we shall see when we examine this text in more detail in Chapter 5, the world of Master F.J. is one of passion and deceit whose medium is writing. The narrative takes the form of prose introductions and explanations to written epistles and verses sent by the lover, or sung aloud, or occasionally written for his private pleasure. Verse functions as the medium through which the illicit affair is conducted, and as an indicator of the lover's prowess. The poet-lover is eventually bested by the mistress's secretary whose pen/penis clearly pleases the lady more than his own:

> It fell out that the *Secretary* having bin of long time absent, and therby his quils and pennes not worn so neer as they were wont to be, did now prick such faire large notes, that his Mistres liked better to sing faburden under him, than to descant any longer uppon F.J. playne song. (p. 199)

The narrative of F.J. is spun entirely from the erotic connotations and cultural fears of courtly amorous verse; such verse might win F.J. the sexual favours of the aristocratic but unstable lady Elinor, but true to its factitious nature it leads to his betrayal by female trickery and faithlessness.[56]

'The Adventures' serve as a kind of warning allegory of the dangers of writing amorous verse throughout *A Hundreth*. The story of F.J. and faithless Dame Elinor repeats itself over and over again in the volume's narratives of courting through verse. Typical is a brief narrative ascribed to one of the anonymous 'sundrie gentlemen' who is given the motto '*Si fortunatus infoelix*' ('If I am fortunate, I am unhappy').[57] The head notes group a number of these poems together in a sequence: '*written to a Gentlewoman whom he liked very well, and yit had never any oportunity to discover his affection, being always brydled by jelouse lookes ... he wrot in a booke of hirs as foloweth*' (p. 229). The verses, written in her manuscript album, are answered by an encouraging line from the lady. The lengthy head note tells us:

> You shall now understand, that soone after this answer of hirs, the same Author chaunced to be at a supper in hir company, where were also hir brother, hir husband, and an old lover of hirs by whom she had bin long suspected. Nowe, although there wanted no delicate viands to content them, yit their chief repast was by entreglancing of lookes. For G.G. being stoong with hot affection, could none otherwise relieve his passion but by gazing. And the Dame of a curteous enclination deigned (now and then) to requite the same with glancing at him. Hir old lover occupied his eyes with watching: and hir brother perceyving all this could not absteyne from winking, ... But most of all hir husband ... was constreyned to play the fifth part in forward frowninge. (pp. 230–1)

This is a scenario that overgoes Gascoigne's master, Ovid.[58] From looking, the clandestine lovers progress to riddling, and from there to 'better acquaintance'. But this lady, like so many of her sisters in these early Elizabethan volumes, is also of Cressid's kind; one day '*(groping in hir pocket)*' he discovers a new letter of her old lover's, and thus he discovers his mistress's faithlessness and his own betrayal. As so often in Gascoigne's verse, intimacy reveals yet more unreliable writings.

A curiously paradoxical dynamic works itself out in Gascoigne's amorous sequences. The high society amours with morally loose courtly dames legitimize the courtly credentials of those who take part in such games. In the case of this particular sequence, Gascoigne himself is implicated, not only through the prominent appearance of his name as a contributor to this supposed manuscript in print, but veiled behind the lover whose initials, we are told, are G.G. The poet who uses this discourse is, however, also constructed by it. Although represented as the male initiator of seduction narratives, the poet-lover is doomed always to re-enact the scenario of deception and female perfidy that constitutes this courtly world in so many poems in these miscellanies. By his very participation in an amorous courtly discourse, the poet-lover inscribes himself as marginal, powerless and insubstantial, a player in a game of charades, a user of a language which is never his own and can never be trusted. Like his amorous balets and sonnets, he is a 'toy' a mere trifle, a 'jeast'.[59] The sense of presence, of 'real' secrets and actual occasions, that the head notes and narratives of *A Hundreth* strenuously try to produce, is continually undermined by the themes of deception and game playing that the narratives continually enact. By casting himself as victim in amorous narratives of his own telling, in which power is attributed to untrustworthy women, the poet-lover paradoxically produces himself as both effeminate and tainted.

It is possible that the G.T. who figures in *A Hundreth* as the gentleman who lends H.W. the manuscript and who provides the 'very proper occasion' for each verse (p. 145) alludes to George Turbervile, who published two volumes of miscellaneous verse, *Epitaphes, Epigrams, Songs and Sonets* (1567, but with a possible earlier edition in 1565), and *Epitaphes and Sonnettes* (possibly first published in 1574 or 1576).[60] Turbervile was a well-connected gentleman in need of patronage who belonged to the same Inns of Court literary circles as Googe, Gascoigne and a number of others who published poetry in this period.[61] He is less coy than Googe about his own part in publishing his own poems, although, like Gascoigne, he both exploits, and playfully undermines, the stability of the autobiographical 'I' especially in relation to love poetry. In 'The Author's excuse' at the end of *Epitaphes and Sonnettes*, he explains that living where 'sundry gallants every day' discoursed of their amours, he pretended to do the like: 'And being there although my mind were freé: | Yet must I seéme loue wounded eke to be' (p. 455). Like other early Elizabethan poets he presents himself to the public and to potential employers, through his miscellanies, as participating in the social and manuscript exchange of poetry within a privileged coterie in which both sober humanist and witty courtly discourses are both common currency.

Like Gascoigne, although more embryonically, Turbervile develops Tottel's use of verse titles to produce extended narrative sequences. Like Gascoigne also, these narratives of courting call into question the very stability of writing and voice on which the more moralistic self-presentations of the author depend. A verse sequence in *Epitaphes, Epigrams, Songs and Sonets*, presents fictional protagonists, Tymetes and his lady Pyndara, but it develops motifs that reappear in a more explicitly autobiographical sequence in *Epitaphes and Sonnettes*, and I shall therefore consider it briefly.[62] Poems relating to the Tymetes sequence are scattered throughout the volume in which it appears, and it is often hard to distinguish verses belonging to the sequence from others attributed simply to a 'lover'. The rather predictable narrative of Tymetes' affair is outlined in a prefatory 'Argument to the whole discourse and Treatise following.' In it we are told how Tymetes loves Pyndara whose beauty 'farre exceeded Helena'. He 'plide his Penne and to his writing fell | And sude as did the man [Paris] to Helena', eventually achieving the same success:

> *Then ioyd he, and cherefull ditties made*
> *In praise of his atchiued* Pyndara:
> *But sone (God wote) his pleasure went to glade,*
> *Another tooke to wife this* Helena. (p. 36)

The 'Argument' does not tell us whether Pyndara is deliberately faithless or is merely a pawn, but the insistence, throughout the 'Argument' on the similarity of Pyndara to Paris's Helena, strongly implies that she too will prove faithless and cause havoc. The fragmentary unfolding of the narrative in the volume (leading one critic to suggest it has been assembled in the wrong order), and the uncertainty about which poems may or may not belong to the sequence may testify to Turbervile's indifference to the precise details of how his narrative of betrayal and vanity is played out and whether it refers to a particular lover or all lovers. The story of Tymetes' love for Pyndara is paradigmatic, its outcome already implied for the mid-century mind in the dangerous combination of fancy, passion and dependence on female favour integral to amorous courtly verse. Having 'plide his Penne' and fallen to writing, thus producing copious amorous matter, Tymetes, or the reformed lover-poet, can then, equally copiously but more aphoristically, 'Applie my Pen, and tell the troth' about women's perfidy and the treachery of passion ('The Louer finding his Loue flitted from wonted troth leaues to write in prayse of hir', p. 211).

Turbervile published verse translations of Ovid's *Heroycall Epistles* in 1567, and the epistle from Helen to Paris may have provided a model for one of the most unusual, and rhetorically destabilizing, aspects of Turbervile's narrative of Tymetes and Pyndara. In a couple of poems Pyndara's voice is heard giving a female point of view. In the first of her verse letters to Tymetes, she cites the examples of Aeneas, Jason and

Theseus to illustrate her assertion that 'we Women are | more trustie than you men':

> They brake their vowed hestes,
>   by ship away they went:
> And so betrayde those siely soules
>   that craft nor falsehood ment. (p. 71)

Tymetes also departed by ship. His absence produces doubt and misunderstanding foregrounding the instability of writing, its lack of a seemingly authenticating voice and presence. Tymetes' first letter from abroad is in his own blood, bringing his bodily presence as a proof of his sincerity to his lady. His second, written in ink and charging Pyndara to avoid the shame of Cressida by remaining faithful to him, produces, rather than assuages, distrust. Each lover doubts the other's writing; 'For some doe weepe that feele no wo', Pyndara tells her lover:

> The more you seeme to me
>   in wofull wise to playne,
> The sooner I perswade my selfe
>   that you do nought but fayne. (p. 92)

Turbervile uses a woman's voice to throw doubt on the stability of male promises and male writing. Pyndara reverses the standard masculine exploitation of Cressida as a figure of faithlessness and female corruptibility, using her deception by Diomedes to accuse men of telling 'To sundrie women sundrie tales':

> Was neuer woman false,
>   but man as false as shee
> And commonly the men doe make
>   that women slipper bee. (p. 94)

However, in spite of Pyndara's accusation, Turbervile's verse does not seriously threaten male self-assurance. After all, the introduction to the sequence has assured us that it is Pyndara who will betray, not Tymetes, however much she may be given the language of moral counsel, and warn women of the falseness of men:

> If she that reads this rime,
>   be wise as I could wishe,

> She should auoyde the bayted hooke
> that takes the biting fishe. (p. 94)

Turbervile's readers are left to negotiate as best they can the *mise en abyme* that opens when the language of moral counsel is offered to us as truth in a poem by a male poet ventriloquizing a female character who will prove a second Criseyde or Helen.

Similar anxieties about the uncertainty of language detached from an authenticating voice or presence are evident in a sequence of amorous verses in *Epitaphes and Sonnettes* in which the poet seems to figure himself as protagonist. This collection of verses with its own title page probably appeared appended to *Tragical Tales*, thought to have been printed in 1574 or 1576, although the only surviving edition is dated 1587. Here, too, the narrative is one of male faithfulness and probable female betrayal, but in this case the setting is the lover-poet's journey to Russia. As the volume includes three verse epistles in Turbervile's own voice to male friends, written from Russia where he had travelled in 1568–9 as secretary to Elizabeth's emissary, Lord Thomas Randolph, the inference is that the lover is a version of Turbervile himself. The first-person poems belonging to the amorous sequence are introduced by third-person titles, such as 'From the citie of Mosqua, to his friend in England' but, like the Tymetes sequence in the previous volume, they are interspersed with other first-person poems in the voice of a lover who may or may not be part of the Russian narrative, and with aphoristic verse, elegies and epitaphs explicitly in Turbervile's own voice.

Epitaphes and Sonnettes begins with an epistle sent by the lover-poet to his mother in which he represents his journey as an enterprising venture to escape the lack of opportunity at home:

> My countrey coast where I
> my Nurses milke did sucke,
> Would neuer yet in all my life
> allowe me one good luck. (p. 348)

Russia, however, provides little comfort. The landscape and the climate provide striking metaphors for themes of exile, separation from the beloved, the cold and heat of despair and desire, and the experience of amorous desolation. The 'frozen floodes where sliding Sledds doe goe' and its 'sauage men' and 'women foule to sight' (pp. 351–2), provide a cheerless setting for the poet's longing thoughts of his mistress and home:

> In Russia where I leade my life,
>   and long againe at home to be.
> No force shall cause me to forget
>   or lay the care of loue aside. (p. 361)

The mistress and his feelings towards her seem inextricably linked to his feelings for his motherland: his homesickness, his anger that it has not offered him 'one good luck', still less a living, and his fear of losing the sense of belonging that it bestows. In what appears to be one of the last poems of the sequence, 'Trauailing the desert of Russia, he complayneth to Eccho' (pp. 373–4), the lover describes his sense of deracination and, particularly, the ineffective power of his voice:

> But now (Alas) she is alacke,
>   helpe Eccho, helpe, I am vndone
> Besides mine absence from her sight,
>   another doth possesse my place
> And of my harvest sheares the sheaues,
>   helpe Eccho, helpe, lament my case. (p. 373)

The conceit of the echo in the deserts of Russia figures the lover's isolation and the insubstantiality of his voice.[63] In the following poem, 'He craues his mistresse to accept his wryting being otherwise insufficient to winne good liking from her' (p. 375), the lover contrasts his own position with those who can impress their mistresses by their physical presences: through their singing, or dancing, or martial appearance. Writing from abroad may prove the writer to be worthier than the factitious displays of the 'carpet knights' at home, but as in the Echo poem that precedes it, this poem figures the lover-poet's existence as insubstantial and bodiless, an echoing sound or a trace on a page.

As in the Tymetes/Pyndara sequence, Turbervile seems here to develop amorous verse into a fragmentary narrative that betrays anxieties inherent in a persona constructed from writings, especially the writing of amorous trifles. Abroad in a strange and hostile land, his pen and voice become signs of absence, both his own and that of his lover/home. The lover finds himself unanchored, a floating signifier without a presence at home or abroad, betrayed by the familiar, and unheard among the echoing wastes of Russia. Even more than in his epistles of counsel and news to male friends from abroad, included in *Epitaphes and Sonnettes*, and which we shall consider in Chapter 3, Turbervile's narrative of amorous exile and betrayal suggests deep anxieties about the stability and self-sufficiency of the masculine self and its grounding in language. Crane argues that because print abstracts verse from 'the control of the body', anxiety about alienating meaning from its production by the body 'would be particularly acute in poems that purport to express directly the voice produced by a suffering body, thus necessitating the addition of a narrative to supply the missing "bodily" context'.[64] Interestingly, in the amorous sequences of both Gascoigne and Turbervile, narrative serves precisely to foreground anxiety over the control of meaning in writing. The central motif of many of their sequences is the exchange of letters, sent from abroad, left in a chamber or found while groping in a woman's pocket. Writing, easily detachable from 'originating' occasions and the bodily presence of voice, is, as Derrida has famously argued, the form in which the fundamental instability of meaning becomes most readily apparent.[65]

A woman's voice: Isabella Whitney

For Gascoigne, Turbervile and the early Elizabethan poets we have been examining, instability of meaning and loss of the gathered self are to be found most acutely in the writing of courtship, a discourse of desire in which male autonomy is threatened by a fantasy of women as powerful, faithless, irrational, and emasculating. When Turbervile attempts to imagine sympathetically a female perspective by writing Pyndara's complaints, he associates her with her Ovidian and Chaucerian models, Helen and Criseyde, and carefully places her in a narrative in which the female, whatever her words may appear to say, will betray the faithful man. In Gascoigne's narratives, although the men do the writing, women are identified as the source and cause of the instability of courting and courtly language. In this discourse of a feminized courtly world, males who succeed become by definition lady's men, abandoning a stable male use of language for an unstable female one.

   The printed miscellanies that we have so far examined are distinctly gendered, written to present gentlemen poets to, in the main, gentlemen readers.[66] The single-author miscellanies thus follow the example of *Tottel's Miscellany*, in which the emphasis is on male authors and male points of view. The genre did, however, produce one remarkable female contributor, Isabella Whitney, who published two miscellanies of her own, *The Copy of a Letter* (1567), and *A Sweet Nosgay* (1573). Whitney exploits the easily imitated and adaptable quality of Tudor and early

Elizabethan verse to construct a female voice and identity with which to enter and turn to her advantage what had become an almost exclusively masculine discourse.

In doing so, she draws on manuscript traditions of female-voiced verse, particularly answer poems, or defences of women, that were not printed in *Tottel's Miscellany*. Such answers and defences sometimes use a female voice although they are by no means always written by women. On occasion the same author composes both the attack and the defence.[67] Some striking examples of female-voiced answers and defences, or adaptions of male-voiced material, can be found in the courtly Devonshire MS (BL Additional 17492) belonging to the 1530s and early 1540s. Among the verses in the Devonshire Manuscript that seem to participate in such a game of slander and retaliation are stanzas copied into some folios at the end of the manuscript (fols. 89^v–91^v). These stanzas are all borrowed from the handsome printed edition of Chaucer's *Workes* published in 1532 by William Thynne.[68] Some, from *Troilus and Criseyde*, are spoken, significantly, by Criseyde, that universally vilified example of inconstant femininity in male poetry of the early to mid sixteenth century. In one of the stanzas, Criseyde voices a point of view typical of woman-voiced defences and answers:

> Also wyckyd tonges byn so prest
> To speake us harme eke men ben so vntrewe
> That right anon as cessed ys ther lest
> So cesseth loue and forth to loue anewe.[69]

Another of the Devonshire MS stanzas deliberately rewrites as praise of women its misogynist original:

> Yff all the erthe were parchment scrybable
> Spedy for the hande and all maner wode
> Were hewed and proportyoned to pennes able
> Al water ynke, in damme or in flode
> Euery man beyng a parfyte scribe or goode
> The faythfulnes yet and prayse of women
> Cowde not be shewyd by the meane off penne.[70]

In the text from which the stanza is copied, the penultimate line read: 'The cursydnesse yet and the disceyte of women'. Much as one might like to imagine a woman writing these lines, a man may as easily have copied the stanzas as a woman. The slippery gendering of many of the discourses of courting, fidelity and defence, is well illustrated by the fact that three of the stanzas copied on these folios, are from the 'Letter of Cupid', included among Chaucer's works in Thynne's edition, although more usually included among Thomas Hoccleve's works. The 'Letter' is in fact Hoccleve's translation of a poem by Christine de Pisan in defence of women, although it seems to have acquired an anti-feminist reputation by the sixteenth century.[71]

Whitney's *The Copy of a Letter* (1567), contains two poems ascribed to Is.W., *'I.W. To her unconstant Lover'* and *'The admonition by the Auctor, to all yong Gentilwomen: And to al other Maids being in Love'*.[72] Entirely typical of the contexts in which such defences of women appear, is the fact that following Is.W.'s poems, two attacks on women are printed: 'A Loueletter, or an earnest perswason of a Louer' by W.G., a male-voiced poem blaming a mistress who 'swerue[d] from her former promise without occasion', and a poem by R.Witc. 'warnyng … all Yongmen to beware the fained Fidelytie of vnconstant Maydens'.[73] Critics have noted Whitney's debts to Turbervile's translations of Ovid's *Heroides*, but the language of her poems in this volume is more strikingly close to some of Turbervile's verse in the voice of Pyndara in *Epitaphes, Epigrams, Songs and Sonets*.[74] The only extant copy of Turbervile's miscellany is dated 1567, the same year as the probable printing of Whitney's volume, but Turbervile's title page describes the volume as 'Newly corrected with additions' implying an earlier printing.[75] As we have seen (pp. 30–1 above), Pyndara invoked Aeneas, Iason and Theseus as examples of men that 'brake their vowed hestes, | By ship away they went.' Whitney invokes the same examples for the same purposes. Jason, for example:

> when he by MEDEAS arte,
> had got the Fleece of Gold
> And also had of her that time,
> al kynd of things he wolde.

> He toke his Ship and fled away
> regarding not the vowes:
> That he dyd make so faithfully,
> unto his loving Spowes. (pp. 30–1)

In Pyndara's 'aunswere of a woman to hir Louer, supposing his complaint to be but fayned', Turbervile has Pyndara warn other women, 'Yf she that reades this rime, | be wise as I coulde wishe', not to trust men's crocodile tears and the 'bayted hooke' of men's false words (p. 94). Whitney, in her *'admonition … to all yong Gentilwomen'*, finds the same tropes useful, comparing men's words to 'the teares of Crocodiles', and concluding:

> And since the Fish that reason lacks
> once warned doth beware:
> Why should not we take hede to that
> that turneth vs to care. (p. 37)

Whether Whitney is directly borrowing images here and there from Turbervile, or using a common language, she is doing exactly what the other mid-century writers have done in their borrowings from Tottel's authors and each other.[76] Out of the fragments and phrases of the flexible discourses of courting and aphoristic counsel, she, like them, constructs a voice and point of view that is then presented as personal and autobiographical. In the case of *The Copy of a Letter*, this effect, attached as it is merely to two initials, seems designed less to make her name known in the world, than to authorize her female complaint by suggesting a narrative of personal experience. Is.W.'s implied presence is a rhetorical device to stabilize a conventional discourse as true speech. Nevertheless, the presentation of Whitney's poems undermines this rhetorical effect. Placed alongside two male-voiced poems that, accusation for accusation, and complaint for complaint, match her own, the volume places her verse in the context of social jesting and witty exchange implied by, for example, the Devonshire MS verses. Where Turbervile's narrative of female faithlessness presented Pyndara's complaints of male faithlessness as the unreliable words of women, Whitney's plea that her faithless lover keep her letter 'in store' as the last expression of her faithful mind (p. 33), is presented merely as a witty reply by its context in a volume of jesting exchange.

Whitney's *A Sweet Nosgay* appeared in 1573, the same year as Gascoigne's collection. Whitney's publication of her own secular poems in the form of a miscellany was a remarkably bold act. The title page is missing but she is identified as Is.W. in her dedicatory letter to George Mainwaring, and a commendatory poem identifies her name as Whitney. Whitney demonstrates great skill and wit in adapting the normally male-gendered conventions of the early Elizabethan single-author collections to serve her own female-gendered self-presentation.[77] The first part of the volume is devoted to a long series of aphoristic poems versifying selections from a collection of ready-made aphorisms, Hugh Plat's *The Floures of Philosophie* (1572). Male writing and wisdom thus authorize Whitney's humble gathering, a task she has undertaken, she tells us, in a time of sickness and enforced idleness to put her time to good use. Whitney presents herself as gathering blossoms and herbs from Plat's 'plot', his garden, and using them to make a medicinal posie for her friends to protect them, as she found they protected her, from infective smells. Here the 'herbs' and 'flowers' metaphors, so popular with early Elizabethan miscellanists, are neatly gendered to represent Whitney as engaged in a woman's task, gathering medicinal herbs for the care and health of friends and family. This section in fact closes with 'A soueraigne receypt', such a one as a woman might put in her household book:

> The iuce of all these Flowers take,
> and make thee a conserue:
> And vse it firste and laste: and it
> wyll safely thee preserue.[78]

Following this section, the volume becomes more self-assertive. Like other miscellanists, Whitney presents her collection as a printed private manuscript. Instead of aphoristic verse to male companions and poems of gentlemanly courting, however, she gathers verse epistles exchanged within a close family network and with a few male friends to whom she turns for counsel. Through these Whitney situates herself and her family with some precision socially. She has been in service 'unto a vertuous Ladye' (p. 9) but has lost her place. Her sisters are also in service, but in a position in which they also have 'teachers and governers' (p. 10), suggesting lady's companions rather than menial servants. Whitney's brother (G.W., the emblem writer Geoffrey Whitney) rides forth from the City at vacation time, apparently to help with the harvest (p. 8), indicating that he is a student at the Inns of Court. By thus presenting herself as maintaining a family network through her verse epistles, Whitney wittily genders the effects of manuscript exchange central to the self-presentation of her male peers. In the final poem of the volume she uses the conceit of her own death, albeit a metaphorical one, to write a last '*WYLL and Testament*'. As Wendy Wall argues, this conceit was to prove enabling for women in the next century who wished to leave traces of their wills, whether to their own children or to the world at large, without violating gender decorums.[79]

Carefully as she adapts the male conventions of single-author miscellanies to mitigate the boldness of her undertaking, the authorial Whitney that is carefully produced by her volume persistently challenges gender stereotypes of the period. While her verse epistles represent Whitney as enmeshed in family relationships, Whitney also defines herself as detached from female domestic interests. Writing 'To her Sister Misteris A.B.', she asserts:

> Had I a Husband, or a house, and all that longes therto
> My selfe could frame about to rouse, as other women doo:
> But til some houshold cares mee tye,
> My bookes and Pen I wyll apply. (p. 13)

As she makes clear in her '*WYLL and Testament*', she is reluctant to leave the freedom she has to wander abroad through the public streets of London to return to the country on her '*Friendes procurement*' (p. 18). Her preference for, and familiarity with, the normally masculine world of printers and book stalls is made clear when, using the conceit of bequeathing aspects of London to its inhabitants, she leaves

> To all the Bookebinders by Paulles
>   because I lyke their Arte:
> They e[ver]y weeke shal mony have,
>   when they from Bookes departe.
> Amongst them all, my Printer must,
>   have somewhat to his share:
> I wyll my Friends there Bookes to bye
>   of him, with other ware. (p. 25)

Whitney's '*WYLL and Testament*' is an extraordinarily vivid poem, evoking mid-sixteenth-century commercial London in all its material specificity with a cornucopian delight in contemporary terms and details: 'Hoods, Bungraces, Hats or Caps' on sale in Cheapside, hose of all kind in Birchin Lane 'For Women stitchte, for men both Trunks I and those of Gascoyne gise' (p. 21), and 'Bootes, shoes or Pantables' in St Martins (p. 21). In spite of the fun of the poem, there is a savage irony. The vivid voice of Isabella Whitney who records this teeming London in such loving detail, has no presence; as a woman without means, she flits ghost-like through London, able to leave (or bequeath) its shops and shopkeepers with as much store as they had before her arrival because she cannot afford to take any of it away.[80] Passing by Ludgate prison, she remarks:

> I dyd reserve, that for my selfe,
>   yf I my health possest.
> And ever came in credit so
>   a debtor for to bee. (p. 24)

So marginal is her economic significance in this public world that she cannot even aspire to sufficient credit to get into debt.

Like the other mid-century authors that we have examined, Whitney uses the borrowed materials of mid-century verse to construct a written version of herself, a name and fragments of a personal history; sufficient to make herself known in the world in order, perhaps to gain some patronage in the face of possible rustication to the country, perhaps to leave some trace of herself in the masculine world of the city.[81] Her version of her female self, economically marginal and without a secure domestic place, but able and willing to assert that self publicly through her pen, gives us the most unusual example of a new kind of autobiographical self-presentation and narrative that emerges from the mid-century miscellanies. More self-reflexively than most, Whitney's 'WYLL *and Testament'* constructs her autobiographical self as a trace on paper, a ghost-like absence in the living world of London unable to buy or even bequeath anything but fantasies.

2
The 'outward marks' and the 'inward man': Thomas Whythorne's 'songs and sonetts'

Thomas Whythorne participated enthusiastically in the fashion for single-author miscellanies that we discussed in Chapter 1. In 1571, he published a collection of settings for his own verses in *Songes, for three, fower and fiue voyces* in five part-books. This volume is one of the earliest surviving examples of printed music in England.[1] In approximately 1576, he put into its present form a manuscript collection of his verse accompanied by often lengthy prose explanations of their occasions within the narrative of his own life, and it is this volume, never in fact published by Whythorne, that is the subject of this chapter. This manuscript, named as an 'Autobiography' by its modern editor James M. Osborn, is in fact entitled 'A book of songs and sonetts, with longe discoorses sett with them, of the chylds lyfe, togyther with A yoong mans lyfe, and entring into the old mans lyf. devysed and written with A new Orthografye by Thomas Whýthorne, gent.'[2] Its title thus unmistakably echoes Tottel's *Songs and Sonnettes* of 1557, but also points to Whythorne's desire to narrate his life not only as a context for the verse, but in terms of a conventional model, that of the ages of man.[3] In the process of reviewing his life in terms of this, and other, conventional models, the manuscript volume also, on occasion, becomes a commonplace book in which Whythorne copies out salutory quotations from a variety of biblical, classical and contemporary sources.

There are contradictory signals about who might be the implied addressee(s) of the manuscript. A prefatory poem addressed to 'yee yowthfull Imps' at the start of the manuscript claims that in the volume, 'yoong yowths, are learned lessons large'. This may suggest that Whythorne initially had some thoughts of preparing the manuscript for print, but the intimate and personal nature of much of the narrative makes publication unlikely. Following the prefatory poem, Whythorne opens his narrative with a direct address to 'My good frend' and claims the manuscript is a gesture of reciprocity:

> Recalling to mynd my promyse made vnto yow, I have heer sent yow the copies of such songs and sonetts, as I have made from tyme to tyme vntill the writing heerof. And becaws that yow did impart vnto mee at owr last being togyther, sum of yowr pryvat and secret affayrs past, & also sum of the secret purposes and entents the which have lyen hidd and byn as it were entombed in yowr hart, I to gratifye yowr good opinion had of me, do now lay open vnto yow the most part of all my pryvatt affayres, and secrets accomplyshed from my childhod vntill the day of the date heerof. (p. 3)[4]

The suggestion of 'pryvat and secret affayrs' and Whythorne's use of explanatory prose narratives recalls Gascoigne's presentation of his verse in *A Hundreth*, and especially his erotic romance, 'The Adventures of Master F.J.'.[5] Similarly, the prefatory poem claiming that in his volume 'yoong yowths, are learned lessons large' may echo Gascoigne's preface addressed to 'al yong Gentlemen' in his 1575 *Posies* in which he expresses the hope that 'yong blouds' reading his volume will learn from example.[6] If Gascoigne is a model, however, Whythorne misses or finds uncongenial the playful game of apparent self-exposure and veiling so characteristic of Gascoigne's miscellany volumes. Gascoigne's preface mocked naively autobiographical readings of verse that '(being written in jeast) have bene mistaken in sad earnest'. Gascoigne pressed home his ridicule of such literal readings, 'laugh not at this (lustie younkers) since the pleasant dittie of the noble Erle of Surrey (beginning thus: *In winters just returne*) was also construed to be made indeed by a Shepeherd.'[7] Inviting just such literal readings, Whythorne tells his friend, that the prose explanations have been provided 'becaws I do thinke it needfull, not onlye to shew yow the caws why I wrote them, but also to open my secret meaning in dyvers of them aswell in words and sentences, as in the hole of the same, lest yow shuld think them to be made to smaller purpose then I did mean' (p. 3). Whythorne takes to an extreme the tendency begun by Tottel's circumstantial titles, to fix the verse as the product of specific occasions.[8] His verses are presented as direct expressions of their author, their worth and truth ultimately authorized by reference to 'secret' intentions which need prose explanations to be known. If Whythorne is following Gascoigne, his model is not the wily poet of the prefaces to the 1575 edition, but the shadowy G.T. of *A Hundreth* who gives H.W. his manuscript of verse by sundry authors, remarking that the poems have some worth and wit 'especially being considered by the very proper occasion whereuppon it was writen (as they themselves [the authors] did alwayes with the verse reherse unto me the cause that moved them to write)'.[9]

In G.T.'s case, as we shall see in Chapter 5, the pretence of explanation is one more in a series of veils that point to inaccessible secrets. In Whythorne's case, explanation is part of a drive towards clarification, everywhere visible in the manuscript. It is not only 'a means of imposing order on a state of mental and emotional turmoil' in Shore's words, but an attempt to fix meaning and thus fix and regulate the self and its shifting identities.[10] The framework of the 'ages of man' that Whythorne announces in his title provides one paradigm for such self-regulation. The 'ages', according to Burrow, envisaged the life of man as 'a series of transits from one distinct age to another', in each of which 'a certain stable set of characteristics would normally appear'.[11] The tension between the notion of a normal 'set of characteristics' somehow naturally belonging to each age, and the need to frame the self to conform to such ideal behaviours and attitudes, is frequently evident in Whythorne's prose and verse. Typically, as we shall see, it is at the point of transition between 'ages' that Whythorne chooses to have a portrait of himself painted (see below, p. 52). The 'ages' paradigm is just one among a number of ideal identities by which, in spite of contradictions and conflicts, Whythorne seeks to frame and explain himself.[12]

'The lẏf of A water spannell'

The self or selves constructed within the pages of Whythorne's 'songs and sonetts' share the contradictory aspirations promoted by the early Elizabethan miscellanists. The manuscript's very title, pointing on the one hand to the songs and sonnets of courtly dalliance and on the other to the moralized three ages of man, indicates Whythorne's sense of the need to perform as a gentleman writer of verse in both courtly and moralizing genres. The tensions of performance on both fronts, visible in most of the mid-century miscellanies in which the moralist shows considerable unease with the suspect passions of the lover, are particularly apparent in Whythorne's narrative. Embarking on his career as a teacher of courtly musical skills (playing on the lute and the virginals) to the daughters of gentry and nobility, he gathers, in good schoolboy fashion, pages of proverbial and aphoristic warnings against the treachery of women (pp. 23–8). So formative in his early years are these gathered sayings that he 'cowld … by no means kontent my self to brook and abẏd in þe servyses of *Cupid* and *Venus*' (p. 22).

His head well-stored and framed with warnings in dispraise of women, Whythorne depicts himself as spending, ironically, most of his career in their company and service. Hired by a nobleman to teach his wife the lute, he finds himself among 'dýverz 3entilwomen, who waited vpon her in her hows, and my lot waz lýwyz to bee her cheef waiting man' (p. 83). Hired by a Privy Counsellor, he has to go to their house in the country to be with the children, his scholars, who were with their mother (p. 86). Over the course of twenty or so years of teaching, Whythorne seems to have been, with only one exception, primarily in the service of the lady of the household.[13] Almost invariably Whythorne's narrative eroticizes his service to his various gentlewomen. Whythorne teaches courtly skills and prides himself on his courtly proficiency in the fashionable modes of music, the writing of verse, and courting skills: 'when tým served to bee in company with women, to talk with þem, to toy with þem, to 3ýb and to 3est with þem, to discoors with þem, and to be mery with þem (all þe which sum do kawll koorting) I kowld yvz þe tým with þem sumwhat aptly and fitly' (p. 33). Whythorne boasts of his proficiency in the mastery of the covert signs and ambiguous messages of elegant courting, singing coded songs, inscribing rings with posies, and leaving billets in chambers. Nevertheless, we are repeatedly assured he is no Cupidian. Whythorne's fascination with courtly arts is accompanied by a deep discomfiture with uncertainty and innuendo. He proves an inept interpreter of others' codes and an eager explainer of his own.

In Whythorne's narratives, women are the employers, the mistresses to whom he owes service, and the sexual predators; they are figures of frightening power and social glamour. Whythorne casts himself in a role familiar to the male miscellanists, that of the manipulated victim of female deceit and inconstancy. His role in the various courting narratives that punctuate his text, is defined by contradictory aspirations and fears. On the one hand the predatory gentlewomen are represented as deeply desirable, widows with large incomes, or sexually experienced courtly ladies, on the other hand, they threaten and offend male autonomy and status. Whythorne's fear of moral and physical contamination is an expression of the threat women seem to pose to the purity and dignity of his identity as a gentleman. The lecherous, he reminds himself, 'do not only bekum beggarz in þe end but also be filled with most horribull, filthy and inkiurabull diseazes, and siurly þe dowt of þe evels þat I miht hạv gotten by þe folloing and keeping kumpany with *Venus* darlings, kawzed mee aswell az þe other kawzes affọrsaid to strýv with fraill natiur very much ... for þat I wold not looz þe lạt liberty & freedom þat I had gotten' (p. 34).

Whythorne's ambivalence towards his gentlewomen employers is well illustrated by his account of his employment in the household of a married lady who had 'bin sum tẏm A koortier' (pp. 93–113). The narrative of this employment begins and ends with lengthy descriptions of the lady's wit and boldness, her sophistication, and her charm. She is, for Whythorne, the very embodiment of courtly knowledge and behaviour:

> shee had A great witt, and A 3oly ready toong to vtter her fantazy and mynd she took pleaziur many tẏms to talk and diskoors of such things az shee by experiens had had sum knowle3 of, az sumtẏms of reli3ions, shee wold argew in matterz of kontroversy in reli3ion. sumtẏms of profan matters. sumtẏms shee wold towch matterz of þe kuntrey, with þe good husbandry & huswẏfrey þerof. sumtẏms shee wold towch þe sytty, with þe tradz of sittizens, and not leav vntowched, þe fynes of þe delikat dams, and þe nẏs wẏvs of þe sitty. sumtẏms shee wold talk of þe koort, with þe bravery, and vanitiez þerof, and of þe krowching and dissimiulasion with þe *bazzios las manos* þat þar iz ywzed by on koortier to an oþer. and sumtẏms shee wold minister talk of þe koorting of ladiez and 3entilwomen by þe gallants, and kavallierz. (p. 93)

Such courtly discourse is for Whythorne a form of coded speech, full of innuendo, challenging his own courtly interpretative skills. He struggles to unravel what the codes may mean for him, and to respond prudently: 'both by wordz and frendly behavor shee seemed þat she wold hav mee to think þat shee bar mee sum goodwill, þe which I mad nomor þen an ordinary akkownt of, bekawz I did perseiv by dyverz means þat shee had A gloriowz head, and þerwithall delyted to hav such az shee lyked of to be in loov with her and to be at her kommaundement' (p. 95).

Whythorne's writing dwells both erotically and anxiously on the intentions of the court lady. Returning from a period away, he finds his chest transferred to a new chamber 'so ny her own chamber az shee miht hav kum from þe on to þe oþer when shee list withowt any suspision' (p. 100). She gives him an exceptionally valuable New Year's Gift, and seems to use a language of innuendo and erotic suggestiveness (for example, pp. 100, 112–13). A friend in London claims to be able to read the signs more clearly than Whythorne: 'Tush man quoþ hee, yee ar but A novis in such kases, ... I did perseiv by her fas, her komplexion, kooler of eyez, and demeanour when I waz at her hows, what her inklẏnasion iz þat way' (p. 111). Whythorne responds with a sermon on the evils of adultery.

Like Elinor in Gascoigne's 'The Adventures of Master F.J.', the court lady embodies the attractions and perils of courting for a socially aspiring, humanist-trained gentleman of modest means. The behaviours associated with the court lady are those of fluency and wit, the graces of mind, of language, and of performance (that Whythorne himself teaches to others), but they are contaminated by all that is implied by the feminine for Whythorne and so many others. Whythorne's continual aphorisms in dispraise of women, 'þei be az slippery az ẏs, and will turn az þe wynd and weþerkok' (p. 23), inculcate a masculine superiority that is founded uneasily on the assumption that women are cleverer than men, more slippery and deceitful, and thus difficult to interpret and control. The attribution to women of greater craft in the manipulation of signs, and the fact that for Whythorne his gentlewomen employers are his social superiors leads to a nefarious combination, well-studied in the more exalted context of Elizabeth's court.[14]

Whythorne's Protestant morality and humanist prudence preserve him from moral contamination in the face of the court lady's attractions. It is, of course, that morality and prudence that mark him as for ever ideologically excluded from and opposed to the Italianate *sprezzatura*, that aristocratic insouciance he so much admires and fears. To become part of the courtliness that fascinates him and whose behaviours he teaches, Whythorne would have to abandon the Protestant–humanist identity to which he clings. The imagined rewards of such abandonment are evident from his account of the court lady with her charm, her easy familiarity with and mastery of the discourses of commerce, politics and relationships, and her exotic, sexualized mystery. But Whythorne cannot abandon his carefully-framed moral self and the lady's secrets must remain forever ungraspable.

Whether due to prudence, or his horror of adultery, or an unwontedly modest sense that his courtly verse is not up to the standard familiar to this experienced woman, the verse Whythorne writes in relation to this episode is not on the whole addressed to the lady, but used instead to bolster Whythorne's moral fibre. The one exception is a verse he sends her when he is away from the house for a period, in which the potentially erotic language of friends, remembrances, and tokens of goodwill, is carefully steered by the dependent Whythorne to remind the lady of her obligations to him as a patron:

> *Remember him þat hath not yow forgot,*
> *ne yowr promẏz owt of remembrans blot,*
> *what tẏm az frendz wold hạv þeir frendz þem mynd,*
> *þen sum konseit for þem þei will owt fynd.* (p. 101)

When some time later, Whythorne claims her 'promyz' to help her 'frend' and asks her to intercede with her husband to obtain a gentle-woman in the household for Whythorne as a wife, she refuses, although she says she will grant anything else he asks. The poem Whythorne writes on this occasion illustrates the way in which his non-courtly verse is often used to fix and control a situation that he finds distressing or perplexing – an attempt to order it into manageable shape through aphorisms or the pattern of metre:[15]

> *Lo. if þe hart doth think þe sam, which now þe toong hath said*
> *of all on lýv. I may þen say, þat I am well apaid.*
> *If kontrary I fynd þe sam, þen piur pasiens parfors,*
> *must bee þe remedy wherwith, to salv my sory kors.* (p. 110)

The patterning of alternatives, 'If ... If kontrary ...', of his happiness 'on lýv' or the misery of 'my sory kors', or the juxtaposing of thinking heart and speaking tongue, in the first quoted line, all provide a patterning, a visible control into which Whythorne's experience can be fitted. Both the verse to the courtly lady and this meditative verse on her refusal of his request, illustrates the close and complex relationship between prose narrative and verse. Whythorne claims the prose exists to explain the verse, laying open the 'secret purposes and entents' (p. 3), but in the moral poems especially, the verse seems to function to clarify and shape the frustrations and confusions of experiences narrated in prose.

The rifts and fissures that threaten Whythorne's attempts to construct a coherent version of himself, open up not only around his competing courtly and moral selves, but also around his sense of his own social status as a gentleman, a tutor of music in private households, and a professional musician. The manuscript constantly returns to the question of his status with an anxious insistence.[16] Whythorne's claim to social status seems primarily based on his education, with an account of which the manuscript begins in preference to details of family or ancestry. On a number of occasions he repeats authorities for the view that true nobility lies in knowledge and virtue, not only in ancestors and lands, and indeed that the gifts of the mind are superior to those of fortune or body (for example, pp. 132 and 177). It is ironic therefore that he continually finds himself, as we have seen, employed as a household servant to assist gentlewomen in bringing up their children '3entilwomen lýk' (p. 97). No doubt the number of misogynist jokes and sayings throughout the manuscript may have much to do with the perceived effeminacy and social stigma of Whythorne's dependent association with women and children. His representation of his relations with female employers (his mistresses) primarily in terms of a covert amorous courtship with them may serve to reassure himself and his 'reader' of his own male potency.

Whythorne particularly relished a period spent in entirely male company in Cambridge as the music tutor to Bromfield's son during his studies there (pp. 114–34). Even there, however, he spends much mental effort and ink on the vexed question of his relative social position *vis-à-vis* Bromfield's Cambridge tutor (pp. 114–18). Characteristically, Whythorne's writing brings his resentments about his social and gendered status into order by means of gathered sayings that simultaneously confirm his low opinion of women and upstart tutors, and impose on himself patience and a properly forgiving mind. The manuscript is a record of Whythorne's repeated painful submission to the approved moral authorities, with his verses frequently marking the achievement of that submission. Falling out with a young 'shrewish' woman on one occasion, he ponders his anger in his manuscript, understands it in terms of his progress through the ages of man, 'so þe hiumour named koler doth cheef rain in þis sekond and last part of þe yoongmans a3' (p. 80), and having found the commonplace into which to put his disruptive emotion, writes himself a verse: '*In weall and wo be pasient | let not fiury þi hart posses*' (p. 81).

Whythorne's efforts to defend his status as a gentleman of education and a master of music seem to get a better hearing on the pages of his manuscript than in the country houses of his employers. Employed by one rich widow 'to bee both her servant and also her skoolmaster', he answers that 'A skoolmaster I did not mislẏk, but to bee A serving kreatiur or serving man, it was so lẏk the lẏf of A water spannell þat must be at kommaundement to fetch or bring heer or karry þar, with all kẏnd of drud3ery, þat I kowld not lẏk of þat lẏf' (p. 37). The uncertain status of the serving-man, required to be both courtier-like and servile, is a recurring theme in the writing of those who, like Whythorne, occupied this role. Thomas Howell's friend John Keeper wrote on the miseries of service in Howell's *Newe Sonets*, and I.M lamented the down classing of service in the 1590s, 'the Seruingmans pleasure, is turned into seruile toyle, and droyling drudgerie'.[17]

Nevertheless Whythorne has to submit because 'I waz behynd hand of my welth' (p. 37). When he subsequently feels mistreated by the widow, he expostulates to the manuscript:

> I for my part seing þat my profession hath bin and iz to teach on of þe sevan sienses liberall, þe which iz also on of þe mathematikall sienses, ... I do think þat þe teacherz þerof (if þei will) may esteem

somuch of þem selvs az to be free and not bownd, much les to be mad slav lyk. (pp. 58–9)

The summit of Whythorne's professional ascent is his appointment as Master of the Chapel to Doctor Parker, Archbishop of Canterbury from 1571 to 1575, an employment that had come to an end due to Parker's death just before the composition of the manuscript. Whythorne prefaces his record of this climactic achievement with a long discourse outlining his carefully worked out scheme for degrees of musicians: doctors, bachelors, and 'miuzisians vnkomenced ... of þe which sort þer hav byn and bee sum þat hav setfoorth az great maestriez in miuzik az ever did any doktor or bachelar of miuzik' (p. 233), among whom he would include himself. Below come singers and at the bottom itinerant minstrels, against whom he tells a scornful jest to distinguish them clearly from such as himself (p. 244).

'To mak my self to be known of many'

The conflict between Whythorne's sense of his own abilities and dignity and the constraints of social inferiority leads directly to his decision to publish his verse with musical settings. At the table of one of his employers, he is subjected to an aggressive verbal attack by a guest, whom Whythorne answers back: 'wee wer lyk to hav had A whot skirmish, but þat owr betterz wer in plas, who took on þem to bee moderatorz between vs' (p. 171). In spite of calling on his stock of sayings and authoritative counsels, this incident, particularly his need to be silent at the command of his superiors, clearly ranckles:

> when I kald to mi remembrans how, when az heer to for at sundry týms I had bin in þe kumpanies of þoz who be wurshipfull, riht wurshipfull, and also honorabull, and saw þat þe meaner sort (in komparizon of þeir estats) wer dryven to put vp quietly sum in3iuriez at þeir hands. also how such things which þe inferiowr sort eiþer said or did in þe prezens of þeir greatterz or betterz, waz but to bee allowd of az it pleazed þeir siuperiors to tak it [... here he rehearses a saying by the apocryphal Jesus Sirach] Þez with many oþer perswazions ... learned mee þat I shiuld not keep kumpany with my greatterz. (p. 172)

Having distilled this lesson in a verse, Whythorne looks more broadly back over his career, 'how I had bin many týms in hop of prosperite, and þen prezently owt of sekiurite, and þe tost from post to piller, now vp, now down, by þe illliuzions of flattering & fikkl fortewn' (p. 173), and makes a 'sonett' on the theme of the mean estate:

> *Till tým had tawht mee how to 3u3 of lat*
> *I did but dream þe siur and quiet stat*
> *at first I thouht þe simplest lýf did best*
> *but seing þat mad A thrall unto þe rest*
> *I chain3ed mýnd to 3u3 þe best of powr*
> *On whom knoing þat hi dizdain did lowr*
> *I turned my sentens and dekreed*
> *þe mean (with mýnd kontent) þe best whoz seed*
> > *Yeeldz raþer sweet þen sowr.* (p. 173)

Praise of the 'mean estate', so popular with the gentlemanly poets of *Tottel's Miscellany*, acquires new meaning when used by someone like Whythorne, whose 'mean' estate is no literary fancy, but a state of financial and prudent balancing, beyond the ken of a Wyatt or a Surrey.[18]

As a result of his humiliating experience at his hosts' table, Whythorne decides to 'gýv my self wholy to þe profession' of music and publish his verse and settings to 'mak my self to be known of many in þe shortest tým þat miht bee' (p. 173). The decision to publish his verse and music and perhaps to win himself a reputation for his music, may be a form of independent self-assertion and self-presentation, at least partially outside the patronage system. It is notable that when he considers the prefatory material for his book, Whythorne acknowledges that some dedicate their books 'to men and women of hy honour or of wurship' (p. 177), but does not follow their lead.

Whythorne's account of the preparation of his 1571 *Songes* indicates that he saw the volume and its verses as intimately related to himself. Such self-display through the medium of print both attracts and terrifies Whythorne. Meditating on the evils of women, he particularly associated them with the inability to keep secrets (p. 29). Now Whythorne finds himself contemplating 'blabbing forth' his own secret self to anyone with the money to buy the book:

> do I not daily see how þei who do set owt books, be bi þeir wurks mad
> A kommen gaz vnto all þe world? and hang vpon þe blasts of all folks
> mowths, and vpon þe middl finger pointings of þe vnskilful and also
> vpon þe sever 3ud3ments of þe grav and deep wits. ... þe fourm of þeir
> bodies ar not seen to be better set foorth in A glas þen in and by þeir

speech, so þat þerby þe som of þe fond affeksions of þeir myndz be setfoorth and displaid. (p. 174)

Whythorne's terror of a secret and shameful self that might be revealed fights it out in his prose with the humanist Thomas Whythorne gentleman, the end-product of years of labour and discipline, an object to be displayed with pride. In order to control how readers might approach his songs, he carefully frames a version of himself to stand in the frontispiece:

and bekawz þat þe ywzerz of þos books shiuld see þat az in þe beginning of þem I do ad vnto my nam þe týtl of A 3entilman, so I mean to shew my self to be on azwell in þe owtward marks, az in þe inward man ... þerfor I will set with my kownterfet such armes, az I hav fownd to be left vnto mee by my poor Aunseterz ... A remembrans þat I am az free A man born both by faþer and moþers sýd, az hee þat mai dispend thowzandz of powndz, of yeerly inheritans. (p. 211)

The book's 'kownterfet' (frontispiece portrait) will display his gentlemanly appearance, his arms display his social status, while his songs show the inward man, the cultivated inner self that confirms the outward appearance. The volume represents a perfected work of self-fashioning in which every sign has been censured and ordered.

Whythorne's fascination with his own image in the eyes of others is apparent in the numerous occasions on which he has his portrait painted. As a young man, his first act on acquiring independence and his own chamber in London is to have a portrait of himself playing on a lute painted in a pair of virginals with the admonitory verses:

> Þe pleaziurz þat I tak
> Now in my yowthfull yeerz
> Þe sam shall mee forsak
> When hoery a3 appeerz (p. 20)

Ostensibly, it is as *momenti mori*, reminders of his steady progress through the ages of man, that Whythorne's subsequent portraits are also made (pp. 49 and 133–4). However, his minute concern with the detail and the effect of his portraits, as we saw in my Introduction (pp. 7–8 above) suggests that his interest goes beyond that of a salutary reminder of the passing of time, and that he has thought long and carefully about the purpose of a portrait. A mirror reflection will not do because it does not show a man how he looks to others, and it captures only a transitory reflection: 'so soon az hee looketh of from þe glas hee forgetteth þe dispozision and gras of hiz fas' (p. 134). The painting delivers a permanent image that will record his achieved self at the stage at which it is made, whether in the 'first part of þe yoong mans a3' (p. 20), after the first intimations of mortality with a bout of ague when the second portrait is made (p. 49), or when 'growing toward þe a3 of forty, at þe which yeerz begins þe first part of þe old mans a3' when his third portrait is made (p. 135).

The painted 'kownterfetts' have the same function for Whythorne as his printed *Songes*, and indeed his aphoristic verse; they fix the transient disorder of experience into ordered and memorizable patterns. Once made permanent in colours, the portrait acts as a wise saying or an epigrammatic verse, something that objectifies the inner man in a speaking picture that the onlooker can then read and use to frame him self. Whythorne's sense of himself as both author of whom he is and what he writes, and at the same time part of a process of inheritance and expectation in which each generation is framed by the values and models that went before, is poignantly expressed in terms of offspring:

> þe books with þe miuzik in þem shiuld bee, az my childern, bekawz þei konteined þat which my hed brouht foorth ... Also bekawz þei shiuld bear my nam, I kowld do no les þen sett in evry on of þem, þeir faþerz piktiur or kounterfet, to reprezent vnto þoz who shiuld ywz þe childern, þe form and favor of þeir parent. (p. 211)

The manuscript autobiography in which he explains the occasions of all his own carefully preserved verses, from the merest graffiti scribbled on a wall in Rome to his own version of Psalm 86 presented to Archbishop Parker, is a product of Whythorne's double desire to record what has been achieved in the framing of self and verse in often adverse circumstances, and the need to control and fix, for his own satisfaction at least, the significance of what he has done and written. Everywhere evident in his writing is a deep anxiety about the anarchic power of language to escape authorial control and reveal more secrets than it should: 'Befor þat wordz be spoken, þe speker of þem hath þem at hiz own will to rewl but if þey be ons spoken befor witnes, þen iz hee no mor þe master of þem' (p. 62). The occasion of this reflection is the indiscretion of a drunken Dutch friend, for whom Whythorne helpfully writes a verse on the theme '*of wordz tak heed*' (p. 62).

The manuscript is a testimony to Whythorne's untiring efforts to form himself on the best models and eschew idleness. It is a record of virtuous 'travail' with all that word's connotations of pain and suffering as well as hard labour (see p. 57 below). For all his admiration for the courtly arts, Whythorne's representation of his own self-formation and verse writing is not that of the aristocratic courtier defined by Castiglione, whose art 'appeareth not to be arte, neither ought a man to put more diligence in any thing than in covering it'.[19] Whythorne admires his first master, the court poet and musician John Heywood, for the sheer quantity of effort that had gone into his verse:

> *If all hiz Rithms, wer set togẏþer now*
> *No English po'et somuch þis day kan show*
> *Az hee, in sort, az hee þe sam hath doon*
> *Az from hiz brain, and not from elswher woon.* (p. 17)

Idleness, 'þe root or moþer of all sin' (p. 104), must be guarded against, and copying and meditating on sayings and proverbs are, for Whythorne, strong bulwarks. To this way of thinking, it is honest effort that is worthwhile, not the aristocratic gestures of effortlessness:

> not to lẏv az dronz and katerpillerz, þat lẏv altogyþer vpon þe swet of oþerz browz. ... wee ouht not to hẏd owr talents vnder þe ground az þe unprofitabull servant did, lest wee be fownd frewtles figtreez, and so kalled to akkount for owr bailiwiks. (p. 176)

The manuscript serves Whythorne somewhat as the boxes and ledgers into which he puts all his transactions when in 1562–3 he acts as the London agent for William Bromfield, Lieutenant-General of the Ordinance, away serving in Le Havre. Fearing Bromfield's imminent death might cause him to be called to account:

> I sorted my wrytings and layd evry sort by þem selvz in severall boxes, in my kownting hows or desk mad for þe purpoz. to þe end þat when I shiuld be kalled to mẏn akkownt I miht þe redilier fẏnd þem. (p. 143)

Ordering, clarifying, producing the written evidence of effort, these are all, for Whythorne, visible signs to himself and others of active virtue and of the laudable labour of framing oneself to conform to the best models, whether biblical, humanist or courtly, however internally inconsistent such models might sometimes prove to be.

Whythorne's uncertainties and strenuous submissions to ordered commonplaces exist in the manuscript alongside a continual self-assertion.
The manuscript is the record of his achievements, carefully composed and
gathered over a lifetime. Although there is no evidence that the manuscript was ever intended for publication, or to be read by anyone other
than Whythorne himself, and possibly his unnamed 'frend', nevertheless
it is prepared with extraordinary care and thought. It has, as we have seen,
a prefatory poem, and it is written throughout in Whythorne's carefully
worked out orthography, a system that he considers rational and which,
like every other aspect of his life is both idiosyncratic and framed out of
existing authorities (pp. 4–6). Reviewing the slow selling pace of his 1571
Songes, a thoroughly innovative enterprise as this publication was the first
set of part songs printed in England, Whythorne suggests to his printer
that it would sell better if he brought out yet another book containing the
full text of the songs.[20] Whythorne is proud of his achievements, and his
ordered, and on the whole, virtuous self is narrated through the ages of
his life with as much satisfaction and sense of personal worth as he man-
ifests when contemplating his engraven image, with its coat of arms, at
the head of his published *Songes*: 'az ... I do ad vnto my nam þe tŷtl of A
3entilman, so I mean to shew my self to be on azwell in þe owtward
marks, az in þe inward man' (p. 211).

Nevertheless the uncertainties remain, in spite of the strenuous effort
with which Whythorne strives to contain them within his store of commonplaces and counsels. His account of his service to Bromfield is particularly revealing in this respect. It ends with Bromfield's sudden death
which deprives Whythorne not only of a place of some estimation in the
male world of London merchants, but of the promise of an annuity which
would have rendered him independent of his life of service in households. His work as Bromfield's deputy seems to have given Whythorne
much satisfaction, bringing him 'in þe kompaniez not only of þe cheefest
of þoz who did depend on þe sam offis þat my frend did, but also of
dyverz of þe wurshipfull marchaunts of London' with affairs in Russia,
Africa and the New World (p. 138). Whythorne's satisfaction is, however, lessened by unease at the morality of this world:

> I miht hear sumtŷmz & perseiv also þat all waz not gold þat glistered
> in hiz siht, neiþer evry on hiz frend þat bar him A frendly kountenans
> when hee waz in England ... þen quoþ I to my self, what hap hav
> I? ... peradventiur þoh I do know nothing of hiz doings þat way, I may
> be mad to smell of þe smok of þat fier wherwith my frend iz lŷk to be
> sin3ed and trŷd. (p. 137)

Whythorne's unease becomes 'desperasion' as the news arrives of Bromfield's imminent death and finally, the coming of the plague to London where Whythorne is trapped by his duties in Bromfield's affairs. Faced with the imminent possibility of death Whythorne wrestles with despair in a scenario familiar to many other Protestants facing death and judgement: 'so þat now þe fear of death did greatly trobull mee, and I being at þat prezent much vnquieted with so many krosses at ons, began to enter into þe 3iu3ment of mўn own konsiens' (p. 145). Protestants were thoroughly familiar with preparation for death and judgement and the biblical consolations that could be called upon.[21] Whythorne copies out a sermon into his manuscript 'to rehers vnto yow sumwhat of þat which I did read' (p. 145). He then copies out numerous biblical passages such as the warning that he understand his desperation as the work of 'owr old enemi þe Divll' (p. 141). Finally having 'kollekted and written all þez forsaid sentenzes to gўþer' he makes a metrical paraphrase of Psalm 51, one of the five penitential psalms, *'O good Lord hạu mersi on mee'* (p. 151). In the course of this narrative, we move from Whythorne's first-person fear and 'trobull' to the collective 'wee' as he seeks to frame himself to the standard consolations and submissions. The final 'I' of the psalm paraphrase is that of the voice of David, and with him all penitential sinners, whose voice and point of view have now been internalized in Whythorne himself. The discipline of framing is to cast off the difference of the 'I' and be absorbed into the collective, ordered 'we'.

Whythorne's manuscript is, however, all about the 'I' which in spite of innumerable submissions and orderings, persistently reasserts its plaintive voice: 'þen quoþ I to my self, what hap hạv I?' It is the persistent self-assertion of Whythorne's 'I', its refusal to be absorbed into the generalized patterns and remedies of 'we' or 'he that', and thus quietened, that drives the manuscript's narratives forward from one dilemma to the next. Each time the disorderly 'I' seems to be absorbed into a satisfactorily ordered verse, it reasserts its insatiable difference in the next episode. The narratives Whythorne tells, for all their strenuous efforts to conform to prestigious patterns, do not fit the commonplaces. Contrary to 'owr old proverb ... which saith. Þis world iz but A skaffold for vs to plai owr kommediz and tra3ediz vpon' (p. 210), the story Whythorne wishes to tell is one of virtuous effort rewarded in this world, and of the dignity and 'wurship' that should accompany a lifetime of careful moral and intellectual schooling. Whythorne records his uncle's counsel as he sets out on his career that, as his parents could not leave him enough to 'lўv idelly and at eaz', then he must 'ply yowr learning so az yow may lýv þerby' (p. 12), which, in characteristic fashion, he encapsulates in a verse:

> *Pithagoras (I read) doth also say*
> *Þat when A man iz entred on þe way*
> *Past þe first brunt, and ek difficulty*
> *Of Vertewz, þen, all after be eazy.* (p. 18)

Finding himself entering into the first part of the old man's age, without a wife or children (apart from his five part song books), with only a chamber in London of his own, with no annuities or settled income, and broken in health, Whythorne's narrative of his life in fact seems to tell of the way in which humanist virtue and godly piety are repeatedly thwarted by the aberrant outcomes of a disorderly world in which wealth takes precedence over worth, in which vain women have authority over chaste men, and in which inner integrity is persistently subject to misinterpretation or indifference.

As we have seen, Whythorne's manuscript account of his life records double and conflicting achievements; on the one hand repeated submissions to authoritative commonplaces, on the other authorial self-assertion of himself as an individual of worth and dignity. Whythorne's career narrative is unusual in terms of its length, its private manuscript form, and the fact that it is written in prose. Printed career narratives in verse, however, constitute a popular genre written by most of the poets of the 1560s and 1570s. These secular narratives of aspiration and frustration, asserting the persistent difference of an authorial 'I', unable to settle among collective pronouns, will be the matter of my next chapter.

3
Narratives of experience

In Chapter 1, I argued that the appropriation of socially elite verse by the single-author miscellanists who wished to advertise their skills in print, subtly altered the significance of the verse they imitated. Among the many contradictions implicit in their careful mixing of courtly and aphoristic verses was that between the implied writer of courtly verse, for whom insouciance and effortlessness (*sprezzatura*) were crucial effects, and the writer of aphoristic verse whose effort and prudence were distinguishing characteristics. In this chapter, I examine verse in which the self-production of the writer as a man of enterprise and 'travail' becomes central. The poets' 'travail' encompasses both hard and painful labour (*OED* 'travail') and, as we shall see later in the chapter, actual travel abroad, as soldiers, factors or agents (*OED* 'travel'). Through such verse the writer characteristically presents himself as both deserving and unfortunate. Like Whythorne, others found that even after the 'first brunt, and ek difficulty | Of Vertewz' all did not become easy as the precepts suggested should happen (see p. 56 above). Enterprise is often associated with failure to thrive in these verses; an ideology of effort accompanies a reiterated sense of the self as marginal to, and excluded from success, power, and privilege.

The mean estate

A favourite topic for amplification and variation in *Tottel's Miscellany* is 'the mean estate', that is, a middling social position neither too prominent nor too lowly (*OED* 'mean'a.^{2}.5).[1] Such poems, when written by socially and politically prominent courtiers such as Wyatt or Surrey, become gestures of political wisdom. The poem printed as 'Stond who so list vpon the slipper whele | Of hye astate' by Tottel, for example, was probably written by Wyatt on the occasion of the execution of his patron, Cromwell and signals lessons learned by a chastened climber.[2] For the single-author miscellanists who had some personal experience of what a mean estate might be like (*OED* 'mean' a.[1].2 = inferior, badly off, abject), the theme held fewer attractions. The narratives of personal failure to thrive that they wished to tell rarely bore out the truisms about contented sufficiency recycled from Horace and Martial by Wyatt, Surrey, and the rest. Thomas Howell, for example, disdainfully rejects the ideal of the contented 'mean estate' as fit only for those who know no better:

> ... a man from byrth brought vp,
> In meane estate that neuer knew, the taste of wanton cup,
>   Doth holde himselfe so well contente, with his degree,
> That he in life doth seldome seeke to craue more greater fee.
>   But I as byrde vnlike, that flew hir timely flight,
> Throughout the groues and fertill fielde, in ioyes and great delight,
>   Which shall no sooner feele hir selfe, to be restrainde,
> From her such wonted libertie, as some time she retainde:
>   But forth withal she doth, such inwarde thought conceaue,
> That yelding up hir pleasures past, hir life therewith doth leaue.[3]

For Howell, the 'mean estate' signifies a lowly, reduced estate, and he is eager to make clear that he is used, like the bird, to 'wonted libertie'. The term no doubt has resonances of the 'fredome' that Surrey claimed was an inseparable part of the self-determination of the aristocratic mind, or the 'liberty' that Wyatt claimed was his although confined on his estate in Kent.[4]

Howell's new situation in life may well have been, as we have seen, one of service (see p. 18 above). Like Whythorne, he seems to have had reservations about the role of a gentleman's, or even worse, a gentlewoman's serving-man. Even the anonymous writer of *A Health to the Gentlemanly Profession of Serving-Men* (1598), ostensibly defending the calling of a serving-man, mocked attendance on a mistress, who riding abroad 'must haue. vi. or viii. seruingmen to attende her, ... one to carrie her Cloake and Hood, least it raine, an other her Fanne' and so on.[5] Howell's *Newe Sonets and Pretie Pamphlets* (c.1567) has verse that worries about the freedom, manliness, and prospects of preferment, of service.[6] It is as well that he could not have read Thomas Churchyard's disparaging contrast between serving-men, who follow the heels of their master and are well rewarded for such servility, with honest soldiers who 'knewe not how to flatter and faune, or crouche and coursie for commoditie' and yet are allowed to fall into neglect:

> Suche as serues at home, and can not goe out of the vewe of a faire
> house, and Smoke of a foule Chimney, snatcheth vp good tournes,
> and steales awaie preferment priuilie. [7]

The potential unmanliness of a mean estate that entailed loss of gentlemanly liberty is compounded in Howell's volume by the unmanliness
of complaint and despair. His friend John Keeper bracingly tells Howell
after the latter's opening 'autobiographical' complaint on his 'great
mishappes', to 'rise from couch ... Haue stronger hart then simple Birdes
on tree, I Let manly corps, a manly minde embrace' (pp. 119–20). Howell
needed to complain of his lot as part of a strategy to establish himself as
a born gentleman, the victim of undeserved social misfortune. However
the very act of complaining brings its own threats to his status. The
stance of powerlessness inherent in complaint taints Howell's medium
with a feared effeminacy.

If Howell's complaint reinterprets the 'mean' estate as a life of service
and the loss of gentlemanly freedom, Thomas Tusser's verse, by contrast,
cheerfully presents his own mean estate as a subject for imitation in his
extremely popular versified tract *A hundredth goode pointes of husbandrie*
(first printed by Tottel in 1557). 'The Authors Life' was first appended to
the second edition of 1570.[8] Tusser's 'miscellany' is designed to encourage householders in the crafts of the 'mean' estate, the honest labour of
the resourceful man cultivating his farm and family:[9]

> A competent living, and honestly had,
>   makes such as are godlie both thankfull and glad:
> Life never contented, with honest estate,
>   lamented is oft, and repented too late. (p. 15)

While Tusser shapes his advice to reinforce godly humanist commonplaces of the mean estate, the need for prudence, and dutiful labour,
he is eager to authenticate the very detailed practical advice he gives to
husbandmen and housewives about wood-felling and sheep-shearing,
candle-making and sowing, as the fruit of his own hard-earned experience,
much of it gained from his own mistakes:

> By practise and ill speeding,
> these lessons had their breeding,
> and not by hearsaie, or reeding. (p. 5)

It is this 'ill-speeding' that becomes the theme of 'The Authors Life'. The poem shifts between contentment with a mean estate, an ideology of self-help and resourcefulness, and a tale of misfortune and stoic resignation. It begins with the claim that the poet lives contented with his lot 'as Bee in hive' (p. 202), but the narrative tells a tale, characteristic of the career narratives we shall consider, of the writer as someone without a fixed place in society, on the intersection between a range of possible roles and identities none of which quite fit. Tusser claims to be 'Of linage good, of gentle blood' (p. 202), although a younger son (p. 210). At an early age he is sent across the country from his native Essex to become a singing scholar at the collegiate church at Wallingford. This proves a painful experience but it begins a promising musical career that takes him to St. Paul's, then to Eton school where he is well beaten by Nicholas Udall, and from thence to Trinity College, Cambridge. There, among 'learned men' he feels in heaven until sickness makes him 'glad | To leave my booke' (p. 204). His talents as a singing man gain him a place in Lord Paget's household at Court where he spends ten years. Tusser knows that the Court is a topic for moral warning, but he wants to offend no one, so his poem characteristically faces both ways with two stanzas whose morals are pointed by marginal notes: '*The vices of the Court*' followed by '*The court commended*' (pp. 204–5).

In confirmation of its proverbial uncertainty, the Court eventually 'frowns' on Tusser and he has to start a career anew, this time with a wife and a farm in Suffolk:

> There was I faine my selfe to traine,
> To learne too long the fermers song,
> For hope of pelfe, like worldly elfe,
>   to moile and toile. (p. 205)

Tusser's narrative is typical in its listing of a succession of attempts to thrive, none of which succeeds. Tusser's own experience as a farmer scarcely bears out the up-beat, self-help ethos of the volume in which it is embedded:

> To carke and care, and ever bare,
> With losse and paine, to little gaine,
> All this to have, to cram sir knave,
>   what life it is. (p. 205)

There is a succession of rented farms of ever diminishing returns, until Tusser finds protection from the Dean of Norwich, perhaps gaining a living again as a singing man. However, sickness again forces him 'Away to flie, or else to die, I To seeke more helth, to seeke more welth' (p. 208). He returns to husbandry, this time as the collector of tithes for a parson, but this yields little and is anyway dependent on the uncertain life of his employer. The 1570 edition ended with Tusser in London, indefatigably attempting to make poetic capital and avoid offence at the same time, with a stanza in which '*London [is] commended*' and another on the dangers of unthriftiness (p. 209). The 1574 edition adds a further step in Tusser's career with the plague causing him to quit London to take refuge again in Trinity College, Cambridge, apparently turning to his 'courtly gifts' and his music.

Concluding his account of his life, Tusser turns to moral commonplaces. The marginal note indicates '*A true lesson*' against a stanza that teaches 'In world is set, ynough to get'. How to get enough is less clear: some by learning, some as sailors, some as farmers, some by wiving (p. 210). Those who are brought up strictly 'with knowledge wraught' live 'to shift and shove, I among the best' whereas those with indulgent Dads are likely 'to beg in age, I Or else to fetch a Tiburne stretch' (p. 210). Tusser might have reflected, at this point, that his own hard childhood, being beaten into knowledge at Wallingford and Eton, had scarcely taught him 'ynough to get' either by learning, farming, or wiving, but instead had brought him close to beggary.[10] Certainly the lesson of resignation in the face of an uncertain world with which he ends the poem offers a more appropriate moralization of his narrative:

> When all is done, lerne this my sonne,
> Not friend, nor skill, nor wit at will,
> Nor ship nor clod, but onelie God,
>   doth all in all:
> Man taketh paine, God giveth gaine,
> Man doth his best, God doth the rest,
> Man well intendes, God foizon sendes,
>   else want he shall. (p. 211)

The contrast between this placid conclusion and 'The Author's Life' that precedes it, a narrative of man taking pain and doing his best with little sign of God's 'foizon', encapsulates the contradictions that run throughout Tusser's volume and, to some extent, the other narratives of 'travail' and failure to thrive that I examine in this chapter, and that we also found in Whythorne's autobiographical narrative. On the one hand, the writers strive to frame themselves as properly submissive to the protestant and humanist ideologies of discipline and effort that should bring reward, and on the other, their narratives construct their writers as men unjustly afflicted and unrewarded.

'Pitie the tale of me'[11]

George Whetstone tells us in his prose tract, *A Touchstone for the Time* (1584), that he figured himself as hero of a sequence of poems printed at the end of his verse miscellany *The Rocke of Regard* in 1576:

> No man was euer assaulted with a more dangerous strategeme of cosonage than my self, with which my life & liuing was hardly beset. No man has more cause to thanke God for a free deliuery than my self, nor anie man euer sawe, more suddaine vengeance inflicted vpon his aduersaries, than I my selfe of mine: as liuely appeareth in the ende of my booke intituled *The rocke of regarde*, imprinted many yeares past.[12]

The sequence to which he refers, 'Inventions of P. Plasmos touching his hap and hard fortune' is a series of alternating prose and short poems in which prose by 'The Reporter' comments on and provides a narrative context for, the lyric 'inventions' of P. Plasmos. *The Rocke of Regard* is greatly indebted to Gascoigne's *The Posies* of 1575, and imitates strategies used by Gascoigne in his sequence 'Dan Bartholmew of Bathe' in which the complaints of Dan Bartholmew are interspersed with verse narrative and commentary by a 'Reporter'. In Whetstone's case, 'The Reporter' comments on a narrative of the seduction, entrapment and impoverishment of the young man, P. Plasmos.

Plasmos's narrative is an entirely unremarkable account of a prodigal reformed with little to suggest that the protagonist is anything other than an exemplary figure. Nevertheless, two details suggest to the reader that something more than an entirely fictional narrative is being told. At one point 'The Reporter' coyly demurs from naming some of those who cause Plasmos's downfall: 'whose names and doings, for that it was supposed some of them were alive, according to my commission, I have lefte unreported' (p. 298). A more intriguing detail concerns a wound to Plasmos's hand got in a brawl, a detail entirely marginal to the narrative, but which produces a poem 'P. Plasmos to his Mishap' (pp. 286–91) in which the wound comes to symbolize the self-destructiveness of the speaker's misspent youth, the betrayals of trust by both his mistress and his supposed friend, and the loss of his inherited lands.

Readers of *The Rocke of Regard* would have recognized the wounded hand as a detail explicitly connected with Whetstone himself in another poem in the collection, 'A breife discourse of the discommodities of quarrelling'. There the maimed hand, apparently Whetstone's own, serves to authorize the moral of the poem by personal experience (p. 223). In 'Inventions of P. Plasmos', the detail of the wounded hand associates the prodigal youth with apparently autobiographical aspects of Whetstone himself, but an authorial voice may also be heard in the comments of 'The Reporter' who in plain prose reflects on the lyric outbursts of the unstable truant. Platitudinous in theme the 'Inventions' may be, but the sequence constructs a complex relationship between author and personae, and between moral paradigms and autobiographical incident. The subjective lyric voice of personal, if erring, experience, is given space alongside the moralizing prose of an older and wiser Whetstone. Such doubling of the authorial voice to give simultaneous expression to both youthful passion and sober commentary anticipates, in spite of its lumbering verse, the relationship between Sidney and Astrophil.

The 'maimed hand' is an easily overlooked sign that 'Inventions of P. Plasmos' may be read autobiographically. The conventional prodigal topos is appropriated by the addition of an idiosyncratic detail to produce a narrative that the writer claims as his own story. In such a case, an autobiographical 'I' is scarcely distinguishable from the exemplary 'I' of a type. Easy slippage between the exemplary and the potentially autobiographical is particularly evident in a group of poems that use the conceit of a farewell to the world, or its variation, the last will and testament. Whetstone uses this conceit for another of his failure to thrive narratives: 'The honest minded mans adventures, his largesse, and his farewell to the world; a worke discovering the subtilties of all sortes of men', also printed in *The Rocke of Regard* in 1576 (p. 186). In this, the first-person speaker, 'a crooked peece with withered age forworne' reviews the narrative of a life of failure to thrive, from disillusionment at Court, to unrewarded soldiering, and, finally, to farming which turns him into a beggar. As it is probable that Whetstone was in his twenties when he wrote this piece, and since he claimed at the time of his publication of *The Honorable reputation of a Souldier* in 1585, that he had no experience of martial service, the apparently autobiographical effect of the poem is entirely spurious.[13] Nevertheless, the rhetorical strategy of the poem in which an exemplary first-person voice of experience authorizes, through personal witness, the truisms the poem rehearses, illustrates the way in which the first-person voice of moralizing experience creates a template within which autobiographical narratives may be developed.

The farewell to the world format proved particularly useful for early Elizabethan poets who wished to tell tales of personal economic and social misfortune in a way that represented the self as victim, and that mitigated elements of protest and complaint within the poem by pretending that the complainer was on his/her deathbed and therefore no real threat. Lorna Hutson has described a popular tradition of mock wills and testaments 'in which unreliable travellers or dying festival fools expose the madness and hypocrisy of "things as they are" in the real world'.[14] While satire and mocking wit are certainly present in the last wills and testaments produced by the early Elizabethan miscellanists, they also introduce, through a real or spurious autobiographical reference, an element of staged pathos and self-pity.

We saw in Chapter 1 that the last farewell conceit is used with particular wit by Isabella Whitney to dramatize her failure to thrive in London: '*The Aucthour (though loth to leave the Citie) upon her Friendes procurement, is constrained to departe: wherfore (she fayneth as she would die) and maketh her WYLL and Testament, as foloweth.*'[15] Whereas Tusser, and Whetstone's 'honest minded man', could move between a number of roles in the public world – musician, farmer, client, husband – Whitney, as a single woman of small means, represents herself as having no substance at all. She leaves the public streets and commerce of London, as she found them, untouched by her presence:

> I M[e]rcers leave, with silke so rich,
> as any would desyre.
> In Cheape of them, they store shal finde
> and likewise in that streete:
> I Goldsmithes leave, with Juels such,
> as are for Ladies meete. (p. 20)

The only trace of Whitney's presence in London is her own writing:

> To all the Bookebinders by Paulles
> because I lyke their Arte:
> They e[ver]y weeke shal mony have
> when they from Bookes departe.
> Amongst them all, my Printer must
> have somwhat to his share:
> I wyll my Friends these Bookes to bye
> of him, with other ware. (pp. 24–5)

The extraordinary detail, however casually thrown off, that Whitney, a woman, has a printer and urges her 'Friends' (presumably not the same ones who are procuring her departure from London) to buy her own books at his shop, helps to undermine the conceit of her last will and testament as an act of self-effacement:

> And let me haue a shrowding Sheete
> to cover mee from shame:
> And in oblivyon bury mee
> and never more mee name. (p. 26)

The paradoxical self-negation and self-assertion inherent in autobiographical uses of the last farewell format, is wittily exploited by Whitney. Her ostensibly modest, female self-effacement is rendered deeply ironic by her act of placing it in a poem which explicitly dramatizes the author's own circumstances and gender, published in a volume of secular lyric poems written by a woman in her own name (or at least under her own initials, Is.W.), an unprecedented event in England in 1572. Her poem is a graceful complaint against the economic and social circumstances that force her to abandon the relative freedom of her life in London (perhaps, like her sisters, that of domestic service), where she has been able to explore the streets and publish her poems, to the domestic constrictions of a return to her 'friends' and guardians in the country. Her trajectory exactly reverses the complaint of Howell. For a woman, home seems more of a cage than does a position of service in London.

Where Whitney exploits her economic and social marginality through the conceit of the last farewell, to construct a vivid version of her life in London, signed with her own initials, Gascoigne, that most chameleon of writers, plays, in his most recent editor's words, a game of 'autobiographical hide and go seek' with a number of personae who claim to be quitting the world and its pleasures. The narrative sequence of the unfortunate Dan Bartholmew, imitated by Whetstone in 'P. Plasmos', builds up to 'His last will and Testament', but Dan Bartholmew's hopes revive and he finds a new lease of life. Dan Bartholmew is close kin, his 'owne Fathers Sisters brothers Sonne' we are told, to another Gascoigne persona, the Green Knight, whose 'farewell to Fansie' is one of a sequence of Green Knight poems, '*The fruite of Fetters*', first printed in *The Posies* in 1575.[16] Gascoigne identifies himself as 'the Greene knight' in his explicitly autobiographical poem, 'Dulce Bellum inexpertis', also in the 1575 *Posies*.[17] Not only may Gascoigne be glimpsed in the Green Knight, but, like the 'Dan Bartholmew' sequence, the narrative of *'The fruite of Fetters'* is split between the Green Knight and 'the Author', providing yet another voice for Gascoigne himself. While mocking, in the preface *'to al yong Gentlemen'*, the 'childish skill' of readers who, unable to understand verses figuratively, naively assume the speaker is the poet, Gascoigne clearly delights in exploiting the ambiguous possibilities of the first person in order to tell tales of misfortune and betrayal that may or may not be stories about himself. The Green Knight makes his *'farewell to Fansie'*, listing a familiar sequence of failed trades: courtiership, farming, hunting, poetry, music, fruit-growing, and finally soldiering (pp. 452–3). All his projects are 'harebrayndly' produced, irrational attempts at success in an unsympathetic world in which the only rational demeanour is philosophy and patience. Through his 'autobiographical hide and go seek', Gascoigne is able both to claim and disclaim as his own the Green Knight's misfortunes and his naïve, aspiring optimism. He thus taps our sympathy for himself as possible subject while also positioning himself as 'the Author', who mocks the gullibility and self-deceptions of his subject.

In his best-known tale of a failed career, Gascoigne invests the speaker with his own name. *'Gascoignes wodmanship written to the L. Grey of wilton'* was printed in the 1573 *A Hundreth Sundrie Flowres*. Some of the topoi of this poem are by now familiar from other failure to thrive narratives, such as those by Tusser, Whetstone, Whitney, and Gascoigne's own Green Knight. Typical is the sense of social displacement, and, in the case of the male writers, the attempts at a series of careers, including, in Gascoigne's case, the law, courtiership, and soldiering. Typically, again, none provides 'the meane which may the man mainteine' (p. 398). As with the other failure to thrive narratives we have considered, a tale of the self as economically powerless and unfortunate is used, paradoxically, to construct the writing self as a figure of moral and intellectual strength; instructed by experience, the writer casts himself as our wise guide.

Gascoigne's poem is a particularly complex and sinuous example of the 'failure to thrive' genre. A prose introduction by G.T., the putative editor of *A Hundreth*, alerts the reader to a precise social occasion:

> *The sayde Lord Grey delighting (amongst many other good qualities) in chusing of his winter deare, and killing the same with his bowe, did furnishe master Gascoigne with a crossebowe cum Pertinenciis, and vouchsafed to use his company in the said exercise, calling him one of his wodmen. Now master Gascoigne shooting very often, could neuer hitte any*

deare, yea and often times he let the heard passe by as though he had not
seene them. Whereat ... this noble Lord tooke some pastime. (p. 312)

The occasion is precisely calculated. Hunting was a noble pastime and
thus places Gascoigne, since he is invited to hunt, on the edges of a
social elite. But Gascoigne is a bad hunter, either missing because he
'stands amased like a sot' (l. 3), or likely to hit a 'carren' doe, that is, a
nursing deer, rather than one of the more desirable 'barren' does.[18]
Gascoigne thus places himself on a lower rung than the aristocrats
for whom natural prowess in the sport is a sign of 'masculine aristocratic
virtue'.[19] Given a joke on the sexual chase often present in verse
on hunting deer in this period, it is possible Gascoigne's rueful anticipation of getting a deer already encumbered with offspring may be a self-
mocking allusion to his notorious marriage to the widow Elizabeth
Bacon Breton.[20]

Gascoigne at first deflects his shortcomings of class and masculine
prowess evident in his hunting failures by adopting the comic persona
of a kind of kept fool, Lord Grey's 'wodman', a huntsman but also a
madman (*OED* 'wood' a. lunatic, or rash and reckless) whose job it is,
since he cannot hunt successfully, to entertain his patron with his
'tedious tale in rime, but little reason' (l. 150).[21] The buffoon Gascoigne,
like the 'melancholy fool' Jacques in *As You Like It*, uses venery to phi-
losophize. Referring to his authorial self in the third person as the 'wodman', Gascoigne reviews his repeated failures to thrive, attributing them
at this stage in the poem to his own foolishness; each time he tried to
shoot the 'white' of economic success 'he proved but a dawe' (l. 23) or
'winked wrong' (l. 31) or lacked 'the fethers of discretion' (l. 40). He
appears as a naïve courtier, absurdly prancked out with his

> bonet buttened with gold,
> His comelie cape begarded all with gay,
> His bumbast hose, with linings manifold,
> His knit silke stocks and all his queint aray. (ll. 49–52)

From courtier he turns to soldier 'As though long limmes led by a lusty
hart, I Might yet suffice to make him rich againe' (ll. 65–6). It is possible
to detect at this point a shift in Gascoigne's self-representation. The
lusty-hearted soldier is not a figure of fun in the same way as the clown-
like huntsman and courtier. Gascoigne's apologia turns at this point
from self-mockery to satire on a world that will not allow men who are

honest and true to thrive:

> He cannot climbe as other catchers can,
> To leade a charge before himselfe be led,
> He cannot spoile the simple sakeles man,
> Which is content to feede him with his bread.
> He cannot pinch the painefull souldiers pay,
> And sheare him out his share in ragged sheetes. (ll. 73–8)[22]

It was consideration of these matters, 'My mynde … rapte in contempla-tion' (l. 93) that led, we are now told, to his failure to shoot the deer, not, as was earlier suggested, his sottishness. Not only is Gascoigne's foolishness properly understood as sober introspection, contemplating 'my youthfull yeares myspente' (l. 90), but his failures are now ascribed less to personal failure of application or virtue, than to the foolishness of aspiring at all in a world governed by fortune and injustice. As the poem progresses, Gascoigne sheds the persona of the buffoon, the 'he' of the 'wodman', and appears increasingly as a man of many talents and skills, the 'I' of the poet: 'For thus I thinke, not all the worlde (I guesse), | Shootes bet than I, nay some shootes not so well' (ll. 99–100). By the end of the poem Gascoigne adopts the role of a man of godly wisdom and patience. The 'carren' doe, he tells his patron, should be seen as a lesson from God, so that

> I myght endevour to amende my parte,
> And turne myne eyes that they no more beholde,
> Suche guylefull markes as seeme more than they be … .
> And when I see the milke hang in hir teate,
> Me thinkes it sayth, olde babe now learne to sucke,
> Who in thy youthe couldst never learne the feate. (ll. 140–3, 145–7)

Gascoigne strives on many fronts in this poem. Above all it is a patronage poem, a witty begging letter to Grey or some other who 'might bee incouraged to employ my penne in some exercise which might tende both to my preferment, and to the profite of my Countrey'.[23] To this end, the poem carefully displays the skill and social tact of the poet, rehearsing his misfortunes, but also his various talents and his experience, with a self-deprecating and self-mocking acknowl-edgement of his social inferiority to his patron. While Gascoigne the 'wodman' teeters on the edge of economic and social ignominy, Gascoigne the poet holds the floor as a man of courtly skills, an honest soldier, a man who knows himself, a man of many parts, and, finally, a man of god. It is the socially inferior client-poet who, through the poem, produces not only himself, but the silent audience of aristocrats whom he entertains and instructs. As Jonathan Crewe comments:

> Gascoigne's ... explicit foregrounding of his authorial 'entitle-ment' ... [signals] the advent of bourgeois authorship, and thus an incipient, fundamental change in the form of property and hence in the forms of cultural production and self-production.[24]

Soldiers' tales

Soldiering was one form of enterprise with clear attractions for those who failed to thrive elsewhere. It could be represented as a manly pro-fession, offering potential status and glory, as well as at least the possi-bility of regular pay and the hope of booty. For the captain, there might be elaborate swindles involving the pocketing of pay of notional mem-bers of the company.[25] Gascoigne and Thomas Churchyard served as soldiers, and Whetstone served as a muster master for the English army in the Netherlands, where he was killed in a brawl.[26] The main arenas for war in the 1570s and 1580s, as far as Englishmen were concerned, were the Netherlands and Ireland. In both, warfare could be represented as a religious fight against Catholicism and a number of Englishmen may have been attracted to fight for religious reasons.[27]

Soldiering could be seen not only as a godly profession and the soldier an instrument of God, but, above all, it was a manly profession in which the brave and enterprising could rise, theoretically, by their own efforts and courage. Whetstone begins his treatise on soldiering, *The Honorable Reputation of a Souldier* (1585), written before he went to the Netherlands himself, by repeating the Italian proverb, 'le parole son femine, & i fatti son maschi' to which he gives a chauvinist spin: 'gli spanioli son femine, e gli Inglesi son maschi'.[28] He thought it 'a highe incouragement to bee valiant, when valour, by gouernment, is able to raise a man from the Carte, to be a Soueraigne Captaine' (sig. Bi^r) and compared the life of the soldier to that of the sluggard at home:

> The Souldiers that carrieth, subduing minds ... will (no doubt) dyet their bodies for to indure paine, as faulkeners do their flying Hawkes: and he that wayeth, what dangers, dishonors, & ouerthrowes, haue followed feastings, drunkennesse, and idle dalliaunce, will (if he

regard his honour) be more affrayd of a wanton banquet then a bloody battaile. (sig. Diii^v)

Thomas Churchyard is at one with Whetstone in his view of the deserts and the manhood of soldiers:

> Shall not a man that hath coped with Champions, buckled with Conquerers, and abidden the hazard of the cannon, stande on his Pantoffelles, and loke to the steppes he hath passed. Yes sure, and suche a member of the state ... deserueth place and preheminence, and is no companion for punies nor meete to be matched with Milkesoppes, whose manhoode and manners differs, as farre from the graue Soldiour, as a Donkite in courage and condition, differs from a Jerfaucon.[29]

Of the four 'sortes of true Nobilitie, or Gentlemenne' the second, Churchyard asserts, after governors but before lawyers or merchants, 'are Soldiours, whose venter and valliance hath been greate, seruice and labour not little, and daiely defended with the hazarde of their liues, the libertie of their Countrey' (sig. Miiii^v). However Churchyard also registers dissatisfaction with the treatment actually meted out to soldiers who return home to be 'rewarded as common persones, and walke like a shadowe in the Sunne, without estimation or countenaunce' (sig. Mii^r).

In the narratives of failure to thrive with which we are concerned, soldiering proves one in a long line of unrewarded travails. Like Gascoigne, Churchyard experiments with autobiographical personae in a number of narrative poems. 'A storie translated out of Frenche' is an account of the life of a soldier from Picardie who, it soon becomes clear, shares aspects of Churchyard's own life.[30] The narrative traces the soldier's career from his upbringing as the son of an honest farmer who, having done well at school, leaves home and comes to Court with his patrimony in his pocket, through an inevitable trajectory to disillusionment as a soldier. Wit is all very well, the poem concludes, but wealth is better: 'Wealth hath the waie the cappe and knee, and twentie at his taile, | When witte hath nere a restyng place, no more then hath a Snaile' (p. 6^v).

The repeated pattern of this narrative, going to the wars, disasters, returning home in the hope of thriving, failure to thrive, and return to the wars, is typical of all Churchyard's many 'autobiographical' narratives. Another transparently autobiographical poem is 'A tragicall Discourse of the vnhappy mans life', printed in *The Firste parte of Churchyardes Chippes* of 1575.[31] This takes the form of a farewell to the

world, concluding with a mock distribution of his goods. The poem
gives a very circumstantial account of the various battles and campaigns
in which Churchyard has served for 'full thirty yeers' (p. 58ʳ). The marginal notes assist the detail of the poem itself; 'First at Wark with George
Lawson', 'In Fraunce serued vnder captayne Crayer', 'Eight yeres vnder
my Lorde Grey', and so on. Many of the incidents parallel those
described in 'A storie … out of Frenche'. In 42 stanzas, the soldier
Churchyard manages to go on approximately ten campaigns in
Scotland, Ireland, France, Flanders, France (again), the Netherlands,
with the Prince of Orange in Germany, back to the Netherlands, then
back through France to Guernsey. As he tells us

> my minde, could neuer rest at hoem
> My shues wear maed, of running leather suer
> And boern I was, about the world to roem
> To see the warres. (p. 59ᵛ)

To some extent, as this quotation indicates, the effect is one of restless-
ness, of a man who cannot settle. The ethos of the willing soldier, eager
for honour, or simply for battle, is the same as that which he describes
in 'The Prayes of our Souldiers' elsewhere in *Churchyardes Chippes*:

> Your harts are sutch, you haet at hoem to bied
> When any bruet, or voice of warrs is hard
> A shaemd in street, on foet cloeth heer to ried
> Whan forward minds, in feele shuld be prefard [feele = field?]
> And skorning pomp, and piuishe pleasurs vain
> For true renowme, ye troedg and toyill a main. (p. 99ʳ)

The indefatigable toil of the soldier epitomizes manly enterprise, the
'forward mind'.

However, competing with an ideology of enterprise and manly
courage is a longing for rest and a home that runs throughout
Churchyard's 'autobiographical' poems. Each time he returns from the
war, he desires to settle down, and this desire is frequently bound up
with getting a wife. In 'A storie … out of Frenche', he twice sets out
to woo: 'a wife shall now content my mynde, suche as the Gods assigne'
(p. 4ʳ). On the first occasion, the widow he chooses tells him in plain
terms he is not rich enough (p. 4ᵛ). On the second, he seems to get more
than be bargained for, '*for he was wivd in deede*, | God sende all Soldiours

in their age, some better lucke at neede' (p. 6ᵛ). 'A Tragicall discourse'
deals with the topic in a similarly confusing way:

> Had I possest, the giftes of Fortune heer
> A house a wyf, and children therewithal
> And had in store (to make my frendes good cheer)
> Sutch common things, as neighbours haue at call
>   In such dispayre, perchaunce I would not fall. ...
>
> Yet for to beare, a peece of all my woes
> (And to impart, the priuie pangs I felt)
> From countrie soile, a sober wife I choes
> In mine owne house, with whom I seldom dwelt
> When thousandes slepte, I waekt I swet I swelt
> To compas that, I neuer could attaine
> And still from hoem, abroed I braek my braine. (p. 68ᵛ)

Whatever Churchyard's actual status, marriage seems to offer the desired
comforts and security of a settled place in society, while the wives seem
to figure either the unwelcoming and ungrateful attitudes of that society, or an entitlement forever beyond the soldier/poet's enjoyment.

Churchyard's rueful presentation of himself in 'A Tragicall discourse'
as an example of woe, shifts as the poem proceeds, to a bitter attack on
the injustices of a society in which the rich and the slothful gorge themselves full and deny anything to the deserving and the needy:

> Of cormrant kinde, some crammed capons aer
> The moer they eat, the moer they may consuem
> Some men likewise, the better that they faer
> The worse they be, and sicker of the ruem
> And some so chaef, so frowne so fret and fuem
> When others feede, they cannot God he knoes
> Spaer any time, the dropping of thear noes. ...
>
> Which snodges swell, and loke like greisie wull
> They puffe they bloe, yea like a baited bull
> And shoue them backe, that on small croems would feede
> Whose pashent harts, maks vertue of a neede. (pp. 65ᵛ and 66ʳ)

Elsewhere the poem attempts to redefine ill fortune and bad luck as
aspects of god's providence; we must wait till 'Harvest come, and God
hath blest the soile' (p. 64ʳ), but it is clear, as the poet-speaker figures

himself lying on his deathbed and looking back on his life, that there is to be no harvest for this soldier, and none, the poet implies for the hard-working honest man in a world as unjust as this one is.

Churchyard's presentation of soldiers is not a simple one. He presents them in 'The prayes of our Souldiers' as 'forward minds' but he also describes them in 'A storie... out of Frenche' as living 'as though ther were I Ne God nor man' (p. 2^v). Gascoigne is similarly ambivalent about soldiering in his '*The fruites of Warre*' (1575), a first-person narrative of the chaotic travails abroad of the soldier. Gascoigne's artful account of his experience as a mercenary soldier in the Netherlands is written '*uppon this Theame*, Dulce Bellum inexpertis'.[32] The Erasmian adage (which Gascoigne translates as '*warre seemes sweete to such as know it not*' (130.7), and the genre, that is, the amplification of a set theme, both appear impeccably humanist. Nevertheless, Gascoigne's self-presentation in the poem is characteristically ambivalent, shifting between the study and the field.

In the first half of the poem Gascoigne speaks as a scholar who knows about wars only from books:

> And herewithal I cannot but confesse,
> Howe unexpert I am in feates of warre:
> For more than wryting doth the same expresse,
> I may not boast of any cruell jarre (2.1–4)

The fruit of this scholar's studies is another commonplace, that war is a scourge of God. It is not until stanza 91 in a poem of just over 200 stanzas, that the speaker suddenly turns to his own experience of foreign wars to 'prove this true' (91.1). The speaker metamorphoses from scholar to a 'Miser', that is, a miserable soldier who goes to the wars to improve his fortunes, 'to advaunce I His staylesse state, by sworde, by speare, by shielde' (73.5–6).

The sense of scholarly certainty, of carefully ordered truisms and stable moral commonplaces established by the first half of the poem disappear entirely once we embark upon Gascoigne's first-person narrative of service in the Netherlands. If previously he had disclaimed knowledge of wars, it now seems this was because what he has experienced does not come within any bookish definition of wars; it is all too chaotic and unheroic:

> For I have seene full many a *Flushyng* fraye,
> And fleet in *Flaunders* eke among the rest,

> The bragge of *Bruges*, where was I that daye?
> Before the walles good sir as brave as best,
> And though I marcht all armde withouten rest,
> From *Aerdenburgh* and back againe that night,
> Yet madde were he that would have made me knight. (95)

His travels/travails have not been heroic by any chivalric standards. Absurd and pointless travelling characterizes Gascoigne's account of his experience of the campaign:

> I romed have about,
> In Zeeland, Holland, Waterland, and all,
> By sea, by land, by ayre, and all throughout,
> As leaping lottes, and chance did seeme to call. (99.1–4)

The Netherlands figures as a list of strange place names located in a confusing geography where normal order is perverted. The taking of Middelburg is described as a chaos of inversions; the 'bravest bragges' prove most cowardly, and when the drums beat the attack, those that follow go backwards, and sailors lead the soldiers:

> Such triumphs chance where such Lieutenants rule,
> Where will commaundes when skill is out of towne,
> Where boldest bloudes are forced to recule,
> By Simme the boteswayne when he list to frowne,
> Where Captaynes crouch, and fishers weare the Crowne. (108.1–5)

In this upside down world, friends prove foes and foes friends. At Leiden, Gascoigne and his English troops find themselves locked out of the city they are meant to be defending:

> They neither gave us meate to feede upon,
> Nor drinke, nor powder, pickax, toole nor spade,
> So might we sterve, like misers woe begone,
> And fend our foes with blowes of English blade. (163.1–4)[33]

Forced to surrender to the Spanish, Gascoigne and his fellow officers paradoxically find themselves supplied with all they could wish, able

> To eate and drinke at Barons borde alwayes,
> To lie on downe, to banquet with the best,

To have all things, at every just request,
To borowe coyne, when any seemde to lacke. (176.3–6)

Not that we should trust the Spanish any more than the Dutch he hastens to add: 'We might soone sell, all freendship found in Spaine' (178.7).

But friendship, it seems, is also in short supply at home. The occasion of the poem seems to be self-defence against accusations from his own soldiers. Gascoigne tells us that having selflessly negotiated the release of his English troops, he finds he is the victim of their slanderous gossip at home:

> we that were their defence,
> With armes, with cost, with deedes, with eloquence:
> We that saved such, as knew not where to flie,
> Were now by them accusde of trecherie. (188.4–7)[34]

Travailing abroad in the wars, it seems, can contaminate home as well:

> And who in warre hath caught a fatall clappe,
> Might chaunce at home to have no better happe. (189.6–7)

Or was home already contaminated? The *Peroratio* returns to the earlier theme that war is the scourge of God with which he punishes the commonwealth whose prince or whose members cease to be virtuous. Gascoigne, the writer/scholar/soldier reviews the estates of the English commonwealth, nobility, clergy, lawyers, and merchants, finding in each, in spite of the virtue of a few exceptional (named) individuals, evidence of vice and corruption.

The apparent distinctions in Gascoigne's poem, between the moralizing scholar and the contaminated soldier, and between English peace and the chaos of continental war, are collapsed. Gascoigne claims for himself the perspectives of the scholar and the bitter experience of the soldier. Neither is sufficient in itself. The scholar's commonplaces are inadequate and platitudinous, but there is no idealization of the soldier's life. In 'L'envoie', the speaker identifies himself again as a 'Miser', one of 'those that in dystresse | Do drive their dayes, till drummes do draw them out' (ll. 25–6). The suggestion of enforced soldiering is nevertheless contradicted by the following lines 'If drummes once sounde a lustie martch in deede, | Then farewell bookes, for he will trudge with speede' (ll. 29–30). Like Churchyard, Gascoigne the soldier seems riven between a desire to portray the soldier's life as one of travail and bitterness, unrewarded by a thankless nation, and a desire to represent himself as a man of courage and enterprise, ready and eager to follow when the drum beats.

'Travailing' abroad: the writer as adventurer

Unlike the narratives we have been considering in most of this chapter, Gascoigne's 'Dulce bellum' does not narrate a whole career, but only one episode in it, Gascoigne's service in the Netherlands from 1572 to 1574. The two sets of poems I shall consider in this section, George Turbervile's three verse epistles from Moscow, dated 1569, and Robert Baker's two epic accounts of his adventures off the 'Guinie' coast of Africa in 1562 and 1563, similarly deal with episodes in each writer's life. Nevertheless, the poems share many of the characteristics of the career narratives we have been examining. In each case, the author figures in his verses as both the frustrated or disillusioned subject of bitter experiences, and as a voice honed by that experience to speak with unique authority. Written for self-promotion or self-justification, these accounts of the chaos and failures that attend the honest travails of the enterprising man in an unsympathetic world, figure the writing self as chastened and wiser, a man more sinned against than sinning.

In a poem celebrating that epitome of Elizabethan enterprise, Sir Humphrey Gilbert, explorer, speculator, colonial undertaker, and mercenary soldier, Churchyard draws an analogy between his own travails as a writer and the heroic toil of the adventurer he celebrates:

> The man that trauels much,
>   with mind and body both,
> (Whose restlesse lims, & labring thoughtes,
>   through heapes of hazards goth)[35]

'Trauels' includes here all its senses of 'to make a journey', 'to labour, toil' and 'to weary, tire' (*OED* 'travail' v. and 'travel' v.). Gilbert's voyage is not a recreational excursion, but a speculative enterprise, with the straining of 'restlesse lims, & labring thoughtes' a sign of heroic virtue. Although the meanings of the word 'travel' were becoming separated in the sixteenth century, travel (journeying) and travail (toil, pain) are still interchangeable terms with the meanings closely associated. Gilbert's heroic travels testify to his virtuous choice of toilsome but manly adventure abroad rather than slothful, effeminate ease at home:

> Abroade where seruice is,
>   much honor may be wonne,
> At home our gay vayneglory goes,
>   like shadow in the Sunne.
> Abroade bare robes are best,
>   and Manhoode makes the showe,
> At home yong Maister must be fine,
>   or all is lost you know. (sig. l. iii^r)

As the poem progresses the anaphora mutate from the oppositon 'abroade' / 'home' to 'toile' / 'rest'. Travel abroad is a sign of manliness while resting at home is to be, in Churchyard's scornful phrase, 'ruld by loue of babes, |... [and] womens willes' (sig. k. iii^r).

The ideology of manly travail manifest in the enterprise of travelling abroad is bound up both with an idealization of endurance and hard work, and with heroic mastery of the monstrous and dangerous. That such dangers and threats may be found in the familiar as well as the foreign, is indicated in Sir Henry Sidney's awed praise of the intrepid adventurer abroad:

> We shall live and rest at home quietly with our friends, and acquaintance: but hee in the meane time labouring to keepe the ignorant and unruly Mariners in good order and obedience, with howe many cares shall hee trouble and vexe himselfe? ... We shall keepe our owne coastes and countrey: Hee shall seeke strange and unknowen kingdomes. He shall commit his safetie to barbarous and cruell people, and shall hazard his life amongst the monstrous and terrible beastes of the Sea.[36]

It is not at all clear whether the 'barbarous and cruell people' are the English mariners or the inhabitants of 'unknowen kingdomes'. Implied in Sir Henry's prose, is a view that to exchange the known for the unknown may be a brave, but is scarcely a sensible, course of action. George Turbervile, in a poem printed in 1567, appears to share the same view:

> In rotten ribbed Barck to passe the Seas
> The forraine landes and straungie sites to see,
> Doth daunger dwell: the passage breedes vnease,
> Not safe the soyle, the men vnfriendly bee.

> Admit thou see the straungest things of all:
> When eie is turnde the pleasant sight is gone:
> The treasure then of trauaile is but small,
> Wherefor (Friend P.) let all such toyes alone.[37]

According to such thinking, the enterprise of travelling abroad could be not only dangerous but vain, breeding unease, and exposing the English traveller at best to insubstantial and treacherous pleasures, and at worst to danger. What was collected and known, the very integrity of the civilized English self, could be scattered abroad. Once embarked, the familiar became strange, stabilities threatened to collapse, and national virtue became susceptible to contamination.[38]

In the year following the publication of his epistle to his 'Friend P.', Turbervile found himself travelling abroad as secretary to Lord Thomas Randolph, Elizabeth I's emissary to the Emperor of Russia. Turbervile's three verse epistles from Moscow were probably first printed in 1574 in *Epitaphes and Sonnettes*.[39] The theme of living in Russia runs through much of the collection that opens with a poem bidding farewell both to his mother and to his mother country:

> My countrey coast where I
>   my Nurses milke did sucke,
> Would neuer yet in all my life
>   allowe me one good lucke ...
>
> From thence tis time to trudge
>   and hire the hackney post
> To shift to ship, to leaue the land
>   and seeke a better coast. (p. 348)

Such enterprise differentiates him from

> The slouthfull Groome that sits,
>   at home and tels the clocke:
> And feares the floud because therein
>   lies hidden many a rocke. (p. 349)

This spirit of hopeful enterprise has evaporated by the time we get to the three verse epistles from Moscow appended to *Epitaphes and Sonnettes: 'The Author being in Moscouia, wrytes to certaine his frendes in Englande of the state of the place'* (pp. 424–4). In these verses, the writer tells his friends that in leaving his native soil 'ful like a retchlesse man' he has emphatically moved from 'blisse to bale' (p. 424). The emphasis throughout is on the outlandishness of the country and the uncouth incivility of the Russians. Even their ingenuity is a sign of barbarity: their buildings are made of wood caulked with moss, their windows of translucent slices of stone sewn together (pp. 433–4), and they stack up their dead in winter because they cannot break the frozen ground (p. 431). Above all he returns again and again to the bodily grossness of the Moscovites: they have fat bellies, drink vast amounts, have greasy wives smoked tawny by the stove fire, and worst of all, the Russian leads a 'bowgards life' (buggers), preferring 'a boy within his bed' to his greasy wife. In a word, Russia is as bad as Ireland:

> Wild Irish are as ciuil as
>   the Russies in their kind:
> Hard choice which is the best of both,
>   each bloodie rude, and blind. (p. 443)

The uncouth grossness of the Russians is represented as both deeply alien and threatening to the writer's integrity. He is forced to join his hosts in drinking, to lie on barbarous bearskins in the same corner as their heathenish idols, and is uncomfortably conscious of and offended by the sexuality of both the men and women. Russia even contaminates the integrity of his speech, as he feels constrained by his part in the trade mission to censure what he writes (p. 435). Turbervile began his travels by differentiating his manly enterprise abroad from the dull-mindedness of the 'slouthfull Groome that sits, I at home and tels the clocke', but ends up sitting idly by a stinking stove in Moscow through the eight-month winter, presumably being tanned by its smoke to the same tawny colour as his hosts. The poet's concluding advice to his friends flatly contradicts the attitude to travel with which the volume began:

> If thou be wise, as wise thou art,
>   and wilt be rulde by mee:
> Liue still at home, and couet not,
>   those barbarous coasts to see.
> No good befals a man that seekes,
>   and finds no better place:
> No ciuil customs to be learnd,
>   where God bestowes no grace. (p. 444)

'Thou were better farre I at home', he tells his friend Parker, 'And wouldst been loath among such loutes I so long a time to dwel' (p. 441). Part of the fascination of the poems is their struggle to maintain the writer's difference, his gentlemanly English urbanity, modelled in these verse epistles on that of Horace, while all the time he is threatened and contaminated by all that surrounds him: the smoke, sexual appetites, the food and drink, the tyrannical encroachments of an outlandish culture.

The confident association of the travel/travails of English enterprise both by ship and with the pen, found in Churchyard's 'Verses to Gilbert', is here dislocated. Travelling abroad proves a barren experience where nothing can be gained or learned, and much is threatened. Turbervile is nevertheless able to make writerly capital out of his apparently barren experiences, presenting himself in print both as a man of bold spirit with news to tell, and as a civil Englishman whose moral difference from the gross Russians is satisfactorily confirmed by his disdainful tone. One hopes this proved a highly sellable combination. The enterprise of travail with the pen is here used to undermine the very travel abroad that enabled the writing in the first place. Nevertheless Russia functions in the volume to subtly disturb Turbervile's attempted constructions of a firmly grounded self, able to carry a fixed and impermeable mind on his travels. An anonymous poem in *The Paradise of Dainty Devices* boasted, 'The noble minde eache where can thriue, I And not be drowned in deepe dispayre'.[40] Turbervile's horrified verse epistles from Moscovia suggest that such a confident differentiation of self from other may not always be possible.

A clear differentiation of the civilized English self from the barbaric other proves even more insecure in the verse narratives of Robert Baker, a merchant's factor trading on ships to the 'Guinie' coast of Africa. His poems about two voyages in 1562 and '63 appeared in the first edition of Hakluyt's *The Principall Navigations* in 1589.[41] According to the account in the opening lines of the first poem, the narratives were written during Baker's imprisonment in France. His motive is, possibly, to tell his remarkable story in the hope of raising a ransom in London, or gaining some celebrity by having the poems printed. Practical as may have been the motives for Baker's painful 'trauels' with his pen (he tells us that 'eke at night I lothe that stile I which I haue writte that day'), he feels his story deserves the full epic machinery of gods and muses. The idea that overseas voyaging was a fit topic for epic verse was later to inspire Luis Camões' epic of Portuguese maritime exloration, *Os Lusiadas* (1572), and

Hakluyt's protégé, the Hungarian Humanist Stephen Parmenius of Buda. In 1582, Parmenius published a Latin hexameter eulogy of Sir Humphrey Gilbert on the eve of a projected expedition to Newfoundland: *De navigatione ... Humfredi Gilberti ... Carmen.*[42] Parmenius' rapturous account of Gilbert's forthcoming voyage invokes the muses and the classical gods, and anticipates the English occupation of America in terms of the scions of one Golden Age (the English) liberating and civilizing the innocent children of another, the native Americans. The contradictions implicit in such a deployment of myth point to only one of the problems of such mythologizing when used of contemporary enterprises. In 1583, Parmenius actually accompanied Gilbert to New Found Land, intending to write another Latin epic poem on the journey. All that remains is a letter to Hakluyt written in a plain prose that seems more suitable for the matter: 'Now I ought to tell you about the customs, territories and inhabitants: and yet what am I to say, my dear Hakluyt, when I see nothing but desolation?'[43] Parmenius and the epic he had undertaken to write were lost at sea in a storm shortly after the letter was written. Established ways of making sense of the world undergo strange subversions when appropriated for their narratives by poets travel/travailing abroad. As we shall see, Baker's epic discourse, modelled loosely on Orpheus's journey to the underworld, proves as inappropriate as that of Parmenius and it is soon abandoned.

Baker set out in 1562 with two merchant ships, the Minion and the Primrose, on a trading voyage to the 'Guinie' coast. He describes his first view of Africans in far from flattering terms:

> Their Captaine comes to me
> as naked as my naile,
> Not hauing witte or honestie
> To couer once his taile. (p. 132)

To divert themselves, the mariners carry this 'wilde man' to their ship and dress him up in European clothes. But the 'wilde man' proves to have a good deal more wit than the English mariners. He uses his opportunity to spy out the arrangements on the English ship and then returns the next evening with some companions and steals all their trading goods. Now the Africans are described as 'fiends more fierce' than any of the devils Orpheus met in Hell (p. 134); they are 'blacke burnt men', followers of Vulcan (p. 134). Baker invents a myth in which Jove lets the Englishmen return to England on one condition: that they go no more abroad. Jove tells Vulcan:

> They haue so fruitfull a countrey
>   that there is none the like,
> But if they can not be
>   therewith content, but still
> Will seeke for golde so couetously,
>   worke then with them thy will. (p. 135)

Jove clearly shares Sir Henry Sidney's and Turbervile's views that it is foolish to leave home. By the following year, however, the adventurous Baker has forgotten Jove's threat, and embarked again on a trading voyage to the 'Guinie' coast. This time the English, as was normal in the period, begin their adventures by ferociously and piratically attacking a French trading vessel. Eventually arriving off West Africa, a crew of nine leaves the larger ships to row a small trading boat to shore. At this point Vulcan wrecks his revenge by sending down thunderbolts while Aeolus sends 'whirling windes' (p. 137). After two days the small boat is irremediably separated from the larger ships that eventually return to England presuming Baker and his crew have perished. Meanwhile Baker and the other eight sailors are left to row in a small boat along the hostile African coast.

At this point in Baker's narrative the mythological apparatus disappears entirely. At the same time, Baker's representations of the Africans change subtly. The Englishmen are now dependent on whatever food Africans on the shore will give them for the small wares they still have. Instead of 'wilde men' and fiends, the Africans are now described as 'Negros' and their food seems wholesome and delicate: 'daintie' dishes of meat and 'wine | much like our whey' (p. 138). However, in spite of such supplies the situation of the English becomes desperate. Confined to their small boat for twenty days, their legs become 'swolne euery ioint' (p. 139), they are scorched by the sun, and are unable to sleep because of the terrible night storms.

By now their boat has strayed into a part of the coast fortified by the Portuguese to protect their trading interests. Although the English are at war with the Portuguese and are bitter commercial rivals, the thought of other Christians nearby offers Baker and his fellows some hope; better to row in a galley and be fed, than row up and down hopelessly as at present, or, worst of all, join the 'Negros'. Baker's terminology reverts to the rhetoric of savagery he had used in the first poem:

> But what fauour would ye
>   of these men looke to haue:
> Who beastly sauage people be
>   farre worse then any slaue?
> If *Cannibals* they be
>   in kind, we doe not know,
> But if they be, then welcome we,
>   to pot straight way we goe,
> They naked goe likewise,
>   for shame we cannot so:
> We cannot liue after their guise,
>   thus naked for to go.
> By rootes and leaues they liue,
>   as beasts doe in the wood:
> Among these heathen who can thriue,
>   with this so wilde a food? (p. 139)

Surrendering to the Portuguese seems by far the more attractive option, but when they try to do so, they are met by cannons and culverin fire and by stones thrown down from the fort on top of their boat. Hastily, the English row out to sea again and reconsider their options. It is clearly time to try the 'Negros' who may prove less savage than the Christian Portuguese.

This seems to be the case. The Africans on whose mercy they throw themselves seem very different from the cunning 'fiends' of the first poem. Their leader, 'the Kings chiefe sonne' is 'a stout and valiant man | In whom I thinke Nature iwis, | hath wrought all that she can' (p. 141). He proves to be noble not only in form but also in sensibility:

> he perceiuing now the teares,
>   which from our eyes did fall,
> Had great pitie on vs,
>   and sayd he would haue nought,
> But streight by signes he will'd vs then,
>   that we should take no thought.
> As one whom God had sent,
>   and kept for vs in store. (p. 141)

Jove has, in these exigencies, been replaced by the plain Protestant God. The Englishmen who a day earlier had decided they could not live 'after [the] guise' of the Africans now find themselves sitting beside them sharing their food, and lying beside them on the ground to sleep.

However, after a few days, the Africans, concluding that nothing is to be gained by aiding these Englishmen, gradually leave them to fend for themselves:

> Some run now in the wood,
> > and there for rootes do seeke, ...
> Our clothes now rot with sweat,
> > and from our backs do fall,
> Saue that whom nature wils for shame,
> > we couer nought at all. (p. 141)

Only a ragged loin-cloth seems now to differentiate an Englishman from the naked, root-eating savages who had previously seemed so beast-like and alien. Not only do the Englishmen scrabble with their nails in the ground for roots and lie at night 'as beasts' on the bare earth (p. 142), but Baker anticipates they may lose the last vestiges that differentiate the civilized Christian from the savage cannibal:

> Perhaps as weake breake our behest
> > which we owe God on high.
> And least we liuing here
> > among this heathen, might
> Perchance for need do that which were
> > right hainous in his sight. (p. 142)

The narrative ends with a final irony. The remnant of three men left alive from the crew of nine, are finally rescued, albeit to be then imprisoned, by a French ship; such a one, no doubt, as Baker and his English crew had begun the voyage by assaulting and robbing.

This extraordinary tale of the travails of travelling abroad only appeared in the 1589 edition of Hakluyt's *Principal Navigations*, and indeed its grimly cautionary description of the outcomes of adventuring abroad for gain does not fit well with Hakluyt's enthusiastic project of recording English enterprise.[44] Cleo, Calliope and the 'muses nine' may be acknowledged by Baker, but he is keen to claim the effort as his own: 'the trauell [is] only mine' (p. 131). The idealizing discourse of epic journeying does not finally fit Baker's project of recording his own survival of an experience that seems to him to fit no moral or generic paradigms.

Travelling abroad offered an opportunity of employment and advancement, seemingly in short supply at home. Writing about going abroad could in turn serve the interests of such men as Gascoigne, Turbervile and Baker because it offered a means of self-promotion, whether for self-justification, or in the hope of making their heroism, talents, and experience known through print to punters avid for news from abroad, or to patrons, or influential protectors. However the tales that get told are often disconcertingly destabilizing. They undermine the assured generic and moral stances of the humanist expounder of commonplaces, the gentlemanly traveller to uncouth lands, or the heroic white colonizer. The first-person observer, loosed from home and the familiar, becomes contaminated by the otherness in which he participates.

Colin Clovts Come Home Againe

Colin Clovts Come Home Againe was printed in 1595, more than twenty years after the narratives we have discussed in this chapter. Nevertheless, I wish to suggest that the poem repeats but redefines many of the themes we have been considering. Like the 'failed career' narratives of Gascoigne or Churchyard, it represents its persona as a worthy but poor man, dazzled by the Court that consistently fails to recognize and reward true worth. Like the travel narratives, it tells of a journey from the familiar to the strange, bringing disillusionment, but endowing the authorial voice with the authority of experience. Like the other narratives we have examined in this chapter, also, the first-person speaker of the poem, Colin Clout, in some sense figures, although not simplistically, the poem's writer, Edmund Spenser. E.K.'s gloss on the figure of Colin in *The Shepheardes Calendar*, 'vnder whose person the Authour selfe is shadowed', is reinforced at his reappearance in *Colin Clovts Come Home Againe* by Colin's location in a fictional version of Spenser's own estate, 'Vnder the foote of *Mole* that mountaine hore ... by the *Mullaes* shore'.[45]

Spenser's poem radically realigns the reader's perspectives on the themes we have been following in this chapter. As many commentators have pointed out, the 'home' of the title, to which Colin 'comes again' is thoroughly ambivalent.[46] Is an English Colin returning to England from the foreign wastes of Ireland to which he had 'banisht' (l. 182) himself? Or is Colin a native or naturalized denizen of pastoral Ireland with the English court a place of contaminating foreignness? From Colin's, and the readers' points of view, which is familiar and which alien, who is at the centre and who on the margins? The Court itself, the place where Colin hopes his efforts may be rewarded, is both unexpected and predictable: unlike Churchyard and his fellows, Colin is bountifully rewarded by the Queen and her ladies, but the English court, and even to some extent the Queen, are sidelined as the objects of ambition and the centre of reward within the poem. Instead the poet's own vatic visions, delivered in marginal Ireland, redefine the meaning of such terms as exile and reward, placing the poet himself at the threshold between the two, providing privileged access into the true courts of beauty and power, and representing himself as the sole source of lasting gifts.

The 'shepheard of the Ocean', a fairly transparent allusion to Sir Walter Raleigh, to whom the poem is dedicated, first introduces the theme of Colin's advancement:

> He gan to cast great lyking to my lore,
> And great dislyking to my lucklesse lot:
> That banisht had my selfe, like wight forlore,
> Into that waste, where I was quite forgot.
> The which to leaue, thenceforth he counseld mee,
> Vnmeet for man, in whom was ought regardfull
> And wend with him, his *Cynthia* to see:
> Whose grace was great, and bounty most rewardfull. (ll. 180–7)

In this view, Colin's resting at home is 'unmeet', implying not only a lack of appropriate recognition, but also a shameful lack of enterprise and ambition. The shepherd's words imply the accusation of a shameful idleness that Spenser in his dedication to Raleigh, seeks to rebut: *'SIR, that you may see that I am not alwaies ydle as yee thinke, though not greatly well occupied'* (p. 344). Spenser carefully balances a challenge to the assumption that the Court is the only locus for the profitable exercise of talent with an indication that, nevertheless, his talents could be put to better use.

Colin does not only seek reward at Court, he also travels overseas. The poem draws on many of the ideas of 'home' and 'abroad' which we traced in the work of Churchyard, Turbervile and Baker, although in a far from straightforward manner. Colin eschews the easy correlation between home and shameful idleness as opposed to travel and virtuous enterprise, developed by Churchyard and so many other advocates of English adventuring in the period, and implied by the 'shepheard of the Ocean' (who figures Raleigh, himself a passionate advocate of overseas adventure). Colin, however, is suspicious of such correlations. Coming to the sea that divides Ireland from England, Colin condemns travaillers abroad as men of greedy and dangerous ambition in terms that recall Turbervile's warning to his

'Friend P.' (see pp. 77–8 above):

> Bold men presuming life for gaine to sell,
> Dare tempt that gulf, and in those wandring stremes
> Seek waies vnknowne, waies leading down to hell. (ll. 209–11)

To the 'shepheard of the Ocean' the seas are a site for the exercise and display of power by his Queen, Cynthia, who has the 'Regiment' (l. 233), and who delegates authority to others including the 'shepheard of the Ocean' himself: 'And I among the rest of many least, I Haue in the Ocean charge to me assignd' (ll. 252–3). To Colin the seas seem, on the contrary, 'A world of waters heaped vp on hie, I Rolling like mountaines in wide wildernesse' (ll. 196–7) where even the land masses seem 'Floting amid the sea in ieopardie' (l. 273). On the one hand, Colin's naivety is a source of comedy, an indicator of his homely ignorance, on the other, it introduces us to Colin's perspective on the foreign world of the Court which for him is unstable and dangerous, a site for the arbitrary and destructive exercise of power.

Colin's fear of the threatening instability of travel abroad is, as we have seen, present in the accounts of Turbervile, Gascoigne and Baker. In their texts, the foreign landscapes seem to confirm the essential and fearful otherness of abroad. Whether in the upside-down geography of the war-torn Low Countries, the inhospitable climate of Africa, or the frozen wastes of Russia, abroad is a god-forsaken place. As Turbervile commented at the end of his epistles from Russia:

> No good befals a man that seekes,
>   and finds no better place:
> No ciuil customs to be learnd,
>   where God bestowes no grace. (p. 444)

However, having, in spite of his reservations, braved the sea, Colin, arrives in a paradisial England: 'There fruitfull corne, faire trees, fresh herbage is I And all things else that liuing creatures need' (ll. 298–9). The outlandish other of this fruitful land of plenty is, in fact, Ireland, Colin's starting point, and the only land Turbervile felt compared in incivility to Russia. The 'shepheard of the Ocean' makes a systematic comparison between the two lands: 'that' (England) and 'this' (Ireland):

> Both heauen and heauenly graces do much more
> (Quoth he) abound in that same land, then this.

> For there all happie peace and plenteous store
> Conspire in one to make contented blisse:
> No wayling there nor wretchednesse is heard,
> No bloodie issues nor no leprosies,
> No griesly famine, nor no raging sweard,
> No nightly bodrags, nor no hue and cries; ...
> For end, all good, all grace there freely growes,
> Had people grace it gratefully to vse. (ll. 308–15, 324–5)

Both places are, it seems, unhomely. If England is a place of peace and plenty, its Court is a place of 'enormities' (l. 665), such that Colin 'Darest not aduenture such vnknowen wayes, | Nor trust the guile of fortunes blandishment' (ll. 670–1). Instead he prefers to return to the 'hardnesse' (l. 673) of his life in Ireland. Spenser utilizes a similar language of travel, enterprise, danger, and disorientation, as that employed by the poets of travailing abroad that we considered earlier, but his verse, more explicitly than theirs, undermines the very sense of home. Colin is in exile both at home and abroad.

Colin's experience of the Court to which he travels to enjoy the grace and bounty of its queen, Cynthia, conforms in many respects to that of his early Elizabethan predecessors. For Gascoigne, the Court is a place where 'lyghte rewarde and recompence [are] founde, | Fleeting lyke feathers in the wynde alofte'.[47] Churchyard, expecting some reward for his years spent in the Queen's service, went to the 'well hedde' herself:

> And in a fewe well couched lines, to make her vnderstande:
> His cace his scourge, loe so he did, and boldly did he tell,
> The same hym self vnto the Prince, who knowes the man full well.
> And gracious words three tymes he gate, the fourth to tell you plain
> Unfruitfull was[,] things were straite laest, faire woords maks fooles full
> fain:[48]

It is, however, no part of Spenser's purpose to represent the poet as a disregarded fool, like the humble Churchyard, probably shadowed in *Colin Clovt* as 'old *Palemon* ... That sung so long vntill quite hoarse he grew' (l. 399). Unlike Churchyard, Colin's verse meets with favour from Cynthia.

Nevertheless the shepherd poet places himself morally and socially outside the Court. It is, above all, a place of verbal deceit:

> Where each one seeks with malice and with strife,
> To thrust downe other into foule disgrace,

> Himselfe to raise: and he doth soonest rise
> That best can handle his deceitfull wit,
> In subtil shifts, and finest sleights deuise. (ll. 690–4)

Colin travelled to Court carrying only his 'oaten quill' (l. 194). He seeks advancement as a poet, but there is no room among such 'lewd speeches and licentious deeds' (l. 787) for the kind of moral truth-teller Spenser conceives the poet to be:

> Ne is there place for any gentle wit,
> Vnlesse to please, it selfe it can applie: (ll. 707–8)

Spenser's strategy of elevating the role of the poet within society, yet setting him apart from the veniality and corruption associated with courtly patronage, entails both recognition and rejection for Colin. The Queen and the more discriminating and virtuous in her entourage recognize his excellence, but he must place himself in opposition to a Court where only flatterers thrive.

In the verse that we have so far considered throughout this study, the writers have placed their authorial selves, implicitly or explicitly, on the margins of social and economic power. They characteristically cast themselves as aspiring courtiers or potential gentlemen clients, eager to display socially prestigious skills and behaviours that they also, paradoxically, represent as deceitful and vain. *Colin Clovt* is also ambivalent about ambition, but it is far bolder and far more innovative in its treatment of the theme. The ambition of the courtier who 'thrust[s] downe other into foule disgrace, | Himselfe to raise' (ll. 691–2) is, of course, condemned, and Colin tells his shepherd audience that he reveals the vices of the court 'to warne yong shepheards wandring wit, | Which through report of that liues painted blisse, | Abandon quiet home, to seeke for it' (ll. 684–6). Colin himself, as we have seen, voluntarily quits the Court to return to the shepherd's life. Nevertheless, Colin is ambitious for a role that places himself, as vatic poet, in an unassailable position of privilege and authority.

Among his fellows shepherds, Colin tells a warning tale of ambition that he first sung to 'the shepheard of the Ocean'. Bregog loved, and was loved by the river Mulla, a tale of dubious ambition on all parts. Mulla's ambitious father, old Mole, 'more carefull of her good, | And meaning her much better to preferre' (ll. 120–1) promises her to a richer stream, the Allo. The 'wily' Bregog nevertheless persists and 'secretly' enjoys his Mulla, until, his secret spied, old Mole 'In great auenge did roll downe from his hill | Huge mightie stones' which scatter the Bregog 'all to nought' (ll. 149–53). Bregog's unsanctioned marriage to Mulla is punished, but her father's ambition, however 'carefull of her good,' to join his daughter to the Allo is also condemned; Colin comments 'loue will not be drawne, but must be ledde' (l. 129). On both sides the wilful assertion of desire leads to disaster.

This simple tale has less simple connotations. The illicit desires of 'my river Bregog' may be a warning to the rustic Colin of the dangers of high aspiration, but it is also a veiled comment on the illicit desires of 'the shepheard of the Ocean'/Raleigh, who had forfeited royal favour by contracting a secret marriage in 1592.[49] The relationship of patron/client is subtly reversed, with the client Colin becoming the moral instructor of the courtly patron. The misdemeanour of Bregog/Raleigh in asserting wilful desire in spite of the law of the father/Queen, is implicitly contrasted to Colin's self-denying humility in relation to the object of his desire, Rosalind. Although she scorns him, Colin takes the blame on himself: 'to my selfe the blame that lookt so hie' (l. 936). Colin's understanding of love is not that venial aspiration that motivates those at Court who profane 'His mightie mysteries' (l. 788), but a transformative service to a higher power:

> So loue is Lord of all the world by right,
> And rules the creatures by his powrfull saw:
> All being made the vassalls of his might,
> Through secret sence which therto doth them draw. (ll. 883–6)

Of this transcendent king, the self-denying Colin is the 'Priest' (l. 832), authorized to declare who the 'outlawes' are, including the amorous sycophants of the English Court, who must 'as Exuls out of his court be thrust' (l. 894).

As with so many poems in this chapter, the poet/author is present in his text as both victim and authority, the subject of experience and a guide to others. In *Colin Clovt*, the shifts in voice and perspective are carefully managed. As a simple shepherd poet, Colin's song is natural and spontaneous, associated with the simplicity and thus innocence of the shepherd community, but also a mark of Colin's special calling. The naivety of the Colin persona may hope to protect Spenser and his song from '*the malice of euill mouthes, which are alwaies wide open to carpe at and misconstrue my simple meaning*' (p. 344, the dedication to Raleigh), but it also places Colin as the native of a pastoral realm that generically lies outside the boundaries of, and in opposition to, the Court.

As the poem progresses, the naïve and simple Colin modulates into a man of experience and weighty judgement, able to hold his own at court among his metropolitan peers and the 'filed toung[s]' of the courtiers. This experienced Colin speaks to his fellow shepherds in the tones of a teacher rather than as a companion:

> Ah *Cuddy* (then quoth *Colin*) thous a fon, [fon = fool]
> That hast not seene least part of natures worke:
> Much more there is vnkend, then thou doest kon,
> And much more that does from mens knowledge lurke. (ll. 292–5)

An observation to be echoed a little later by that scholar Hamlet who sagely warned 'there are more things in heaven and earth, Horatio, | Than are dreamed of in your philosophy' (*Hamlet*, I.v). Colin's new voice as a man of wisdom and judgement lends plausibility to his attack on the court for its failure to recognize true scholarship and learned skills:

> For arts of schoole haue there small countenance,
> Counted but toyes to busie ydle braines,
> And there professours find small maintenance,
> But to be instruments of others gaines. (ll. 703–6)

Colin, it seems, is both an innocent with divine gifts whose purity is in part protected from contamination by his humble distance from the source of power, and also a man of experience and true discernment, one of those perhaps whose 'gentle wit', that is, whose truly gentle-manly wit, deserves reward at court, but who is shouldered out, 'as base, or blunt' by the shallow courtiers (ll. 707–10).

Colin's voice finally becomes that of the vatic poet, inspired by 'some celestiall rage' to pour 'forth these oracles so sage … wherewith thou art possest' (ll. 823–6). Colin's hymn to a transcendent love that is 'Lord of all the world by right' changes the power relations of the poem so that Love's court becomes the true source of power, with the poet as Love's 'oracle' or 'priest'. The marginalized client/writer moves to the centre, constructing a world of language whose authorizing source, however inspired, is his own first-person experience.

4

Spenser as Orpheus

Amoretti and Epithalamion was published in London in 1595, '*Written not long since by Edmunde Spenser*'.[1] Although *Epithalamion* is divided from *Amoretti* by a separate page bearing its title, the marriage hymn provides a fitting development of the sonnet sequence. In both, the first-person speaker is both the lover/groom, and, in some sense, a version of the author, Edmund Spenser, the well-known poet of *The Faerie Queene*, whose first instalment had been published in 1590. This identification is first made explicitly in *Amoretti* 33 addressed to Lodowick Bryskett, a fellow official of Spenser's in Ireland, in which the speaker excuses himself for not getting on with *The Faerie Queene*. Other details in the sequence confirm such autobiographical signals, for instance, the poet-lover is said to be forty in *Amoretti* 60, and his lady, his mother and his Queen are all said to share the same name, Elizabeth (*Amoretti* 74). More esoterically, scholars have found in the sequence, specific allusions to dates in Lent in 1594.[2] It is known that Spenser married, probably as his second wife, Elizabeth Boyle, an Englishwoman, and a kinswoman of Richard Boyle, later Earl of Cork and at that time part of the vice-regal administration.[3] *Amoretti and Epithalamion* thus seems to be designed to refer to Spenser's own courtship of Elizabeth Boyle and his marriage in 1594 on a date which *Epithalamion* tells us was 11th June, St Barnabas's Day, the date of the Summer solstice (*Epithalamion*, stanza 15).

My argument in this chapter will be that while it may indeed be a private memorial for Spenser and his bride, in becoming a public document the volume becomes, and bears all the marks of having been designed to be, an exemplary and instructional text, an instance of that 'delightful teaching' that Sir Philip Sidney said 'was the right describing note to know a poet by'.[4] Spenser dramatizes himself as the hero of a narrative of self-formation both as a moral gentleman and as a member

of a civil commonwealth. In doing so, he voices the concerns and perspectives of a very specific class and place. Edmund Spenser was socially
a gentleman by virtue of his education and his service to the state as an
official of the crown in Ireland. In 1594, he was, as well as a man about
to embark on marriage, an 'undertaker' in Munster, that is, a colonial
landowner, master of a substantial property confiscated from its rebellious owners as part of a policy of pacifying, or as Spenser put it 'reduc-
ing that (salvage) nation to better government and civility'.[5]

Civility

In order to understand what Spenser meant by 'civility' and its central
importance to the 1595 volume, I shall use as a context a prose treatise
by one of Spenser's fellow officials in Ireland, Lodowick Bryskett's
A Discourse of the Civill Life. Richard McCabe describes the *Discourse* as
providing 'a unique insight into the intellectual nature of Spenser's Irish
circle'.[6] The *Discourse* was not published until 1606, but Bryskett sets it
in his house near Dublin sometime in the early 1580s. It claims to record
a discussion over three days at which, among other fellow servants of
the Crown, Edmund Spenser was present.[7] Bryskett summarizes for his
guests material he has been gathering (largely from his Italian source,
Cinthio) about what a good man is and how he is formed. For Bryskett
such good men are such as 'haue aunciently bin called *Heroes*' (p. 207)
because through their own moral virtue and self-discipline they help to
create a civil commonwealth. The following passage, although lengthy,
is strikingly close in a number of its points, I shall argue, to the exemplary poet-hero constructed in Spenser's 1595 volume. According to
Bryskett, the 'good man':

> knoweth that he is not borne to himselfe alone, but to ciuill societie
> and conuersation, and to the good of others as well as of himselfe, he
> therefore doth his endeuour with all care and diligence so to carry
> himselfe in words and in deeds, as he might be a patterne and exam-
> ple to others of seemly and vertuous speeches and honest actions,
> and do them all the good he could in reducing them to a good and
> commendable forme of life. For the performance whereof, he per-
> ceiueth how requisite it is, that honestie and vertue be vnited with
> profite and pleasure, that by a iust and equall temper of them, both
> himselfe and others may attaine that end which is the *summum
> bonum*, and the thing wherupon all our discourse hath bin grounded.
> This end is not to be attained but by the meanes of morall vertues,

which are the perfection of the minde, & setled habits in ruling the appetite which ariseth out of the vnreasonable parts of the soule: for vertues are grounded in those parts which are without reason, but yet are apt to be ruled by reason. (pp. 208–9)

For Bryskett, the good man recognizes his duty is to further the good of the community not only of himself. This duty is fulfilled primarily through his ability to make a 'patterne and example' of himself, displaying himself to others as a civilized man, that is, a man able to 'temper', or rule, his own desires and appetites through the control of a reason perfected by the moral virtues. By so doing, both the good man and others attain the '*summum bonum*', what Bryskett elsewhere calls 'ciuill felicitie' (p. 40).

Bryskett's listening guest, Spenser, does not comment on his host's definition of this civil hero, but I suggest that the process of forming the private self so that it can be openly and shamelessly displayed in public as the basis for a civil commonwealth, is central to his use of himself as protagonist in *Amoretti and Epithalamion*. His highly distinctive rewriting of the Petrarchan sonnet sequence in *Amoretti*, figures a process of binding what is shamefully secret and selfish, 'ruling the appetite which ariseth out of the vnreasonable parts of the soule', in Bryskett's terms, so that the state of man may be 'tempered' or 'settled'. This process is analogous to, indeed for Spenser and Bryskett, instrumental in, tempering, settling and binding the larger commonwealths of people and landscapes imagined as sharing Spenser's personal celebrations in *Epithalamion*.

Bryskett's concern with the formation of a civil society acquires particular significance in Ireland, inhabited by 'wilde Irish' who, in the words of Sir Philip Sidney 'choose rather all filthiness then any law'.[8] Bryskett's guests were, like Spenser, all part of the Elizabethan colonial establishment in Ireland, either as soldiers, officials, or, in one case, John Long, a clergyman shortly to become Primate of Ireland.[9] Spenser's programme in *A View of the State of Ireland*, written just two or three years after the 1595 volume, designed to reduce 'that (salvage) nation to better government and civility' is in many respects typical of what were termed the 'New English' views of the Elizabethan settlers and government officials in Ireland.[10] Civility for the 'New English' was defined in English terms, specifically imitating English patterns of government and belief. The Council in England instructed the Lord Deputy in 1583 to repeople Munster, devasted by rebellion, with 'obedient people... governed by the laws of the realm, as the people in the civil countries of the pale are, that is, by distributing the territories into baronies, and those into hundreds, and those into townships and parishes'.[11] That done, the importation of 'obedient people' with their reformed faith, organized in parishes and towns, might, it was hoped, by law and example, succeed in 'civilizing' Ireland. The 1595 volume, significantly located in a cleared and resettled Munster, offers through the exemplary courtship and marriage of its protagonist, just such an example of a godly, English civility. In fact, in order to achieve such civility, Spenser like other English colonial theorists and practitioners, advocated first the use of savage force to extirpate savagery. As McCabe has pointed out, the terms 'civility' and 'savagery' prove unstable in Spenser's writings on Ireland, and 'intended contrasts collapse all too easily into unintentional comparisons, betraying the common heritage of "civil" and "savage", the embarrassing kinship of self and other'.[12]

It is no accident that Spenser is concerned with the larger civil ordering of the commonwealth in a volume of verse celebrating courtship and marriage. Metaphors that link the private with the public, the microcosmos with the macrocosmos are, of course, everywhere to hand in Elizabethan thought. In the process, distinctions tend to disappear. The private becomes public and the public depends on the private. Thus in *A Discourse*, Bryskett gathers authorities to support the view that unruliness of the appetites, and particularly sexual looseness in the individual can have macrocosmic effects:

> *Architas* the Tarentine was of opinion, that the pestilence was a lesser euill among men then pleasure of the bodie: from whence came treacheries, and betraying of countries, destructions of commonweales, murders, rapes, adulteries, and all other euils, euen as from a spring or fountain. The cause whereof *Pythagoras* desiring to find out, said, that delight first crept into cities, then satietie, next violence, and lastly the ruine and ouerthrow of the Commonwealth. (p. 198)

If disorderly sexuality could destroy commonwealths, marriage was represented as a bond that held unruly elements together. Indeed it was often described as the central bond of civil society, ordering the selfish sexual appetites of men. For William Perkins, Elizabethan churchman and theologian, matrimony 'was made and appointed by God him-selfe, to be the fountaine and seminarie of al other sorts and kinds of life, in the Common-wealth and in the Church'.[13] Heinrich Bullinger, the reformer who wrote an influential treatise on marriage which was translated by Miles Coverdale, and frequently reprinted, described its effects as being 'to comforte / mainteyne / helpe / counsaill / to clense / to further vnto good maners / honestie & shamefastnesse to expel vnclennesse / to avaunce the honoure of god and the publike weale'.[14] Not only could the binding of individual appetites figure the wider bonds of civil society, but *vice versa*, a disordered state could be figured in terms of private appetites. Nowhere was this more true than in representations of Ireland. John Derricke, for example, in 1581 described Ireland as a peverse bride:

> I meruailde in my mynde,
>   and therepon did muse:
> To see a Bride of heauenlie hewe,
>   an ouglie feere to chuse.
> This Bride it is the Soile,
>   the Bridegrome is the Karne,
> With writhed glibbes like wicked Sprits,
>   with visage rough and stearne.
> With sculles upon their poules,
>   in steade of ciuill Cappes.[15]

If the lack of civil bonds renders individuals and nations 'wilde', loose, disordered, and unproductive, notions of civility in both the individual and the state are described in Bryskett's and Spenser's texts in terms of ruling, ordering, 'tempering' and balance: 'ciuill felicitie' writes Bryskett, 'is atchieued by the temper of reason, ruling the disordinate affects stirred vp in vs by the reasonable parts of the mind ... and guiding vs by the meane of vertue to happy life' (p. 40). The 'meane of vertue' is not only the 'means' or agency of virtue, but also a reminder that virtue itself, as defined by Aristotle, and Spenser in Book 2 of *The Faerie Queene*, is a mean or mid-point between two extremes. As with ideas about marriage, the virtuous mean is sometimes represented as a dynamic bridling of unruly elements, entailing constant vigilence, with order and reason continually having to 'measure out a meane' (*FQ*, 2.i.58) between extremes, and sometimes as an ideal state of achieved balance. In *A View*, Irenius holds out the tantalizing possibility that one might lead to the other in Ireland where with 'moderation ... in tempering and managing, this stubborne nation of the Irish [might be brought] from their delight of licentious barbarisme unto the love of goodnesse and civilitie' (pp. 20–1).

Civility and language

Whether conceived of as a dynamic binding of unruly elements, or the recovery of an ideal godly harmony, civility was often described as the product of the civilizing arts of language. Bryskett cites Socrates as the authority for the view that,

> verses and Poeticall numbers are the perfectest Musike, and that they enter like liuely sparkes into mens minds, to kindle in them desires of dignitie, greatnesse, honor, true praise and commendation, and to correct whatsoeuer is in them of base and vile affection. In auncient time therfore men caused their children to be instructed in Poesie before all other disciplines, for that they esteemed good Poets to be the fathers of wisedome, and the vndoubted true guides to ciuill life, and not without cause. (p. 148)

The type of the civilizing poet was the mythical Orpheus who through his playing on the lyre was thought to have moved trees and rocks and calmed human strife. One of the most popular allegorized compendiums of myth in the sixteenth century, Natalis Comes' *Mythologiae*, summarizes the myth:

> Before Orpheus came among mortal men, they were barbaric, living without chosen customs or laws, roaming the fields like wild animals, without so much as a roof over their heads. But Orpheus's words and the sweetness of his speech had so great an effect that he converted men to a gentler way of life, calling them together into one place, teaching them to build cities, to keep civil laws, and to accept the institution of marriage. Such was believed to be the vocation of ancient poets and is intrinsic to the art of poetry.[16]

As we shall see, Comes' interpretation of the significance of Orpheus is strikingly similar to the civilizing programme implied in Spenser's 1595 volume. If the good Orphic poet could civilize unruly men, then bad poetry bestialized them. Such, in the eyes of the 'New English', were the verses of the Irish bards who, in the words of Fynes Moryson, 'allure the hearers, not to the love of religion and Civill manners, but to outrages Robberies living as outlawes, and Contempt of the Magistrates and the kings lawes':

> Alas how vnlike vnto Orpheus, who with his sweete harpe and wholesome precepts of Poetry laboured to reduce the rude and barbarous people from liuing in woods, to dwell Ciuilly in Townes and Cittyes, and from wilde ryott to morall Conuersation.[17]

Moryson's views chime with those of Irenius in the *View*, who accused the Irish bards of praising 'whomsoeuer they finde to be most licentious of life' unlike those 'Poets as in their writings doe labour to better the manners of men, and thorough the sweete baite of their numbers, to steale into the young spirits a desire of honour and vertue' (pp. 75–6). The poet of the 1595 volume emphatically places himself in the latter group. His culturally and politically freighted language constructs an exemplary courtship and marriage, by an exemplary civil gentleman, in Munster in 1594, as an exemplary image of civility.

Spenser twice alludes to Orpheus in the 1595 volume and on both occasions the allusions register the failure of language as much as they celebrate its power.[18] *Amoretti* 44 compares the effect of the poet-lover's verse to that of Orpheus:

> When those renoumed noble Peres of Greece,
>   thrugh stubborn pride amongst themselues did iar
>   forgetfull of the famous golden fleece,
>   then Orpheus with his harp theyr strife did bar. (ll. 1–4)

The 'ciuill warre' which the lover's 'selfe against my selfe doe make' (l. 6) cannot however be so pacified:

> But when in hand my tunelesse harp I take,
>   then doe I more augment my foes despight:
>   and griefe renew, and passions doe awake,
>   to battaile fresh against my selfe to fight. (ll. 9–12)

As protagonist in his own history, the poet-lover has not, at least by this stage in the sequence, achieved that tempering of the will that should, in making him a 'good man', also make him a 'patterne and example to others' (Bryskett, *A Discourse*, p. 208).

Orpheus is again alluded to in the first stanza of *Epithalamion*. This is a more unusual and puzzling reference. The poet-bridegroom calls on the Muses to help him sing in praise of his bride: 'So Orpheus did for his owne bride, | So I vnto my selfe alone will sing' (ll. 16–17). It is not primarily the myth of Orpheus's civilizing powers that is here alluded to, but the story of Orpheus the poet-bridegroom whose bride, Eurydice, was stung by a serpent on her wedding day and died. Later, trying to lead her back to life from the underworld, Orpheus was unable to refrain from looking back longingly at her and so broke the injunctions of the gods and lost her a second time. As Loewenstein and others have pointed out, an allusion to Orpheus' songs for his bride is highly problematic at the beginning of a marriage hymn.[19] The Orpheus that is invoked in the 1595 volume as a model for the poet is thus a complex figure, a public poet, able to pacify civil strife and create social harmony, but also a private poet whose inability to bring about and celebrate his own marriage could be interpreted as an allegory of the limitations of a civilizing eloquence, particularly in the face of the unruly potential of desire.[20]

Amoretti

Earlier critical readings of the 1595 volume and especially of the sonnet sequence, as lacking coherence, have given way to a more general recognition of the evidence of plan and sequential arrangement of both the sonnet sequence and the volume as a whole.[21] Alexander Dunlop in particular, in his 1970 study of the sonnet sequence, emphasized the importance of Spenser's 'An Hymne in Honour of Love', published as one of Spenser's *Fowre Hymnes* (1596), for an understanding of *Amoretti*'s programme.[22] My own study of the sequence strongly supports Dunlop's perception, but differs in emphasizing the equal importance of another of the *Fowre Hymnes*, 'An Hymne in Honour of Beautie'. In so doing, I question Dunlop's reading of the sequence in terms of a gradual neoplatonic ascent by the lover 'from desire to a higher form of love'.[23] Erotic desire remains central to the narrative of love in the 1595 volume, culminating in marriage.

Spenser claims in the dedicatory epistle that the two Hymns in Honour of Love and Beauty (to which I shall refer as HL and HB) were written 'in the greener times of my youth' (p. 452). In view of the many parallels between these Hymns, *Amoretti and Epithalamion*, and Colin Clout's vatic exposition of the power of love and beauty in *Colin Clovts Come Home Againe* (also printed in 1595), this statement needs to be treated with some caution. The repeated celebration of love as an elemental force at work within the divine economy of creation, often expressed in very similar terms in all five texts, suggests that the first two Hymns were at least revised in the years immediately preceding their publication in 1596.

In HL, Love is figured as a divinely sanctioned Cupid who 'tempers' the unruly elements out of which matter is made:

> Ayre hated earth, and water hated fyre,
> Till Loue relented their rebellious yre.

> He then them tooke, and tempering goodly well
> Their contrary dislikes and loued meanes,
> Did place them all in order, and compell
> To keepe them selues within their sundrie raines,
> Together linkt with Adamantine chaines. (HL, ll. 83–9)

Cupid's 'tempering' of the irreconcilable elements is here given a kind of permanence through force ('Adamantine chaines'), but the ordering power of love within human individuals works more subtly. Like all living things, man seeks to 'quench the flame' (l. 102) of desire, but in his case the object should not be the simple satisfaction of lust. Instead, he 'for eternitie, | Seekes to enlarge his lasting progenie' (ll. 104–5) as part of a providential economy. The complex, and divinely-ordained process of courtship that follows is explained through the course of HL and HB. In Spenser's syncretic myth, male erotic desire, if rightly used and tempered, provides the energy through which God's providential plan for the material world is enacted. The feminine beauty that is the object of male desire is, rightly understood, 'a celestiall powre' (HB, l. 50). Those with 'most resemblance of that heauenly light', an inner beauty, are those who are 'most beautifull and braue' (HB, ll. 121–2). It is the desire to possess such celestial beauty, reflected in the outer form, that drives the male lover to endure a long courtship in which, through suffering, he is tested and transformed:

> Such is the powre of that sweet passion,
> That it all sordid basenesse doth expell,
> And the refyned mynd doth newly fashion
> Vnto a fairer forme. (HL, ll. 190–3)

In turn, the lady must also learn to show grace to 'Gentle Love', who

> Will more illumine your resplendent ray,
> And adde more brightnesse to your goodly hew,
> From light of his pure fire, which by like way
> Kindled of yours, your likenesse doth display,
> Like as two mirrours by opposd reflexion,
> Doe both express the faces first impression. (HB, ll. 177–82)

In this universe of reflections, 'Gentle Love' may signify Cupid, who will 'adde more brightnesse' to the lady, or it may signify the love 'faire dames' should feel for their lovers which will illumine their beauty, or perhaps it signifies the heroic love felt by the male lover whose 'pure fire' will augment the lady's beauty and reflect her true self back to her, as she reflects his true likeness to him. The uncertain signifieds indicate a conflation of all three in Spenser's paradigm of love's operation. In the same way, the lovers mirror both 'the faces first impression', that is, the first sight by which the lovers were smitten, but also the originating impression or imprint of a divine 'goodly Paterne' (HB, l. 32). Thus learning to love the other may be, rightly understood, a process of refinding a godly, whole and unified self:

> a celestiall harmonie,
> Of likely harts composd of starres concent,
> Which ioyne together in sweete sympathie,
> To worke ech others ioy and true content,
> Which they haue harbourd since their first descent
> Out of their heauenly bowres, where they did see
> And know ech other here belou'd to bee. (HB, ll. 197–203)

HL and HB develop a myth of erotic love as a dynamic force working through all created things as an agent for a divine pattern of order, but it is a myth that contains contradictory aspects. On the one hand love is imagined as a binding, legalizing pressure that can bring anarchic and selfish desires into a productive balance, on the other hand, it is also imagined as a process of recognition in which the hero-lovers find their preordained place within a divine order. In *Amoretti*, the poet figures himself as the hero-lover of such a narrative of self-formation and discovery. In this process, the ordering of desire is not only of personal significance for Spenser's domestic history, but also for a notion of divine order that embraces all aspects of human life and society; much more than a private '*summum bonum*' (Bryskett's term) seems to depend on the personal conformity of Spenser's hero-lover. However, the heroic agency of the poet-lover striving to make out of his own personal history a pattern that like a seed crystal will precipitate order through society, can also be seen, from a different perspective, as the striving of the individual to conform to a pattern imposed from without. The tension in Spenser's writing between a notion of order that depends on forcing unlike elements together, and one which sees order as the discovery of a divine pattern, betrays the cultural mechanism by which the conformity of selfish desires, required for civil order, is naturalized by being represented as the felicitous outcome of a divinely-ordained dynamic. The individual who, through her or his personal conformity to a divine pattern, produces the civil state, is at the same time, willy-nilly, produced in conformity to the interests of that state through the cultural work of writers such as Spenser.

The process described in the Hymns, whereby the male lover is refined by love, and the lady tempered by showing grace, in order to achieve a mutual love that fulfils a divine 'goodly Paterne', structures the narrative of *Amoretti*. In this process of mutual formation, self and other, subject and object, conqueror and conquest, become difficult to differentiate. *Amoretti* 69, for example, may refer either to a conquest of the lady by the poet-lover, or a conquest of the lover by the lady that implies a conquering of the lower lusts of the lover by his idealized self:

> What trophee then shall I most fit deuize,
>   in which I may record the memory
>   of my loues conquest, peerelesse beauties prise,
>   adorn'd with honour, love and chastity?
> Euen this verse vowd to eternity,
>   shall be thereof immortall moniment:
>   and tell her prayse to all posterity,
>   that may admire such worlds rare wonderment.
> The happy purchase of my glorious spoile,
>   gotten at last with labour and long toyle. (ll. 5–14)

The martial imagery points to a dynamic of conquest and subjection found throughout the *Amoretti*. The poet's self-formation as a moral hero, able to rule his own appetites and schooled in an understanding of the divine nature of love, is imagined as a process of discipline and education by the other, the lady, who is not only luscious virgin territory to be possessed, but, in the terms of HB, the embodiment, in particularly transparent form, of that 'goodly Patterne' of the originating celestial beauty. In order to be formed as a fully 'tempered' and refined man, a hero of civility, and legitimate master of the territory, the poet-lover must show himself able to submit to the discipline of Love as an instrument of divine order:

> By so hard handling those which best thee serue,
> That ere thou doest them vnto grace restore,
> Thou mayest well trie if they will ever swerue,
> And mayest them make it better to deserue,
> And hauing got it, may it more esteeme,
> For things hard gotten, men more dearely deeme. (HL, ll. 163–8)

As the poet-lover of *Amoretti* tells us: 'Onely my paines wil be the more to get her, I but hauing her, my ioy wil be the greater' (51). The passing of a protracted period of trial and suffering is essential in forming the worthy lover and proving the permanence and faithfulness of his love. He who gives up too easily is merely subject to 'loathly sinfull lust' and 'like a moldwarpe in the earth doth ly' (HL, ll. 179, 182). He is not one of those in whom Love, in the words of *The Faerie Queene* 'stirredst up th'Heroës high intents' (3.iii.2).

Able to conquer himself, and refined by a virtuous passion, the lover may in turn conquer the lady, a process that involves the defeat of what Spenser calls her pride or 'selfe assurance' (*Amoretti* 59). Her fierce separateness is as much a threat to the ideal of mutual love as the poet's lust, and it too must be softened and tempered. This process is enacted through the sequence as in part a response to the godly instruction that is audible through the poet's words, and in part a reward for his increasingly godly behaviour and the evidence of his long-term faithfulness. In *Amoretti* 13, the lady is praised for her 'goodly temperature' combining a 'proud port', her 'face rear[ed] vp to the skie' with a 'myld humblesse' as, her eyelids bent to the ground, she 'remembreth her mortalitie'. Nevertheless she 'seems to scorne I base thing', failing to recognize any kinship with the poet-lover. Were she to do so, the lover tells her, 'such lowlinesse shall make you lofty be'. The lover's plea here is scarcely distinguishable from a standard Petrarchan lover's self-interested wooing, but the argument recurs with increasingly explicit Christian overtones. In *Amoretti* 53, for example, she is told:

> Great shame it is, thing so diuine in view,
>   made for to be the worlds most ornament:
>   to make the bayte her gazers to embrew,
>   good shames to be to ill an instrument.
> But mercy doth with beautie best agree,
>   as in theyr maker ye them best may see. (ll. 9–14)

The pleadings of desire become, as the exemplary narrative unfolds, the vehicle of a providential love working through desire, anticipating the lesson given to the lady in HB, 'It you behoues to loue, and forth to lay I That heauenly riches … For else what booteth that celestiall ray'? (HB, ll. 184–7).

The process of persuasion and redefinition that characterizes the process of mutual conquest and formation in the sequence may be illustrated by two sonnets on the theme of self-assurance. *Amoretti* 58 and 59 are clearly a pair with one answering the other. Sonnet 58 is headed '*By her that is most assured to her selfe*'. It has been suggested this may mean the sonnet is '*by*' the lady, but given the theme of the conquest of the lady's self-sufficiency through the sequence, '*by*' is more likely to mean 'concerning'.[24] It is sonnet 59 that is more likely to ventriloquize the lady's voice. Sonnet 58 teaches the lesson that no assurance can be put in anything belonging to this world, least of all beauty:

> Ne none so rich or wise, so strong or fayre,
>> but fayleth trusting on his owne assurance:
>> and he that standeth on the hyghest stayre
>> fals lowest: for on earth nought hath enduraunce.
> Why then doe ye proud fayre, misdeeme so farre,
>> that to your selfe ye most assured arre? (ll. 9–14)

In reply, sonnet 59 defends self-assurance, defining it in terms of a tempered Aristotelian mean between destructive extremes:

> Thrise happie she, that is so well assured
>> Vnto her selfe and setled so in hart:
>> that nether will for better be allured,
>> ne feard with worse to any chaunce to start,
> But like a steddy ship doth strongly part
>> the raging waues and keepes her course aright. (ll. 1–6)

The subject and object of the concluding verb are characteristically ambiguous:

> Most happy she that most assured doth rest,
>> but he most happy who such one loues best. (ll. 13–14)

Is he most happy in his love for her, or as the fortunate object of her love?

The dialogue of the two sonnets contest definitions of self-assurance. In the first self-assurance may be a synonym for pride, a reprehensible self-sufficiency in which the 'proud fayre' separates her (or him) self from the rest of society and its common experience of time and dependency. In the second, self-assurance is a settled inner virtue that guarantees the faith and trustworthiness of she/he who has it. The definitions of the two sonnets echo and mirror each other through a feminine and a masculine voice that cannot be easily differentiated, but which work in relation to each other to modify and redefine common terms into a sharper understanding of what the best happiness and love might be. The process of gradual education and formation of lover and lady, and through them of the reader, evident throughout the sequence, is here enacted in a single pair of sonnets.

The vexed question of whose voice speaks which sonnet reminds us of the illusory nature of this dialogue and the theme of mutual formation in the sequence. The lady is a construct of Spenser's writing and never speaks for herself; she is virgin territory, a blank sheet onto which Spenser projects his own exemplary self-formation. She represents a reflection of divine beauty, a threatening Pandora, gifted by the gods to attract and correct the poet-lover (*Amoretti* 24), but also, more disturbingly, she represents temptations on the poet's own part to self-sufficiency, and, its opposite, lust – desires that threaten in different ways the self-mastery of the 'good man' and hence the civil society of which he is an integral part. Self-assurance may take the form of arrogance, a conscious sense of superiority and of the self as origin of the 'goodly Patterne'. It is the lady who is rebuked for her pride, as we have seen, but she may represent, in her separateness, a seductive hubris that tempts the hero-poet himself who, in rewriting Petrarch's prestigious *Canzoniere*, attempts no less than 'an endlesse moniment' for short time (*Epithalamion*, l. 433), and a transformation of the self into a blueprint for civility.

The lady may embody not only the poet-lover's temptation to an individuality and self-assertion that must be softened and tempered, but also his uncivil appetites, the threatening rebelliousness of desire. As we have seen in HL, desire (Cupid) is imagined as a dynamic force that binds the warring elements and drives men to seek that Beauty that will refine their minds and lead to marriage, that central bond of civility. But erotic desire is also the most powerful of the appetites that must be bound and fettered in civil society. Throughout *Amoretti and Epithalamion* powerful images and narratives of the pleasures and godliness of erotic desire are juxtaposed to other images and narratives that betray fear and suspicion of its perceived anarchic dangers.

The godliness of erotic desire is suggested by the careful juxtaposition of Spenser's wooing with the period of Lent. Alexander Dunlop established in detail that the 46 sonnets from *Amoretti* 22 (the 'Ash Wednesday sonnet') to 68 (the 'Easter Sunday sonnet') imitate the Lenten period of 40 days plus the intervening six Sundays.[25] The alignment of Edmund Spenser's personal erotic trial, however exemplary, with the period of Lent, a time of fasting in preparation for the crucifixion on Good Friday, imitating Christ's forty days of fasting and trial in the wilderness, may at first sight seem sacrilegious, but is part of

Spenser's Protestant authorization of his narrative of courtship and civil marriage as divinely sanctioned. *Amoretti* 22, the Ash Wednesday sonnet, seems to indicate in its idolatrous substitution of the lady as object of worship, that the poet has as yet much to learn:

> This holy season fit to fast and pray,
>   Men to deuotion ought to be inclynd:
>   therefore, I lykewise on so holy day,
>   for my sweet Saynt some seruice fit will find. (ll. 1–4)

By *Amoretti* 68, the Easter Sunday sonnet, the poet's profane love is represented as no longer a distraction from his worship of God, but as an appropriate development of it:

> This ioyous day, deare Lord, with ioy begin,
>   and grant that we for whom thou diddest dye
>   being with thy deare blood clene washt from sin,
>   may liue for euer in felicity.
> And that thy loue we weighing worthily,
>   may likewise loue thee for the same againe:
>   and for thy sake that all lyke deare didst buy,
>   with loue may one another entertayne.
> So let vs loue, deare loue, lyke as we ought,
>   loue is the lesson which the Lord vs taught. (ll. 5–14)

Here two kinds of love normally distinguished are conflated; the charitable love (agape) invoked by Christ in his two commandments: that we love God and that we love each other (John 13, vv. 34–5), and erotic love (eros) which the poet invokes when he turns, after addressing his 'deare Lord' to addressing his 'deare love'. However striking the conflation, the Prayer Book's marriage service, which placed erotic marriage within paradise, lent Spenser sufficient authority.

Spenser's Lenten sequence enacts the poet-lover's suffering, trial and the growing conformity of both lovers to the godly pattern of submission and grace. Sonnet 25, for example, is suitably Lenten, with the lover complaining of the long 'mysery' of his 'lyke dying lyfe'. Even so, the lover recognizes that were his mistress 'to shew me grace', all his 'woes and wrecks' may eventually be a 'meanes of blisse'. By sonnet 35, it is becoming evident that the lover's long misery is beginning to produce signs of the refinement and fidelity that should characterize the heroic lover. The lady's beauty detaches the lover from the vain shows of the world: 'All this worlds glory seemeth vayne to me, I and all their showes but shadowes sauing she.' This may be seen as a first step towards the achieved wisdom and virtue with which he praises, in *Amoretti* 79, the 'trew fayre' of the lady:

> For all the rest, how euer fayre it be,
> > shall turne to nought and loose that glorious hew:
> > but onely that is permanent and free
> > from frayle corruption, that doth flesh ensew.
> That is true beautie. (ll. 5–9)

The lover of *Amoretti* 35 is, nevertheless 'lyke *Narcissus* vaine' in so far as his gaze is unreturned; there is no approving other looking back. This sonnet is part of a developing narrative of sight, transparency and reflection that runs through the sequence. At the beginning of *Amoretti*, the gazing is all on the part of the lover, as is conventional in Petrarchan poetry. In *Amoretti* 8, the poet recognizes that his lady's beauty is 'heauenly' and that, through her, 'Angels come' to 'frame my thoughts and fashion me within' in the disciplines of chastity, faithfulness and patience, but our signal that all is not right at this stage is the lack of reciprocity imaged by the competing gazes of the lover and the lady. Where the lover is content to 'behold you euer', the lady's eyes reflect only the 'liuing fire' that is their source in heaven, or, more ominously, they harbour an unseeing guest: 'Thrugh your bright beams doth not the blinded guest I shoot out his darts to base affections wound?' (ll. 5–6). In this lady's eyes, the lover sees only reflections of heaven and lust; there appears no virtuous place for himself.

In *Amoretti* 45, it is the lady who is Narcissus-like, and who is urged to find her true reflection in the poet:

> Leaue lady in your glasse of christall clene,
> > Your goodly selfe for euermore to vew:
> > and in my selfe, my inward selfe I meane,
> > most liuely lyke behold your semblant trew.
> Within my hart, though hardly it can shew
> > thing so diuine to vew of earthly eye:
> > the fayre Idea of your celestiall hew,
> > and euery part remaines immortally. (ll. 1–8)

As yet, however, there is no reflection of the godly image of the other in either lover; she will not look in the right place and the poet's sorrow has 'dimmed and deformd … the goodly ymage of your visnomy' (ll. 10–11). Anyway, as Dunlop points out, the poet's heart, the seat of the passions, is not the best place for the lady to look for a 'celestiall' image.[26] The lover at this point has as much to learn as the lady.

Not until *Amoretti* 66 do we find an image of mutual reflection and confirmation, 'Like as two mirrours by opposd reflexion' that signals achieved love in HB (l. 181). In *Amoretti* 13 the lady scorned to look on the 'base thing' that was the poet. Now, in 66, she is praised for stooping 'unto so lowly state':

> But ye thereby much greater glory gate,
>> then had ye sorted with a princes pere:
>> for now your light doth more it selfe dilate,
>> and in my darknesse greater doth appeare.
> Yet since your light hath once enlumind me,
>> with my reflex yours shall encreased be. (ll. 9–14)

This image of mutual recognition and illumination is central to the theme of love's civilizing power in the 1595 volume. As her approving gaze validates his virtuous submission to the disciplines of a godly love, so his gaze confirms and rewards her equal submission. The self and the other now reflect each other, narcissus-like, or rather they see in the other their mutual conformity to a godly identity.

Mirror images of each other though they be, their difference remains crucial. The mutual looking in sonnet 66 is a sign of endorsement and approval, of the willing submission of the conquered that validates the conquest. But they remain symbiotically dependent; there is always a lack in the lover figured by the irreducible and desirable otherness of the lady's body. That lack becomes a major theme in the final group of sonnets following *Amoretti* 68. In *Amoretti* 76 the lady's body is a 'bowre of blisse, the paradice of pleasure', but it is a forbidden paradise:

> How was I rauisht with your louely sight,
>> and my frayle thoughts too rashly led astray?
>> whiles diuing deepe through amorous insight,
>> on the sweet spoyle of beautie they did pray. (ll. 5–8)

The lover's 'frayle thoughts' that 'loosely … theyr wanton winges display' (l. 11) cast him as a potential Eve/serpent in this paradise. In *Amoretti* 77, the lady's body is again a stimulus to forbidden appetites, this time through the imagery of food and feasting: 'a goodly table of pure yvory: | all spred with iuncats' (ll. 2–3). But this banquet is enticingly off-limits: 'Exceeding sweet, yet voyd of sinfull vice, | That many sought yet none could euer taste' (ll. 9–10). In its final line the sonnet returns to the erotic thoughts of the poet-lover: 'my thoughts the guests, which would thereon haue fedd' (l. 14). The insistent return of the motif of for-bidden fruits signals the limits to mutually self-reflective and self-validating identity figured by the mirroring gaze of the lover and his lady. The lady's erotic body remains insistently other to the disciplined masculine self, disturbing its self-mastery and emphasizing its lack of completeness.

The thoughts that would have fed on the banquet of the lady's body make another appearance in *Amoretti* 78. Here they are urged to com-pensate for her absence by beholding 'her selfe in mee'. 'Lackyng my loue', the lover seeks her in 'field [and] bowre':

> But when myne eyes I thereunto direct,
>   they ydly back returne to me agayne,
>   and when I hope to see theyr trew obiect,
>   I fynd my selfe but fed with fancies vayne.
> Ceasse then myne eyes, to seeke her selfe to see,
>   and let my thoughts behold her selfe in mee. (ll. 9–14)

The third quatrain in which the lover's inwardly turning eyes enact a kind of sterile narcissism, 'ydly backe returne to me', 'fynd my selfe … fed with fancies vayne', offers little hope that the thoughts, so sensu-ously engaged in the previous sonnet, will succeed in finding a satisfy-ing 'trew object' in the poet's own mind.

The lady's absence foregrounds the poet-lover's lack of self-sufficiency, his need for her confirming presence, and her legitimisation of his oth-erwise vain fancies. Her fleshly resistance to abstraction becomes the guarantee of her difference, that part of her which cannot be mastered by the lover. This difference unsettles Spenser's narrative of mutuality and conquest. The insufficiency of the idea alone of the lady is drama-tized in *Amoretti* 88 in which the lover again attempts to substitute for his lack 'th'Idæa playne' of 'some glance' of the 'image of that heauenly ray' (ll. 7–9). The unsatisfactory nature of such Platonic abstraction is made clear: 'But with such brightnesse whylest I fill my mind, | I starue my body and mine eyes doe blynd' (ll. 13–14).[27] In a sequence that cul-minates in a marriage hymn the inadequacy of substituting for the lady's physical presence an idea of a glance of a ray is appropriate. Nevertheless, it also signals the poet-lover's dependence on the other as potentially troubling and even dangerous. The lady as idealized other, willingly reflecting an approved divine image back to the poet-lover, is a sign of the achieved conquest of self and other, but her irreducible sexual difference, foregrounded by her physical absence, disturbs and disorders the self-conquest her submission seemed to guarantee.

The motif of Narcissus, as we have seen, repeatedly recurs in *Amoretti*, used often to differentiate false images of sterile self-reflection from godly images of mutual reflection. The similarity of these two forms of self-reflection nevertheless lays bare an identity that threatens to collapse Spenser's narrative of exemplary self-formation. Both self and other reflect aspects of the authorial self, spun out, to use another recurring image of the sequence, of the writer's own spider body, but conversely his sense of what he is depends on what he sees in her. This fragile sense of the self, dependent on the reflection that is cast in the mirror into which the poet looks, becomes apparent, appropriately, in a pair of repeated Narcissus sonnets, *Amoretti* 35 and 83. As a number of critics have pointed out the recurrence of the same sonnet, whether an error or not, produces different readings in the two contexts.[28] At its earlier appearance, this sonnet seemed to contribute to the narrative of the gradual refining of the poet through his love for the lady; her true beauty drew him away from the vanity of 'this worlds glory' and the Narcissus image seemed ironic, a misunderstanding on the part of the speaker, analogous to that of Britomart who mistakenly compared her divinely-approved love for Artegall to that of Narcissus' love for a mere shade (*The Faerie Queene*, 3.ii.44). Repeated as sonnet 83, towards the end of the sequence, following a series of poems in which the lover's thoughts seem to loiter dangerously on the forbidden physical delights of the lady, the confession that 'All this worlds glory seemeth vayne to me, | and all theyr shewes but shadowes sauing she' (ll. 13–14), suggests an opening void, 'so plenty makes me pore'. The lover, absorbed in the unpossessable otherness of what he desires, is in danger of losing his self-affirming sense of difference. He sees, like Narcissus, only an identity that denies him existence.

The conquest of self and its appetites was the means through which, according to Bryskett, the good man brought 'both himself and others [to] attaine the *summum bonum*' (quoted p. 93 above). Spenser's poet-lover finds, in the last part of the *Amoretti* sequence, that desire for an other that is unpossessed and cannot be assimilated threatens not only his formation as a fully mastered self, but also his wider roles in civil society. Mutual love is repeatedly imaged in the sequence as a form of bondage, both a place of safety, but also a prison, or a cage.[29] In *Amoretti* 73, two prisons/cages figure in the sonnet: the first is the 'prison' of the poet-lover's responsibilities in the public world of men, and the second his captivity to the lady:

> Being my selfe captyued here in care,
>> My hart, whom none with seruile bands can tye
>> but the fayre tresses of your golden hayre,
>> breaking his prison forth to you doth fly. ...
> Doe you him take, and in your bosome bright
>> gently encage, that he may be your thrall:
>> perhaps he there may learne with rare delight,
>> to sing your name and prayses ouer all. (ll. 1–4, 9–12)

Private and public are here opposed, with the poet-lover asserting that he happily exchanges the prison of public life and responsibility for a life in which like an encaged bird, he learns to sing, taught presumably by the lady. Some sense of what his public duties may entail is suggested by the following sonnet (74), in which the poet-lover does indeed sing Elizabeth Boyle's 'name and prayses ouer all' by elevating her 'of all aliue most worthy to be praysed', not only above Elizabeth Spenser, the poet's mother, but also above Elizabeth I, his queen.

The idea that service to Elizabeth Boyle may compete with other forms of service recurs in *Amoretti* 80 in which 'prison' imagery makes another appearance. Recalling the terms of *Amoretti* 33 in which the poet conceded that he did 'great wrong' to his Queen by neglecting his epic for his private courtship, the poet-lover in 80 asks leave to rest after so long spent compiling the six books of *The Faerie Queene*, in order 'in pleasant mew, | to sport my muse and sing my loues sweet praise' (ll. 9–10). He tells his Queen that praise of Elizabeth Boyle will be 'low and meane' compared to that for her. 'Refreshed' after such 'sport' he will 'out of my prison ... breake anew' (ll. 5–6), like a bird of prey escaping its cage ('mew'), and continue with his epic. As in *Amoretti* 73, the duties of the public man and the pleasures of the private man are represented as being in conflict. In the final sonnet of the sequence, the poet-lover images himself as a female 'Culuer' who, lacking 'her mate', will, in private song, 'mourne to my selfe the absence of my loue'. At the end of *Amoretti*, the absence of the lady, a sign of the limits to his self-mastery, leaves the poet unable to take advantage of his claimed freedom of flight, trapped, it seems in private song.

There is a sense of lost or false directions after the climactic sonnet 68. The lady having been won, the poet anticipates 'entrance ... Vnto thy heauen' (HL, ll. 273–74), but instead of closure, the sequence presents us with images of illicit desire, of absence, and of the potential conflict of private and public service. Unlike HL, *Amoretti* does not give us entry to a 'happie port' (l. 298). The betrothal will not be consummated until two thirds of the way through *Epithalamion* and already a number of sonnets in the last part of *Amoretti* suggest that the lady's otherness, her enticing and never fully transparent difference, is closely bound up with her desirability. Nor, as we have seen, can satisfaction and rest be achieved through a solipsistic contemplation of a disembodied 'Idæa playne' of an 'image of that heauenly ray' (*Amoretti* 88). Unable to move forward, the poet-lover at the end of the sequence cannot either quit his private project in order to celebrate the Virgin Queen, or bring his own private vision of the civil conversation of marriage to completion.

In Bryskett's treatise, the moral formation of the 'good man' precedes the formation of a civil society, imaged as the 'ciuill conuersation' of 'good men'. In Spenser's case the formation of the 'good man' struggles with a perceived lack of autonomy, its dependence on the confirmation and the presence of a conquered and virtuous other. Without the private, inner order and validation which his union with an idealized woman signals for the poet, he cannot go on to form an ideal nation in his epic. *Amoretti*'s celebration of an imagined mutuality and dependence in fact serves to signal a limit to mastery, and the impossibility of autonomy. The lady may be imagined mirroring an idealized version of the poet-lover back to himself by returning his loving look, and validating through her graceful recognition his vision of an ordered society through mutual love and marriage, but in the end her physical difference and separateness remain obstinate and uncontrollable, her absence a sign of that which cannot be wholly known, or possessed by the poet-lover, but on which his civic and godly identity depends.

Epithalamion

The marriage hymn seems at first to position Spenser, the poet-lover-husband, as patriarch, in full control of the events of the day and of his bride, offering his own private union as an instructive model for the wider structures of civil society. Spenser is both bridegroom and master of ceremonies.[30] Each stanza of the poem leads the bride, and we the readers, in an orderly sequence through the ceremonies of the marriage day from dawn to the marriage night. Spenser directs the proceedings at each step: the muses are instructed to 'Go to the bowre of my beloued loue' and 'Bid her awake' (ll. 23, 25); 'Bring with you all the Nymphes' (l. 37); the bride is told to 'awake' (l. 74); the attendant damsels are told to adorn her in stanza 6, and to await her coming forth in stanza 7, and so on. The full ceremony is ordered, open to view, and vigilantly controlled by the poet/master of ceremonies. Nevertheless, I shall argue, traces of imperfection remain, detectable in images and stories of disorder and mutability that threaten to defeat the success of the day, and that disturb the poet's male voice of mastery, of the self and others.

Closely as *Amoretti* and *Epithalamion* are related as parts of the narrative of the poet-lover's courtship, betrothal and marriage day, the shift in mood between the two is striking. This shift is mediated through the group of anacreontic verses that precede *Epithalamion*.[31] The poet-lover of *Amoretti* 89 was, as we saw, a sad figure describing himself as 'disconsolate', joyless and lifeless without his mate, singing his lamenting songs only to himself. The anacreontic verses provide a quite different perspective on love: lively, amusing, and wry. The intensely personalized experience of the poet-lover gives way to a generic discourse that stresses love's universality, absurdity, and indifference to the individual.

In the verses, the lover has 'waxed old' without learning from the lessons of his youth (1). In this and other respects he is not unlike the naughty Cupid of verse 4 who will not heed the warning of his indulgent mother from pursuing the bee and as a result gets stung. But perhaps such stinging is well worth it if the pain is assuaged by the erotic indulgence of Venus who wraps her son in her smock as the lover looks on covetously:

> And then she bath'd him in a dainty well,
> > the well of deare delight.
> Who would not oft be stung as this,
> To be so bath'd in Venus blis? (4, ll. 69–72)

The anacreontics associate erotic love with an anarchist Cupid, a sensuous and irresponsible child who breaks all the rules, but who inhabits a fantasy world in which the repercussions, however dire for humans, are never serious for Cupid, and, indeed, may be rewarded by pleasure. This association of desire with irresponsibility and wilfulness with pleasure provides a mocking perspective from which to view the virtuous poet-lover's privations at the end of *Amoretti*. Its disconcertingly playful perspective on erotic love returns again, as we shall see, at the most solemn moments in *Epithalamion*, that hymn to the social and godly legitimization of desire.

The first stanza of *Epithalamion*, in which the poet-groom asks the Muses to help him sing such songs as 'Orpheus did for his owne bride' (l. 16) seems ominously, to echo the final line of *Amoretti* 89, 'dead my life that wants such liuely blis'. As we have seen, the allusion is to Orpheus's fatal marriage day on which, fleeing from the lustful Aristeus, Eurydice was stung on the heel by a snake hidden in the grass (see my discussion pp. 98–9 above). The sixteenth-century mythographer, Comes, interpreted the story and its aftermath as an allegory of the soul threatened by fleshly desires, and continued: 'she died and descended to hell; she was recalled by the sound of the lute, but on this condition that the body could easily lose her if it did not obey reason and law'.[32] Telling the story of Orpheus's doomed attempt to lead Eurydice back from death to life in *Virgil's Gnat*, Spenser also emphasizes that all is lost through misplaced masculine desire:

> She (Ladie) hauing well before approoued,
> The feends to be too cruell and seuere,
> Obseru'd th'appointed way, as her behooued,
> Ne euer did her ey-sight turne arere,
> Ne euer spake, ne cause of speaking mooued:
> But cruell *Orpheus*, thou much crueller,
> Seeking to kisse her, brok'st the God's decree,
> And thereby mad'st her euer damn'd to be. (*VG*, ll. 465–73)

An allusion to Orpheus's songs for his bride at the start of a processional poem by a poet-lover who will lead his bride through their marriage day, may well imply the well-known stories of her loss and interpretations of those stories in terms of the dangers of unruly desire. It is an indication of the degree to which desire and its temptations are invested in the female body that it is the bride's eye-glances that are controlled lest they let in 'a little thought vnsownd' (l. 237), contributing to the sense of anxious policing and lurking danger hinted at throughout the marriage song.

Critics have located one source of the uneasiness that resonates through *Epithalamion* in the echo motif of the refrain which for sixteen of the twenty-three complete stanzas, plays variations on 'That all the woods may/shall/should answer and my/your/their eccho ring.' In the final seven stanzas, marking the fall of night, the refrain changes to variations on 'The woods no more shall answer nor our/your/their eccho ring.' For Loewenstein, the voice of echo is the 'voice of daemonic accusation', and he suggests that in *Epithalamion* it is used 'to inscribe threat on the very formulae of celebration'.[33] Bates suggests that the echo motif is 'conventionally associated with failed courtship' and is part of Spenser's experimentation 'with humiliation, failure, loss' as well as with 'reward and triumph'.[34] The motif of the woods responding to song refers to the civilizing power of Orpheus's song. Ovid described the woods moving their very roots to come to listen to Orpheus's songs, and Spenser translates Virgil's description of Orpheus's association with listening woods in *Virgil's Gnat*: 'the shrill woods, which were of sense bereau'd, | Through their hard barke his siluer sound receau'd (ll. 455–6).[35] The trees and the quality of the song they echo represent in *Epithalamion*, as in the Orpheus myth, the susceptibility of the uncivilized to civilizing song. The sounds of the poet-groom's celebration of civic marriage may resonate out beyond the walls of the Munster town in which *Epithalamion* is set, but there is some uncertainty about their echoing response.

Spenser was an official of the English crown and an undertaker of the Munster plantation. For such a man to set his exemplary model of marriage, a central civilizing bond of society, in Ireland, is to give that model a very considerable political charge.[36] In stanza 3, Spenser calls on the Muses to bring to his wedding the 'Nymphes... Both of the riuers and the forrests greene' (ll. 37–8). In the next stanza these nymphs are very specifically identified as belonging to the landscape surrounding Spenser's own estate, Kilcolman, in Munster:

> Ye Nymphes of Mulla which with carefull heed,
> The siluer scaly trouts doe tend full well,
> And greedy pikes which vse therein to feed, ...
> And ye likewise which keepe the rushy lake,
> Where none doo fishes take,
> Bynd vp the locks the which hang scatterd light,
> And in his waters which your mirror make,
> Behold your faces as the christall bright, ...
> And eke ye lightfoot mayds which keepe the deere,
> That on the hoary mountayne vse to towre,
> And the wylde wolues which seeke them to deuoure,
> With your steele darts doo chace from comming neer.
>
> (ll. 56–8, 60–4, 67–70)

The nymphs and the landscape they represent seem to need considerable vigilance and ordering: the trouts are in danger from rapacious pikes, the scattered 'locks' of the nymphs who keep the unfruitful and 'rushy lake' need binding up, and the wolves on the 'hoary mountayne' must be kept in order with 'steel darts'.[37]

This language of lurking savagery and predation that requires restraint and order, introduces into the poem, although in the fanciful language of mythology, a discourse that is all too familiar in sixteenth-century English, especially 'New English', accounts of Ireland. The savagery of wolves was an appealing metaphor for the wild Irish in this discourse. Fynes Moryson, for example, begins his account of 'The Meere Irish' with an epigram:

> For foure vile beasts Ireland hath no fence,
> their bodyes lice, their houses Ratts possesse,
> Most wicked Preists gouerne their conscience,
> and rauening Woolues do wast their feilds no lesse.[38]

Richard Venner writing in 1601, makes explicit what is perhaps implicit in both Moryson's epigram and Spenser's poem: the Irish rebels, who 'keepe their Caues: | Amidde the woods', feeding on grass and sham-rocks, are like 'wolves or ravening beasts'.[39] Another of Spenser's images of restraint and order, the binding up of the hanging locks of the nymphs to make their faces clear and bright, suggests the hanging locks, or 'glibs' of the native Irish, a constant source of exasperation to English commentators who saw them as a sign of Irish barbarism and devious-ness. As Spenser explains in the *View*, the Irish 'pulleth [the glib] so low downe over his eyes, that it is very hard to discerne his theevish counte-nance'.[40] As we have seen, John Derricke imaged the degeneration of Ireland in terms of a grotesque marriage in which the land perversely chose as her groom not a decently-cropped, civil Englishman, but the wild Irish 'with writhed glibbes like wicked sprights'.[41]

Spenser's marriage is not of such a perverse kind. For Spenser and those who thought like him, the 'New English' government officials and the 'undertakers' and their supporters, the great debate about Ireland was how to bring it to civility, that is, how to make it conform to a specifically English notion of civility defined in terms of a settled English division of the land into market towns and arable agriculture, inhabited by reformed parishioners obedient to an English hierarchy of authority. As we have seen, marriage was regarded as one of the central symbolic institutions of civility, a public, religiously sanctioned event, signalling the private binding of unruly appetites, in a ceremony that legitimised procreation and thus the ordered progression of the generations. For Bullinger, the public nature of the marriage 'in the face of the church / and of Gods mynistre' was crucial, giving testimony 'that wedlocke is … an holy work of the light / & no foull work of darknesse. For the parties darre lightly come in to the open church (euen in the light) where gods workes onely are practised.' Quite contrary are the 'workes of whordome and dishon-estye / they hyde themselves in the darknesse'.[42] The marriage celebrated in the daylight hours of *Epithalamion*, open to the gaze of all, 'Behold whiles she before the altar stands' (l. 223), demonstrates what a truly civil marriage ceremony should be, epitomizing the civil Protestant culture that Spenser and his fellow undertakers in Munster had been imported to establish. Nevertheless, as the bride is presented openly to the gaze of all, her own eyes are carefully down turned:

> But her sad eyes still fastened on the ground,
> Are gouerned with goodly modesty,
> That suffers not one looke to glaunce awry,
> Which may let in a little thought vnsownd.
> Why blush ye loue to giue to me your hand. (ll. 234–8)

The blush, as Judith Owens suggests 'signals both occludedness and depths of response beyond Spenser's ken and control'.[43]

The Elizabethan 'Homily on Marriage', advised husbands on the management of wives in terms of a husbandman's cultivation of the land:

> Dost thou not see the husbandmen, what diligence they use to till that ground which once they have taken to farm, though it be never so full of faults? As for an example, though it be dry, though it bringeth forth weeds, though the soil cannot bear too much wet, yet he tilleth it, and so winneth fruit thereof: even in like manner, if thou wouldst use like diligence to instruct and order the mind of thy spouse, if thou wouldst diligently apply thyself to weed out, little by little, the noisome weeds of uncomely manners out of her mind, with wholesome precepts, it could not be, but in time thou shouldest feel the pleasant fruit thereof to both your comforts.[44]

A feminized Ireland could also be represented in terms of a peverse soil that must be broken and manured by the colonial husbandman. Sir John Davies described Ireland as a land that must be broken 'before it be made capable of good seed'.[45] In fact, by law, an Irishwoman could not marry an Englishman. The reasons for this prohibition are self-evident to Spenser: 'how can such matching (but bringe forthe an evill race), seeing that commonly the child taketh most of his nature of the mother.'[46] The marriage of an Irish nobleman to an Englishwoman on the other hand could be represented as a civilizing act. When the Gaelic Earl of Tyrone married Mabel Bagenal in 1591, he explained that he had chosen her 'chiefly to bring civility into my house, and among the country people, which I thank God by her good means is well begun, both in my house and in the country abroad'.[47] If the marriage of an Irishman to a virtuous

Englishwoman could produce this effect on the surrounding country-side, how much better a marriage by an exemplary Englishman and Englishwoman, Edmund Spenser and the well-ordered Elizabeth Boyle who by settling in a colonized Munster, might serve as instructional models to educate the 'country abroad' in true civility.[48]

Spenser sets his marriage hymn not only in Munster, but also within a town. The 'boyes run vp and downe the street' (l. 137), the poet-lover asks the 'merchants daughters did ye see | So fayre a creature in your towne before?' (ll. 167–8). In stanza 15, the 'yong men of the towne' ring out the bells (l. 261), and after dark, Silence is invoked to keep the peace like 'trew night watches' (l. 353). Setting the ceremony within a town may reflect, of course, the actual circumstances of his marriage, although there is a puzzle about the actual whereabouts of this event. The most obvious town, close enough for Mulla's nymphs to attend, was the city of Cork. However, Cork was particularly inhospitable territory for a New Englishman and his Protestant marriage service in 1594. The citizens seem to have excluded Elizabethan settlers from owning prop-erty or succeeding to civic office in the city.[49] It was just as inhospitable to Protestant 'New English' culture and politics on the religious front. The Bishop of Cork from 1583 to 1617 was William Lyon, an active and assiduous Protestant, English-born cleric. From the early 1590s on, Bishop Lyon had increasing difficulties with his clergy and congrega-tions. In 1595 he reported that 'within these two years...where I have had a thousand or more at church or sermon, I now have not five.'[50] So serious was the mass defection by both priests and congregations that the few Protestant clergy left were unable to fulfil their functions and as a result, he wrote in 1604, no marriages had been celebrated in the dio-cese of Cork for the past 11 years, i.e. since 1593.[51]

Wherever Spenser may have actually married Elizabeth Boyle, the set-ting of the marriage in 1594 in a town, possibly Cork, is evidently polit-ically sensitive. Walled towns, such as Cork had always been viewed as essential to the English project of subduing, and latterly, of civilizing Ireland. Towns such as Cork were dominated by a merchant oligarchy of Old English extraction, whose very extensive charters and privileges had been given them by the Crown in order to extend and confirm English sovereignty in Ireland. Towns were perceived as a 'medium through which authority and civilization could be imposed'.[52] Irenius promul-gates this strategy in *A View*:

There should bee in sundry convenient places, by the high wayes, townes appointed to bee built, ... to be by their inhabitants well and strongly intrenched, or otherwise fenced with gates on each side thereof, to be shut nightly, like as there is in many places in the English pale, and all the wayes about it to be strongly shut up, so as none could passe but through those townes: To some of which it were good that the priviledge of a market were given, for there is nothing doth sooner cause civility in any countrie then many market townes, by reason that people repairing often thither for their needes, will dayly see and learne civil manners of the better sort.[53]

'Nothing', Spenser goes on, 'doth more stay and strengthen the country then such corporate townes.' Nevertheless, Spenser acknowledges in *A View*, that Cork and its Munster neighbour Waterford were not to be trusted: 'those two cities above all the rest, do offer an ingate to the Spaniard most fitly, (and allso the inhabitantes of them are moste ill affected to the Englishe gouernment and moste friendes to the Spaniarde)' (p. 131). As a result, Irenius suggests the towns should be garrisoned at their own expense:

for indeed it is no reason that the corporate townes enjoying great franchizes and privileges from her Majesty, and living thereby not onely safe, but drawing to them the wealth of all the land, should live so free, as not to be partakers of the burthen of this garrison. (p. 131)

The attitude of the citizens of Cork to such ideas is indicated by the fact that in 1603, the city 'went into open insurrection against the provincial garrison, assaulting and bombarding the castles around the city'.[54]

Spenser represents his own exemplary marriage as taking place in a populous, and joyous civic community, through public expressions of unity and approval: a procession, a church ceremony, communal celebrations, and bell-ringing. Having constructed the courtship as an exemplary narrative of the formation of the good and civil man through *Amoretti*, the marriage of *Epithalamion* takes place in the symbolic space of the *civis*, as part of the 'fabric of urban life'.[55] This marriage functions as a microcosm, and symbolic emblem, of a more general notion of civil society that, with particular point in 1594, echoes out from the walls of this Munster town to the 'savage' hinterland beyond. In its invocation of classical models and its Hellenization of the tutelary deities of this Munster (the Muses, the Graces, Hymen, and the Gods) Spenser brings to Ireland his vision of a pan-European culture in which England and its civilization becomes the culmination of a tradition stretching back to the first poet, Orpheus.

Looking outwards, as well as backwards, A. Kent Hieatt in an argument now widely accepted in its essentials, has argued that the poem has a complex numerological structure that imitates in its 24 stanzas the hours of the day, its punctuating short lines figuring the divisions of the day, and its 365 long lines the days of the year.[56] We are told in the poem that the marriage takes place on St Barnaby's Day, the 11th June, the summer solstice, and Hieatt finds the hour of nightfall on that day coinciding with the coming of night in the seventeenth stanza, or seventeenth hour, of the poem. The marriage celebrated in *Epithalamion* is thus set within the context of the rotating heavens as they create the onward orderly movement of cyclical time through which, in the words of Nature in the Mutabilitie Cantos, all created things

> by their change their being do dilate,
> And turning to themselves at length againe,
> Do worke their owne perfection so by fate. (*FQ*, 7. vii. 58)

The poem's network of political, cultural and cosmological allusions construct a marvellously ambitious and indeed mesmerizing vision of the order implied by Spenser's personal marriage day. But the more steadily we gaze at this complex construct, the less stable become its elements. The poem, indeed, acknowledges its own instability. *Epithalamion*, we are told at the end, in a short coda, is a

> Song made in lieu of many ornaments,
> With which my loue should duly have bene dect,
> Which cutting off through hasty accidents,
> Ye would not stay your dew time to expect,
> But promist both to recompens,
> Be vnto her a goodly ornament,
> And for short time an endlesse moniment. (ll. 427–33)

What seemed to be public, ordered, and illuminating, here becomes disturbed by the private and the imperfect. Quite what has interrupted the song remains unstated. Imperfection, accident, and uncertainty dominate the poem's conclusion, confronting the all-controlling poet-husband-master of ceremonies, with the limits of his Orphic powers. This volume has always been as much about the exemplary poet-lover's willingness to submit to godly disciplines as it has been about his eager instruction of others, and the final stanza enacts the need to submit to summons from outside the poem.

The 'cutting off' of mutability and mortality are undoubtedly implied in this monument 'for short time', but in a poem as haunted by failure and loss of control as *Epithalamion*, other threats to an achieved work abound.[57] One possible summons from without may be Spenser's obligations to another Elizabeth, Elizabeth I not Elizabeth Boyle. Throughout the 1595 volume, the poet-lover's celebration of his own courtship and marriage has been represented as being in competition with, and a kind of vacation from, the poet-lover's public responsibilities in the service of Elizabeth I. Elizabeth may even, in the familiar form of Cynthia, make an ominous appearance in *Epithalamion* itself as one of the deities that needs to be continually cajoled and placated for the poet-groom's day to be his:

> whose is that faire face, that shines so bright?
> Is it not Cinthia, she that neuer sleepes,
> But walkes about high heauen al the night?
> O fayrest goddesse, do thou not enuy
> My loue with me to spy. (ll. 373–5)

However playfully Spenser might represent his marriage volume as a holiday from his epic poem in praise of Elizabeth I, *Amoretti and Epithalamion*, as I have tried to show, is not just a private celebration of the poet's courtship and marriage, it offers its exemplary narrative as a model of civility for all. The competition between the celebrations of the two Elizabeths may in fact be understood as about competing ideologies of service and gender.

As we saw in Chapter 3, it is particularly his dislike of amorous service at court that convinces Colin Clout in *Colin Clovts Come Home Againe* to return to shepherding in Ireland. At court, in Colin's view, they 'prophane' Love's 'mightie mysteries'

> And vse his ydle name to other needs,
> But as a complement for courting vaine.
> So him they do not serue as they professe,
> But make him serue to them for sordid vses. (*CCCHA*, ll. 788–92)

Love, rightly understood is a civilizing god, as Colin Clout explains in terms that closely echo HL, HB, and *Amoretti*. How, but through Love should unlike things: 'Be euer drawne together into one, | And taught in such accordance to agree?'(*CCCHA*, ll. 845–6). In men 'that had the sparke of reasons might, | More then the rest to rule his passion' love should work, as we have seen it doing in exemplary fashion in *Amoretti and Epithalamion*, to allure men, through the love of heavenly beauty, 'for to enlarge his kynd' (ll. 867–72), that is, to marry and have children. All should submit to love's laws:

> So loue is Lord of all the world by right,
> And rules the creatures by his powrfull saw:
> All being made the vassalls of his might. (ll. 883–5)

Elizabeth I's cult of virginity that entails submission by others and power for herself does not conform to such an idea of Love. There is a tension in a number of Spenser's writings between a fear of independent female power entailing male submission, and an ideal of a civil society formed by virtuous individuals who willingly submit to the godly laws of married love and patriarchy in which the self-rule of good men leads to wider civic order.[58] According to Bryskett, all 'ciuill felicitie' has at its core such well-tempered 'friendship' that 'tieth ... the husband to the wife, and the minds of men of valour & vertue fast together' (pp. 225–6).

Closer to home, or at least, to Ireland, in which the poem is set, potential intrusions into the poem's exemplary pattern of achieved order multiply. We have already noted that the ceremony itself, set in the civic space of a consenting Irish town and culminating in the English marriage service in the 'temple', imagines an occasion that, if it took place in Munster at all, was hardly a welcome or uncontested civic occasion. Historians have suggested that it was to a large extent the alliance of Protestant reform with unwelcome 'New English' methods of subjection that stiffened the religious resistance of the towns.[59]

Beyond the recalcitrant towns themselves, the perceived threats of the wild Irish in Munster on the eve of open rebellion that was to break out in 1598, are registered in the poem not only in the wolves, pikes, and unkempt nymphs, but in the refrain's appeal that the poem's message of civility might echo out to, and be echoed by, the surrounding woods, where, as *A View* repeatedly acknowledges, the wild Irish might be lurking, 'hiding ... in woodes and bogges' in order to commit their 'spoyles and stealthes'.[60] Just such 'stealthes' creep in to haunt the poet-husband after dark:

> Let no lamenting cryes, nor dolefull teares,
> Be heard all night within nor yet without:
> Ne let false whispers breeding hidden feares,
> Breake gentle sleepe with misconceiued dout.

> Let no deluding dreames, nor dreadful sights
> Make sudden sad affrights. (ll. 334–9)[61]

The fearful wildness and ungodliness of what lies outside threatens to break into the inside of this civic space in spite of night watches and all the strenuous efforts of the Orphic poet.

But there are also stealths within the bridal chamber itself:

> an hundred little winged loues,
> Like diuers fethered doues
> Shall fly and flutter round about your bed,
> And in the secret darke, that none reproues,
> Their prety stealthes shal worke, and snares shal spread
> To filch away sweet snatches of delight,
> Conceald through couert night. (ll. 357–63)

The 'little winged loues' with their snares and 'filches' recall the anarchic cupid of the anacreontic verses, linking sexual pleasure to wilfulness and illegitimacy. Elsewhere in *Epithalamion*, the poet-groom anticipates his sexual enjoyment of his lady in terms of Jove's adulterous rapes of Maia and Alcmena (ll. 307–10, 328–9). Sexual desire, even in this legitimised time and place, is persistently associated with the imagery of darkness and lawlessness; it escapes the poet-lover's construction of a love characterized by mastery and transparency. The lady's tongue and eyes as signs of her mind may be policed for any evidence of 'thought unsownd' (l. 237) by the poet-lover, but her erotic body and the pleasures it promises continue to be imagined in terms of secrecy, illegitimacy, and otherness to the ordering, rational discourse of the civilizing poet. The imagery of stealths and snatches under cover of night disturbingly anticipates the language Spenser uses of the wild Irish in *A View*: 'hiding … in woodes and bogges' in order to commit their 'spoyles and stealthes'. Elizabeth Boyle, a virtuous Englishwoman, is very different from such a representation of a feminized Irish landscape as that of Luke Gernon in 1620: 'very fayre of visage … [but] somewhat freckled (as the Irish are) [with] some parts darker than others'.[62] Nevertheless, the enticing pleasures of the bride's physical body seem similarly to confound the transparency, order and rational control of 'ciuil conuersation', substituting instead a language of snatches, stealths, and rapes in the 'secret darke'. Not only does the sexual body of the bride offer a private landscape analogous to the disorderly landscape of Ireland, the erotic groom becomes strikingly similar to its lawless and uncivil inhabitants.

The *Amoretti and Epithalamion* volume is a highly sophisticated and significant publication. In it Spenser places himself at the centre as an exemplary godly Englishman, one who is fitted to instruct others because of his own submission to the disciplines of wisdom, virtue and love. Like Bryskett's good man, his own self-formation is seen as the central act in a notion of civility that extends from the virtuously schooled individual, through the civilizing power of the Orphic poet, to society at large. However, this vision of a civic order and felicity emanating from the individual meets at every point with problems. It is not entirely compatible, for example, with his understanding of a court politics dominated by a queen who demands absolute subjection to her will. Even more disturbingly, the poet-lover's own will slips disconcertingly from an instrument of mastery to an instrument of erotic subjection. The poet-lover's mastery, whether imagined in terms of control of a sexual desire invested in the female body, or in terms of the ordering of an unruly and uncivil land, also often imaged as female, proves incomplete, subject to resistances and desires that threaten the whole project. Finally, the volume itself, with its ambitious blueprint for English civility in Ireland, written in a sophisticated English that rewrites European traditions, and anglicizes the classical past, had to be sent to London for publication. It was to be followed just three years later by Spenser himself, forcibly ejected from a land that also rejected his version of civility.

5
Passionate ejaculations and the poetics of presence: Gascoigne's 'The Adventures of Master F.J.' and Sidney's *Astrophil and Stella*

In *Amoretti and Epithalamion*, the passionate sonnets of the poet as lover are set in a narrative of virtuous self-discipline in which the poet figures as both Orphic teacher and exemplary hero. The single dominant voice of the author guides and instructs the reader through his own account of his own courtship and marriage. Even so, I suggested in Chapter 4, that many of the courtship sonnets imply, and sometimes through the admonitory voice of the lady, supply, a double perspective in which the unschooled poet-lover has to learn the disciplines of a godly and virtuous love. In other narrative sequences of verse examined so far in this book, double or multiple authorial voices have been used to complicate the point of view of the first-person subject.[1] Gascoigne and Whetstone's uses of a 'reporter', for example, to comment on the verse of semi-autobiographical versions of themselves in the sequences of 'Dan Bartholmew of Bathe' or 'Inventions of P. Plasmos' (see pp. 62–3 above) problematize the first-person voice of experience. In Whythorne's MS 'songs and sonetts' the relationship between Whythorne's verse and his prose explanations becomes far from simple with the prose taking on some of the characteristics of a language of disordered passions and turbulent humours, while the patterned formality of the aphoristic verse provides a discourse of control and discipline.

   In the texts I examine in this chapter, Gascoigne's 'The Adventures of Master F.J.' ('Master F.J.') and Sir Philip Sidney's sonnet sequence, *Astrophil and Stella* (*AS*), voices of passionately self-expressive subjectivity are juxtaposed, explicitly or implicitly, to alternate perspectives that call the very possibility of self-expression into question. While *AS* tantalizes the reader with the possibility that Astrophil is a version of the authorial Sidney, 'Master F.J.' makes no allusion to Gascoigne who is not named as author in the first printing in *A Hundreth Sundrie Flowers* (1573). It is, however, presented as a secretive *roman à clef*, in which a prose narrative explains events in the life of F.J., the author of the verse it contains. Both texts are centrally concerned with developing new and complex versions of the passionate first-person speaker, while both also foreground some of the problems attendant on such a rhetoric of self-expression.

Anne Ferry in her valuable study of 'inwardness' in the sixteenth century, reflects a widespread critical view of Shakespeare's *Hamlet* when she writes that the character 'shows a sense of inward experience and the difficulty of denoting it truly which makes him a new kind of figure in English literature, and distinguishes him from the speakers in virtually all sixteenth-century verse.'[2] Ferry excepts *AS* from her general dismissal of other sixteenth-century writing, but I shall hope to show that the problems of expressing inwardness are central concerns not only of *AS* and *Hamlet*, but also of 'Master F.J.'. I shall further argue that such a concern arises, at least to some extent, from conflicting sixteenth-century views about the expression of the passionate self, and the nature of the inner man. As part of my discussion, I shall analyse the way in which the texts of Gascoigne and Sidney deploy double or multiple voices and perspectives in ways that call into question the self-expressive claims of the passionate subject, and render problematic any sense of a single controlling authorial and authoritative point of view.

'A straunge discourse of some intollerable passion'

The self-expressive effect of amorous songs and sonnets is, of course, in conflict with their rhetorical artfulness. A poem by Gascoigne entitled '*A Lady being both wronged by false suspect, and also wounded by the durance of hir husband, doth thus bewray hir grief*', purports to be a spontaneous 'betrayal' of the lady's innermost feelings in the privacy of her own chamber.[3] Any reader of *Tottel's Miscellany*, however, would have recognized the poem as an adept imitation of two of the verses printed in that volume, Wyatt's 'My lute awake' and Surrey's 'Good ladies, ye that haue your pleasures in exile'. By the last two decades of the sixteenth century, Petrarch's sonnet sequence, the *Rime Sparse* in which Petrarch figures as both passionate lover and consummate poet, had become the dominant model for English poets seeking to master the techniques of passionate self-expression and artful display.

Success in producing a convincingly passionate speaker seems to have been regarded by both Gascoigne and Sidney as a mark of technical poetic accomplishment; a display of skill that marked the master out from 'common writers'. In *An Apology for Poetrie*, Sidney is contemptuous of most writers of 'songs and sonnets':

> But truly many of such writings as come under the banner of unresistible love, if I were a mistress, would never persuade me they were in love; so coldly they apply fiery speeches, as men that had rather read lovers' writings...than that in truth they feel those passions, which easily (as I think) may be betrayed by that same forcibleness or *energia* (as the Greeks call it) of the writer.[4]

The desired effect of passionate verses is sincerity, showing 'that in truth they feel those passions'. At the same time Sidney points to the rhetorical technique, 'that same forcibleness or *energia*', needed to produce the effect. There is a slippage between artfulness and truth that parallels the description of '*sprezzatura*' in Castiglione's *The Courtier*, as 'a verie arte, that appeareth not to be arte', art masquerading as nature.[5] To write as though 'in truth' is to distinguish the master of rhetoric, one who 'naturally' has the skill, from those who laboriously betray their dependence on others' models.

In his treatise on writing poetry, appended to the 1575 *Posies*, the 'Certayne Notes of Instruction', Gascoigne uses amorous verses to illustrate 'the quicke capacitie' of a master of verse:

> If I should undertake to wryte in prayse of a gentlewoman, I would neither praise hir christal eye, nor hir cherrie lippe, etc. For these things are *trita et obvia*. But I would either finde some supernaturall cause wherby my penne might walke in the superlative degree, or els I would undertake to aunswere for any imperfection that shee hath, and thereupon rayse the prayse of hir commendacion. Likewise if I should disclose my pretence in love, I would eyther make a straunge discourse of some intollerable passion...or discover my disquiet in shadowes *per Allegoriam*, or use the covertest meane that I could to avoyde the uncomely customes of common writers. (p. 455)

Gascoigne is more explicit than Sidney in describing the successful writing of fresh-seeming amorous verse as a matter of technique, but the effects he advises the learner to avoid are similar to those of Sidney: to be '*trita et obvia*' is to reveal too noticeably the reliance on others' writing and thus the labour of the invention. The artist who hides his art finds 'some supernaturall cause wherby [to]...walke in the superlative degree', suggesting effects of inspiration and ecstasy, or makes 'a straunge discourse of some intollerable passion', suggesting something different and uncommon (*OED* 'strange', a. 6 and 8), but also perhaps something extreme and unaccountable to reflect the irrational mind of the lover-poet (*OED*, 9 and 10). Such a 'straunge discourse', might resemble one of F.J.'s verses, about which we are told: 'This is but a rough meeter, and reason, for it was devised in great disquiet of mynd, and written in rage' (p. 162).

Gascoigne, like Sidney, slips between discourses of truth and artfulness in his use of the first person: 'if I should disclose my pretence in love'. 'Pretence' here has both its sixteenth-century meanings of a claim, or intention (*OED*, 2 and 3a), and the more familiar modern meaning, already in use in the sixteenth century, of a false or feigned pretension (*OED*, 3b). The phrase 'I should disclose' suggests autobiographical confession while the word 'pretence' points to the rhetorical art that produces such effects of personal overflowing and ejaculation. Sidney and Gascoigne both strive to explain the techniques of an art that to work properly must seem natural, truthful and autobiographical. In doing so, they disclose a principal motive for the acquisition of that art, the competition to overgo the 'uncomely customes of common writers'.

The effects of an authentic-seeming passion are most convincing when the 'I' is identified as the author, when the suffering body and passionate speech appear seamless. The conflation of author with speaker deflects attention from writing itself and produces the illusion of full presence, of unmediated passionate self-expression. But, as I have already noted in Chapters 1 and 2, in representing themselves as eloquent lovers, sixteenth-century poets put at risk other, more socially orthodox identities, defined in terms of moral virtue and gathered wisdom. Gascoigne can be seen negotiating these contradictory demands in the various prefaces to *The Posies* of 1575. He both appeals to the supposed sophistication of a courtly audience, able to discriminate the writer from the fiction, and at the same time exploits the charisma and scandal attaching to an identification of the voice of the risqué lover with that of the poet himself. On the one hand, he claims 'the most part of [his amorous verses] were written for other men' (p. 370), implying detachment, and, on the other hand, he confesses that 'most of them being written in my madnesse, might have yeelded then more delight to my frantike fansie to see them published, than they now do accumulate cares in my minde to set them forth corrected' (p. 368), thus implying that the poems were direct expressions of the mind of the writer, albeit, he now acknowledges, a morally and physiologically disordered one. A successful poetry of passionate self-expression might bring the male writer a reputation for glamour and sophistication and might even lend him a courtly and sexually-potent charisma, but it could also imply disorder, effeminacy and consequent decay and self-destruction.

As an appetite of the lower body, a function of the senses, desire in man must be subjected to the rule of reason and law, but the human body was often conceived of in the early modern period as an unstable bag of fluids and the volatile spirits they produced when heated. Gail Kern Paster has described this fluid, dynamic notion of the body proposed by the dominant Galenic medical discourse:

> Galenic physiology proposed a body whose constituent fluids, all reducible to blood, were entirely fungible. Not only did blood, semen, milk, sweat, tears, and other bodily fluids turn into one another, but the processes of alimentation, excretion, menstruation, and lactation were understood as homologous and hence were less conceptually differentiated than they may be in popular medical understanding now. ... The humors moved with greater or less fluidity within the bodily container and exited the body with varying degrees of efficiency. The key differentials were heat, which in the mean promoted solubility, and cold, which hampered it.[6]

As Paster explains, semen was understood to be a refined concoction from the blood and in order to keep a fragile equilibrium within the humoural body, the release of seed was part of 'the general economy of bodily solubility'.[7] Even so, the male loss of seed in intercourse, since it is also a loss of blood, 'diminisheth', in Donne's phrase, 'the length of life a day'.[8] Excessive venery could thus be seen as having a weakening, indeed emasculating, effect on men.

If too much venery debilitated the masculine body, turbulent and overheated passions had as terrible an effect on its inner workings, especially on the mind. While the 'body is in health', wrote the physician Timothy Bright in 1586, 'the humors beare no sway of priuate action'. Bright's term 'priuate' is part of an ongoing analogy between the internal order of the body, threatened by the selfishly motivated actions of individual humours, and the public order of the state, threatened by disorderly individuals. The analogy was felt, in the early modern period, to have more than metaphorical force:

> but it [the body] being once altered, and they [the humours] euill disposed, and breaking from the regiment whereunto they should be subiect, are so farre of from subiection to the disposition of our

bodies, and strength of our partes, that they oppresse them, and ...
dispise that gouernment wherto by natures law they stand bound.[9]

A central faculty in such rebellions against the 'gouernment' of reason
was the imagination. This was the image-making faculty in man's mind
that fed information from the senses to the reason. It was considered
easily corrupted by both the senses and the humours, leading to the
misregulation of the body's humoural economy and the overthrow of
reason.[10]

As the image-making faculty of the mind, imagination was particularly intimately connected with verse. As Sidney and Gascoigne were
well aware, verse was often blamed for corrupting the imagination, especially of youth, with its vivid and seductive images and fictions. Sidney
conceded in *An Apology* that, while rationally ordered poetry figured
forth 'good things', '*phantastike*' verse, corrupted by man's wit, 'doth
contrariwise infect the fancy with unworthy objects'.[11] Not only might
verse infect the imagination, it might also, through its language, speak
forth the inner disorders of the mind. Thomas Wright, in *The Passions of
the Minde* (1601) warned that speech betrayed the inner man: 'Thus you
may coniecture by words, the passions of the mind, when speech mani-
festly carieth the coate of pride, choller, lust or gluttony'.[12] Not only
might amorous verse infect the imaginations of others, it might also
reveal to the world the internal disorder of the amorous subject who
speaks literally from an overwhelmed heart or mind.

If the discourses of Renaissance medicine and psychology provide the
terms for one warning narrative of passionate desire, Renaissance misogyny provides another, closely related. The first verse F.J. writes to his
hoped for mistress at the beginning of Gascoigne's 'Master F.J.' seems a
tactless opening gambit in a seduction, but it is certainly proleptic:

> *Fayre Bersabe the bright once bathing in a Well,*
> *With deawe bedimmd King Davids eyes that ruled Israell.*
> *And Salomon him selfe, the source of sapience,*
> *Against the force of such assaultes could make but small defence:*
> *To it the stoutest yeeld, and strongest feele like woo,*
> *Bold Hercules and Samson both, did prove it to be so.*
> *What wonder seemeth then? When stares stand thicke in skies,*
> *If such a blasing starre have power to dim my dazled eyes?*

> L'envoie
> To you these fewe suffise, your wittes be quicke and good,

You can conject by chaunge of hew, what humors feede my blood.
                                                    F.J. (p. 146)

All F.J.'s examples are of masculine strength and wisdom weakened
and overthrown by the 'assaultes' of women. Even Bersabe, guiltless in
the biblical account of David's adultery, here actively bedims her victim's eyes in terms that recall the goddess Diana's sprinkling of water
over the doomed Acteon in revenge for his inadvertent gaze.[13] In the
same way F.J.'s mistress has dimmed her new lover's eyes. Solomon
whose heart was turned to strange gods by his foreign wives and concu-
bines, and Hercules and Samson whose strength was betrayed by their
wives, are even more obvious examples of the damage done to masculine strength and virtue by their passionate enslavement to women.[14] In
such narratives desire is emasculating and destructive to male autonomy
and reason. By enslaving themselves to woman, disordered male desires
reverse the natural order, making men into women so that they become
changeable and subject to the unstable flux of their humours, a condition characteristic of women in early modern thought.[15] Passionate
enslavement to women may also corrupt male language, producing the
potentially effeminate and irrational utterances of amorous verse.[16]

One strategy that mitigates the potential dangers to authorial reputation of a too lifelike performance of first-person lyric passion is the use of
an alternate commenting voice, a technique that we noted earlier was
used by Gascoigne and Whetstone in their use of a narrating 'reporter'.
A striking example of the use of such a double voice, that enabled the
author to exploit the expressive effects of a discourse of amorous autobiography, while at the same time preserve unsullied his well-framed
humanist identity, is Thomas Watson's *The Hekatompathia* or *Passionate
Centurie of Love* (1582). Watson figures in his sonnet sequence 'as both
author and editor of his poems'.[17] His sequence is divided into two parts
somewhat in the manner of Petrarch's sequence, with the second entitled
'My love is past'. Watson provides editorial headnotes to each 'passion',
explaining its content, and commenting on its themes or indicating its
sources. Alongside such editorial signals, the preface 'To the friendly
Reader' coyly, like a dancer with veils, invites us to at least glimpse the
possibility that the first-person verse may be autobiographical:

I hope thou wilt in respect of my trauaile in penning these loue
passions, or for pitie of my paines in suffering them (although but
supposed) so suruey the faultes herein escaped, as eyther to winke at
them, as ouersightes of a blinde Louer; or to excuse them, as idle

toyes proceedinge from a youngling frenzie; or lastlie, to defend them, by saying it is nothing *Praeter decorum* for a maiemed man to halt in his pase, where his wound enforceth him, or for a Poete to falter in his Poeme, when his matter requireth it.[18]

Watson thus displays his skill as a Petrarchan imitator, hints titivatingly at the possibility of his courtly experience of passion, and reassures the reader of his own authorial, learned, and rational control of the whole. It may well be that the sonnet's double effects, of expressive intensity and spectacular formal control, contributed to its attraction for Renaissance writers. Sonneteers could at the same time display themselves as men of courtly sensibility, and as accomplished craftsmen in full control of their wits.

In what follows, I shall explore the ways in which the erotic sequences of Gascoigne and Sidney place lyric ejaculations within narratives and commentaries, explicit or implicit, that problematize the passionate self-expression of the first-person poet-lover. In deconstructing the poetics of real presence, these texts threaten to unravel the very idea of an authoritative author able to control meaning within the text.

'The Adventures of Master F.J.'

As I outlined in Chapter 1, 'Master F.J.' is prefaced with a flurry of letters that introduce not only that narrative but also the verses of 'sundrie Gentlemen' that follow and that make up the bulk of *A Hundreth Sundrie Flowres*. The first prefatory letter is from H.W. who explains that the manuscript of verses printed as *A Hundreth* was lent to him by a friend G.T. G.T. has allowed H.W. to borrow the manuscript with the strict injunction 'that I should use them onely for mine owne particuler commoditie, and eftsones safely deliver the originall copie to him againe' (p. 142). H.W. has violated this injunction by sending the manuscript to a printer, A.B. Following H.W.'s letter are two more from G.T., one addressed to H.W. and the other more generally prefatory to the manuscript. G.T. tells H.W. that he personally prefers such verse as that written by Chaucer who after writing vain love poetry in his youth devoted his age to 'describing the right pathway to perfect felicitie', that is Heaven.[19] Nevertheless, he has 'gathered' the verses and 'reduce[d] them into some good order' (p. 144). Again G.T. enjoins H.W. to keep the manuscript private: 'desiring you as I onely do adventure thus to participate the sight therof... even so that you will by no meanes make the same common' (p. 144). The verses have been collected by G.T. personally, after 'no small entreatie', from the gentlemen authors who also communicated to him 'the cause that then moved them to write' (pp. 144–5). G.T. has thus been able to add notes to each poem indicating the 'proper occasion' of each.

The prefatory letters and G.T.'s introduction to the verse, place the writers and the occasions that give rise to their verse at the centre of a widening circle of communication. G.T.'s manuscript of 'sundrie copies' with his 'tytle[s] ... wherby the cause of writinge the same maye the more evidently appeare' (p. 216) is passed to his friend H.W. with warnings to keep it private ('by no meanes make the same common'). H.W. may make a copy but should then 'redeliver unto me the originall copie' (p. 144). But a copy is passed to the printer and thus reaches the wider reading public. G.T.'s oxymoron 'the originall copie' alerts us to the subterfuge in all this: at the centre of the manuscript(s) lie private events that can only be known from the written traces that point to them but are never the events themselves. The fiction of manuscript circulation marks these private events as those of elite 'young gentlemen' participating in a life of courtly ease; in the case of 'Master F.J.' the location is a castle 'in the north partes of this Realme' (p. 145). This narrative of exclusive privilege is also one of scandalous intimacy. H.W. anticipates that other readers will share his pleasure in the spectacle of the shame of others:

> I my selfe have reaped this commoditie, to sit and smile at the fond devises of such as have enchayned them selves in the golden fetters of fantasie, and having bewrayed them selves to the whole world, do yet conjecture that they walke unseene in a net. (p. 142)

As the written traces proliferate, so does the titivating illusion of private secrets and privileged revelations.

The connotations of secrecy and privacy in the sixteenth century have been usefully explored by Ferry, Goldberg, and others.[20] Ferry argues that a developing 'language of inwardness' in the sixteenth century, in which such terms as 'secret' and 'private' play a part, points to 'a heightened awareness of distinctions within humanity, differences sometimes phrased as what is particular within a general category, or proper to one rather than common to all, or private as distinguished from public'.[21] The construction of ideas of secrecy and privacy in terms of a glamorous elite, in 'Master F.J.', suggests that the 'heightened awareness of distinctions' identified by Ferry, may be motivated at least partly by class anxieties and the need to maintain social distinctions in the face of what is common; that is, the threat to difference represented by the imitative behaviours and illegitimate copying of such 'others' as will read G.T.'s pirated manuscript.

At the same time as 'Master F.J.' constructs intimacy and privacy in terms of the behaviours of an inaccessible elite, it associates such behaviours with scandal and sexual immorality. Both Ferry and Goldberg point to an association between privacy and secrecy in early modern texts with what goes on in closets and inner chambers. Such places were both sites of privilege and danger. Ferry points out that the possession of a closet was relatively rare and a mark of social privilege in the early modern period. Closets are imaged as sources of power and glamour and potential danger whether associated with the secrets of great men or the sexual intimacies of rich women. Such connotations are closely related in, for example, Robert Cecil's comparison, cited by Rambuss, of the private counsels of master and secretary, typically located in the secrecy of the closet, to 'the mutual affections of two lovers, undiscovered to their friends'.[22] The central place of the secretary, with access to such intimate spaces and secrets, but whose writing mediated those secrets to the outer world, is explored by Rambuss who notes that secretaries were often called 'inward men' in the Renaissance.[23] To partake of a world of secrets and privacy is to belong to the socially particular, the elite, as opposed to what is common, but it is also to invoke the dangers of what is private and hidden and may be shameful and inimical to the common good.

The secrets at the centre of 'Master F.J.' are located within F.J.'s heart and in the various closets and bedchambers that figure in the narrative. At the same time as the proliferating prefatory letters and the narrative itself offers us intimate access to elite secrets, full knowledge is teasingly withheld behind ciphers and the mediation of written copies. The way in which the text produces secrets at the same time as it promises to give access to them is illustrated by the playful preliminary matter. Who are H.W. and G.T. and F.J.? G.T. continually tantalizes us with full knowledge only to withhold it. In the case of one of the 'sundrie authors' whose verse follows 'Master F.J.', G.T. tells H.W. 'you may gesse him by his Nature' (p. 205). Of others, known only by their mottos, he challenges H.W. to 'gesse them' (p. 216). When the verses were reprinted in *The Posies* of 1575, it turned out the only name behind all these ciphers was that of Gascoigne himself, who claimed to have written the 'most part' for others. When a somewhat chastened version of 'Master F.J.' was reprinted in 1575, it was entitled 'The pleasant Fable of *Ferdinando Jeronimi and Leonora de Valasco*, translated out of the Italian riding tales of *Bartello*'. Bartello appears elsewhere in Gascoigne's verse, apparently as a cipher for himself.[24] Further, in the proliferating and contradictory prefaces to the 1575 edition, Gascoigne characteristically stokes while appearing to dismiss the possibility of 'real' secrets: 'some busie conjectures have presumed to thinke the same ['Master F.J.'] was indeed written to the scandalizing of some worthie personages, whom they woulde seeme therby to know' (pp. 362–3). The possibility that the narrative is a *roman à clef*, ciphering real personages and a contemporary scandal, is repeatedly encouraged in the 1573 'Master F.J.'.[25]

It is, of course, the rhetoric of ciphers, innuendo, and violations of privilege that produces the teasing possibility of secrets and scandals, of full meaning and apprehension lying just 'beyond' or 'behind' the writing. At the same time as 'Master F.J.' manufactures the illusion of full presence and tantalizes with imminent revelations, the writing exposes the vanity of such a quest by tripping us up and reminding us that we cannot get beyond the writing itself. Nevertheless the tale of F.J. is above all about the desire for full expression and full possession: both F.J.'s desire to bring his full bodily presence into the closet and bed of Mistress Elinor and control all her secrets, and the reader's desire for full possession of F.J.'s secrets. In the first of F.J.'s writings, purveyed to us by G.T., we are given the words of a man who gets directly to the point. Falling into the company of the wealthy and married Mistress Elinor, while a guest of her father's at his estate 'in the north partes', he abruptly writes her a letter to tell her of the 'hotte affection' he feels for her: '*Such is then thextremitie of my passions, the which I could never have bene content to committe unto this telltale paper, weare it not that I am destitute of all other helpe*' (p. 145). Once written, the 'telltale' paper leaves the control of the author and may blab its message out, 'bewraying' F.J. 'to the whole world' as H.W. gleefully anticipates.

The paper may also tell many tales, some of which F.J. tries to manipulate. He suggests Elinor keep it in her sewing box:

> *And let this poore paper (besprent with salt teares, and blowen over with skalding sighes) be saved of you as a safe garde for your sampler, or a bottome to wind your sowing silke, that when your last nedelfull is wrought, you maye returne to readinge therof and consider the care of hym who is*
> More youres than his owne.
>   F.J. (p. 145)

F.J. represents the paper as literally bearing the bodily marks of his passion (sighs and tears) that will bring his bodily self into the presence of the lady. It may also suggest his bodily presence in other ways. For example, it may serve as a 'safe garde' (a protective wrapping), physically enclosing her sampler as F.J. desires to enwrap her body. Imagery of sewing, and of needles whose eye may be penetrated like a vagina or may prick like a penis, commonly carried sexual innuendo in the sixteenth century.[26] If his paper cannot enwrap the pricked body of her sampler, then F.J. offers it as a 'bottom' (*OED*, II. 15: a clew or nucleus on which to wind thread, but also referring to the pubic region).[27] The paper's physical presence in her sewing box offers a surrogate for the lover's bodily presence, serving as an ersatz spindle which remains stiff and bare to remind her of him when her silk is unwound and her needle is empty.

Elinor is not at first as receptive as F.J. might wish: 'she understode not for what cause he thrust the same into hir bosome' (p. 146). Before F.J. can make another attempt in verse, copied 'in legible writinge', the lady gives him a piece of paper in return. Presuming this to be his first letter spurned, F.J. 'began to wreake his mallice on this poore paper, and the same did rend and teare in peeces' (p. 146). But the lady is not as obtuse as she pretends. F.J. notices the torn words are 'not of his owne hande writing' and pieces together from the fragments a letter from 'SHE'. Nevertheless, further deciphering convinces F.J. that the letter is not of Elinor's 'devise': 'For as by the stile this letter of hirs bewrayeth that it was not penned by a womans capacitie, so the sequell of hir doings may discipher, that she had mo ready clearkes then trustie servants in store' (p. 147). Writing is thus, in the first exchanges of the narrative, dramatically foregrounded. Not only is this narrative concerned with writing and its power to produce or seem to produce bodily presences in however mediated a form, but it is also presented as dangerous, deceitful and multiply interpretable. The sexual contest enacted in this narrative is played out through language: on the one hand the male author desires to make his bodily and passionate self present to the lady in her bosom, her private closet and her sewing box, through his pen as well as his penis, and on the other the lady repeatedly confuses interpretation and evades control.

A number of Gascoigne's readers have noted his fondness for the pen/penis pun.[28] It is deployed with particular ebullience in 'Master F.J.'. The lady's store of 'ready clearkes', or secretaries, who may, according to Rambuss have been called 'inward men', do Mistress Elinor's business for her in more ways than one.[29] When F.J. replaces the clerk, who penned Elinor's letter, in his mistress's sexual services, G.T. describes the displaced secretary in a passage worth quoting in full for its playful slippages between sexual and scribal potency:

Hee was in height, the proportion of twoo *Pigmeys*, in bredth the thicknesse of two bacon hogges, of presumption a *Gyant*, of power a

Gnat, Apishly wytted, Knavishly mannerd, and crabbedly favord, what was there in him then to drawe a fayre Ladies liking? Marry sir even all in all, a well lyned pursse, wherwith he could at every call, provide such pretie conceytes as pleased hir peevish fantasie, and by that meanes he had thoroughly (long before) insinuated him selfe with this amorous dame. This manling, this minion, this slave, this secretary, was nowe by occasion rydden to London forsothe: and though his absence were unto hir a disfurnishing of eloquence: it was yet unto *F.J.* an opertunitie of good advauntage, for when he perceived the change of hir stile, and therby grew in some suspicion that the same proceded by absence of hir chiefe Chauncellor, he thought good now to smyte while the yron was hotte, and to lend his Mistresse such a penne in hir Secretaries absence, as he should never be able at his returne to amende the well writing thereof. (pp. 153–4)

Even while G.T.'s language seems to celebrate the masterful agency of F.J.'s pen and penis in the passage quoted above, his description of the secretary undermines it. His gross physicality is matched by his slavish abjection. To serve one's mistress as F.J. now does is to be physically more like a beast, and socially more like a woman ('this manling, this minion') than a man. G.T.'s account implicitly parallels the 'manling' secretary with F.J., his rival and successor as Elinor's penman. It seems that to be in such amorous service to a woman is to be less than a man, to lack that mastery of the well-balanced rational self that defines manhood in humanist discourse. 'Appasionate persons' according to Thomas Wright, 'spend their best houres, and purest spirites, for the most parte, in mere fantasticall discoursing'.[30] The vain expenditure of volatile spirits, whether though intercourse or in 'fantasticall discoursing' will equally diminish and bestialize the body of the penman.

F.J.'s penmanship is, however, significantly different from that of his rival. A 'manling', the latter may be, but he is well-stocked with materials and is notably successful, possessing 'a well lyned pursse, wherewith he could at every call, provide such pretie conceytes as pleased hir peevish fantasie' (p. 153).[31] F.J.'s success with the lady coincides with the secretary's absence and ends with his return: 'it fell out that the *Secretary* having bin of long time absent, and therby his quils and pennes not worn so neer as they were wont to be, did now prick such faire large notes, that his Mistres liked better to sing faburden under him, than to descant any longer upon *F.J.* playne song' (p. 199).[32] The difference between the secretary's penmanship and that of F.J. is a matter of how they tickle the lady's fancy, their deployment of the pen. Where the secretary has a

ready stock of 'pretie conceytes' and is able to write and sing the complementary part harmonies of pricksong, F.J.'s verse is 'playne song' and he
leaves the lady to fit herself to his music as best she can with her descant.

F.J.'s song may be plain and by implication, manly, but it is less successful with Elinor than the secretary's 'prick song'. His attitude to language is
repeatedly figured as rhetorically unsubtle. His attempted insinuation of
his bodily presence into his lady's chamber in his first letter points to a
recurring motif of his use of language. For F.J. the arts of language seem
akin to magical arts in which words are a mere conduit for extra-linguistic
powers, imbued with the real presence of the author. F.J. spectacularly
seems to demonstrate such extra-linguistic powers when he miraculously
cures Elinor's nosebleed, an exploit that seems to lead directly to access to
his mistress's sexual favours. This miracle is achieved through a combination of mock 'oraisons' ('certen words in secret') spoken by F.J. and a
'Hazell sticke' into which his mistress has to cut five nicks (pp. 151–2) as
he mutters. Nosebleeds were commonly interpreted as a sign of sexual
desire. Robert Burton explains that it is those of sanguine temperament
that are most likely to be of an amorous disposition. Those who are enam-
oured have an uneven pulse causing them to blush, suffer from palpita-
tions, 'and sometimes through violent agitation of the spirits bleed at the
nose'.[33] Whatever the possibly phallic symbolism of the nicked hazel
stick, Elinor's staunched nosebleed may be understood as due as much to
her anticipation of imminent sexual satisfaction through F.J.'s bodily intimacy ('hee layd his hand on hir temples, and privily [whispered] … in hir
eare') as to any extra-linguistic potency inhering in his words.

F.J.'s semi-magical understanding of language, as somehow imbued
with real presence and extra-linguistic significance, is most fully elabo-
rated by G.T. in his account of F.J.'s silence during the period when he
most fully enjoys the 'more than speakeable pleasures' of his lady's sexual
favours (p. 178). During this time, F.J. 'being charged with inexprimable
joyes' nevertheless struggles to express, or squeeze them out: 'a lover…
can by no means devise a greater consolation, than to commit it into
some cyphred wordes and figured speeches in verse, whereby he feeleth
his harte halfe (or more than halfe) eased of swelling.'[34] Writing is thus
like a purgative or bloodletting, siphoning off the excessive fluids and
volatile spirits of the body, and giving relief. Such an understanding of
writing draws on the moral/physiological notion of the passionate man's
body as an unruly and turbulent container in which the 'normal' equilibrium and restraint of reason has been overthrown. As Thomas Wright
explained: 'from the aboundaunce of heart, the tongue speaketh: for as a
riuer abounding with water must make an inundation, and runne ouer

the bankes; euen so, when the heart is ouerflowen with affections, it must find some passage, by the mouth, minde, or actions.'[35]

But if the bodily self inheres so inextricably in the words spoken and written, communication implies some loss of self. G.T. explains F.J.'s refusal to let anyone else have copies of the verses he writes as an attempt to retain within the container of his body, essences which would otherwise be lost:

> even so if hee do but once bewray the same [his verse] to any living creature, ... he leeseth the principall vertue which gave effecte to his gladnes, not unlike to a Potycaries pot which being filled with sweete oyntmentes or parfumes, doth reteyne in it selfe some sent of the same, and being powred out doth returne to the former state, hard, harshe, and of small favour: So the minde being fraught with delightes, as long as it can kepe them secretly enclosed, may continually feede uppon the pleasaunt record thereof ... but having once disclosed them to any other, strayghtway we loose the hidden treasure. (p. 179)

Versing, so conceived, is a pouring out or spillage of the self (*OED* 'verse', v. 1 and 2) analogous to the loss of vital spirits in the act of sex, lamented in Shakespeare's 'Expense of spirit' sonnet (no. 129). The danger of such spillage to the early modern masculine sense of self, and its need for reconstitution, are suggested by Mark Breitenberg: 'In a sexual sense, satisfaction represents to the male imagination not just a "little death" but also a moment of loss and vulnerability – it figures an end to the desiring subject that must be resurrected through another "conquest" ... the evacuation of semen meant the loss of the masculine principle.'[36] The dissemination of F.J.'s verses beyond the bed closet threatens to dissipate his inner self, to diminish his real presence through language. The only solution to F.J.'s dilemma, caught between the need for bodily relief and fear of bodily loss, is private writing, verse as a form of auto-eroticism: '*F.J.* swymming now in delightes did nothing but write such verse as might accumilate his joyes, to the extremitie of pleasure, the which for that purpose he kept from mee' (p. 179). Only by keeping his verse within the erotic circuit of his sexual pleasures, stimulating and relieving his masculine body, can the identification of pen and penis be sustained.

The erotic circuit of F.J.'s satisfactions necessarily pass through Mistress Elinor, a porous vessel. F.J.'s notion of language confounds presence and language, but he is unable to master the meaning of his mistress. The return of the secretary disturbs F.J.'s private idyll. Can F.J. be sure that the secretary's penmanship is not again at work in Elinor's words and in her bed? Suspicion and jealousy, those inevitable diseases of the love-sick mind, undermine F.J.'s confidence in his ability to interpret signs. Coming to comfort him in the sick bed to which he has retired, Elinor brings a branch of willow in order, she says, 'to beate you a little' for slothfulness (p. 181). The willow seems to F.J. a 'token that he was of hir forsaken: for so lovers doe most commonly expound the willowe garland, and this to think, did cut his hart in twayne' (p. 184). Unable to decide on the meaning of his mistress, and unable, through words to impose his will on her, F.J. finally abandons language and imposes his meaning by bodily raping her.

Susan Staub has commented on the tendency of writers on 'Master F.J.' to ignore the scene in which F.J. rapes Elinor.[37] This may be due to a modern embarrassment with the way in which, like Leander's rape of Hero at the end of Marlowe's 'Hero and Leander', the violence is presented as part of the wit. The literalism of action suddenly and unexpectedly short-circuits the play of language.[38] Staub in fact deals with the scene by erasing the wit. She describes F.J. as throwing 'the lady unceremoniously to the ground', but in fact Gascoigne places the pair in a bed whose pillows play a crucial part in the erotic titillation of the writing:

> The softe pillows being present at all these whot wordes, put forth themselves as mediatours for a truce betwene these enemies, and desired that (if they would needes fight) it might be in their presence but onely one pusshe of the pike, and so from thenceforth to become friends again for ever. But the Dame denied flatly...adding further many wordes of great reproche: the which did so enrage *F.J.* as that having now forgotten all former curtesies, he drewe upon his new professed enimie, and bare hir up with such violence against the bolster, that before shee could prepare the warde, he thrust hir through both hands, and etc. (p. 198)

The familiar wit of the bed as a field of battle is developed in leisurely and playful detail: the pillows are mediators, the lady has 'gently strip[ped] of hir clothes' (p. 197) for action, the lover desires 'but onely one pusshe of the pike'.[39] F.J.'s sudden phallic literalization of the metaphors seems, disconcertingly, both appropriate and outrageous. At the same time as the conceit is literalized, the status of the act itself as mere words, part of G.T.'s salacious narration, is foregrounded by the 'and etc.' reminding us that the readers, at least, cannot get beyond language.

Elinor's rape may be treated by G.T. as a form of wit but it enacts F.J.'s impatience with a language that thwarts male potency. Unable to control language, either hers, or her reception of his, F.J. abandons it for the real presence of the penis. While there may be some mockery of F.J.'s 'playne song' compared to the secretary's more adept prick song, the narration nevertheless presents Elinor's rape as somehow appropriate. Female language like female desire is duplicitous and teasing, threatening male potency and identity with its prevarications and betrayals. F.J.'s silent assertion of his masculine potency may lose him the lady but perhaps this is the price he must pay for assertion of his plain masculine self. The assertive male is well-rid of the duplicitous feminine. Elinor slips away and comforts herself with the prick notes of her more adept penman, the secretary. Engaging with women, the narrative seems to tell us, is to risk becoming such a penman as the secretary, prostituting language in the service of female pleasures.

We cannot so easily escape the complications of language however. F.J.'s masculine self-assertion is followed by a verse on the renunciation of love, a popular humanist/moralist mid-century genre that entails misogynist abuse of women:[40]

> *Why then (quod I) olde proverbes never fayle,*
> *For yet was never good Cat out of kinde:*
> *Nor woman true but even as stories tell,*
> *Woon with an egge, and lost againe with shell.* (p. 213)

In the way of written verses, copies of F.J.'s renunciation circulate until they reach Dame Frauncis, a woman who figures in the narrative as both virtuous and trusty. Her female virtue belies F.J.'s misogyny: 'I pray you pardon me (quod he) and if it please you I wil recant it ... I was but cloyed with *Surquedry*, and presumed to think more than may be proved' (p. 214). Dame Frauncis not only proves F.J.'s blunt words false, but offers us an alternative model of writing and its interpretation that avoids both the 'manling' secretary's prostitution of language, and F.J.'s masculine 'surquedry'. She is an adept but virtuous manipulator of a playful courtly language of *questioni d'amore*, witty allegories, and opaque stories. Jane Hedley describes her as the mistress of Gascoigne's central trope of allegoria that 'enables ... characters to play in earnest and to meet one another on the ambiguous middle ground between truth and lying'.[41]

Hedley's argument that Dame Frauncis offers us a version of Gascoigne's own voice within the narrative is suggestive and helpfully undermines the simple dichotomies of masculine/effeminate, truth/courtliness towards which concentration on F.J.'s narrative seem to lead us. Nevertheless, Dame Frauncis's sophisticated use of language is not the only alternative model in 'Master F.J.'. There is also G.T., the narrator whose prose 'notes' to F.J.'s verses so expand and proliferate through the work, that gradually it is his narration, claiming knowledge far beyond anything that could have been imparted by F.J., that becomes the main body of the text, while F.J.'s poems, when available, appear as occasional interludes or illustrations.[42] Yet however much G.T.'s prose appears to be the source of the secrets, information and opinions that constitute the narration, he never claims authority. G.T. situates himself, like the reader he addresses, on the outside, peering through a keyhole at the secrets of others which can never be finally known or understood. In this respect his role as the explainer of F.J.'s verses is paradigmatic of the whole discourse of amorous self-expression. F.J.'s lyric spillages of his inner self, the sup- posed source and first-hand evidence of secret events that the narration exists to elucidate, remain resolutely opaque, revealing nothing beyond their own artfulness and conventionality. Of one of F.J.'s verses, G.T. tells us 'it is but a translation ... and Master J. hath a little dylated the same, but not much besides the sence of the first' (p. 178). Of another, that 'hath great good store of deepe invention', he remarks that sung to the lute by F.J. it was a 'pleasaunt diddeldome' (p. 171).

G.T.'s role as a narrator and interpreter who never elucidates is ren- dered farcical by his comments on one set of verses in which F.J. refers to Elinor under the name of Helen (pp. 176–7). They were, G.T. surmises, written 'in an extasie' and given to Elinor, but 'by the negligence of His Mistresse dispersed in to sundry hands'. However, even within the inti- mate circulation first intended, misinterpretation had crept in. F.J. 'had his desire if his Mistresse liked them', but apparently she did not, prov- ing a more literal reader than even F.J. hoped for. Her objection is that since the poem refers to Helen it cannot refer to herself.[43] G.T. reports that there has been some debate about this issue. 'Some have attributed this prayse unto a *Hellen*, who deserved not so well as this dame *Elynor*', others that this Helen was of 'so base condicion' that F.J. would never 'bestow verse of so meane a subject'. G.T. avouches F.J. himself has told him that Elinor was meant, and anyway, he knew Helen six or seven years later than Elinor, and then 'he might adapt it to hir name, and so make it serve both their turnes'. To write is to lose control of meaning – whatever the meaning may have been in the first place.

G.T. concludes his proliferating interpretations, in which F.J.'s own explanation is only incidental, with an ironic apology:

> Well by whom he wrote it I know not, but once I am sure that he wrote it, for he is no borrower of inventions, and that is al that I meane to

prove, as one that sende you his verses by stealth, and do him double wrong, to disclose unto any man the secrete causes why they were devised, but this for your delight I do adventure. (p. 177)

Characteristically, the claim that F.J. is no 'borrower of inventions' is immediately followed by the sonnet G.T. notes 'is but a translation'. G.T.'s multiplication of explanations surrounding the Helen poem claim to clarify but serve only to confuse and undermine. He vouches for his friend F.J. but insinuates subsequent, or perhaps earlier, or even contemporary sexual affairs by F.J. that contrast mockingly with the language of sincerity he elsewhere attributes to his friend. G.T.'s own motives and purposes are fraught with contradiction and obscurity. In the passage above, G.T. hints at dark secrets which he has stolen by 'stealth' for our pleasure, but in the prefatory letter to H.W. he presented himself as a mere detached collector and arranger, one who would rather read 'directions, whereby a man may be guided towards thattayning of that unspeakable treasure' of heaven, rather than 'wanton penning[s] of a few loving layes' (p. 143).

The narrative of G.T. unfolds the doublings and contradictions of early modern discourses of desire and the tropes of a rhetoric of passionate self-expression. Passion figures as a dark secret, glamorous and shameful, accessible only through keyholes and via puns and innuendo giving oblique access to a fantasy world of social elitism. Paradoxically, as a secret within the intimate closets and connecting galleries of the castle, it threatens the social status quo, displacing and cuckolding the host/ fathers and the husbands who enjoy legal possession and represent social responsibility. Desire appears to make the turbulent body speak, threatening to overthrow reason and the restraints of prudence and order, and appearing to express itself through first-person verse that is as ecstatic, raging, and disordered as the passionate inner self. On the other hand what is spoken is always at second-hand, conventional, artful and ultimately indeterminate. Those best able to deploy the discourses of amorous courting turn out within the narrative to be either duplicitous, untrustworthy, and shameful like the pricksong secretary, who nevertheless wins the lady, or female, artful, and sophisticated like Dame Frauncis.

The master of these discourses, G.T. (and beyond him the even more chameleon Gascoigne), is figured as an editor and copier, not an 'author'. He represents himself not as the source, but as a mere conduit of the discourses of others even while it is through his narrative and insinuations that the secrets he reports are constructed. His tale, in fact, calls the whole notion of authorship, of an authoritative originating source, into question. Sir Philip Sidney's *AS* sequence, on the contrary, and beyond it *An Apology for Poetrie* written at approximately the same time as *AS*, focuses our attention on authors, whether *Astrophil* (lover of stars), the poet-lover, or the more shadowy Sir *Philip Sid*ney (*Philisides*, lover of stars). It is to the notion of the self-expressive presence of the double authors of *AS* that I now turn.

The 'feeling skill' of Astrophil

Petrarch's *Canzoniere* has long been acknowledged as the great model for a poetry of the self, 'a score to be performed by generations of readers from the Renaissance to the Romantics ... the model of poetic self-creation even for poets who, in matters of form, thought of themselves as anti-Petrarchan.'[44] In the last twenty years however, through analyses such as those of John Freccero, Giuseppe Mazzotta and Nancy J. Vickers, readers of Petrarch's sequence, and thus those of his successors, have become more aware of the strategies through which effects of expressive coherence are built on absence, elision and fragmentation. Vickers uses the Diana/Acteon myth to point out strategies of Petrarchan self-constitution through fragmentation of the desired woman, a technique that 'becomes the lyric stance of generations of imitators'.[45] Mazzotta focuses on the sequence's endless displacements of signs and their significance: 'language is the allegory of desire, a veil, not because it hides a moral meaning but because it always says something else.'[46] In what follows, I shall analyse how language similarly produces, but also displaces, the desiring voices of both Astrophil and the authorial Sidney in the sequence of Petrarch's English heir.

Celebrating, in sonnet 69, one of his few moments of joy in a narrative of despair, Astrophil's excitement reaches a climax with an ejaculatory spilling of the self onto the page: 'I, I, ô I may say, that she is mine' (l. 11).[47] This moment of climactic joy briefly gives Astrophil the illusion that he and his beloved are one ('she is mine'), the desired end that drives the *AS* sequence forward. That fantasy of union is, as we shall see, in some sense also a fantasy of full self-expression, as what Astrophil strives over 108 sonnets to say is what is in his heart which is also the meaning of Stella, the object of desire: 'now she is nam'd, need more be said?' (*AS* 16). But in such a moment of union, with the desiring self united with its ideal object, language would become redundant ('need more be said?'). Of course, Astrophil never gets further than the stutteringly inarticulate expression of the self-fulfilment that we find in sonnet 69. In the final three lines we learn that Stella is 'mine ... but thus conditionally'.

The imagined union is in fact a matter of covenants, dependent on the mediation of yet more words.

Sonnet 70 takes up the same themes and constructs the gap between language and the imagined fullness of experience as a comically masturbatory fantasy. Astrophil's Muse, elated by Stella's seeming kindness, chafes to be free of the disciplines of complaining sonnets that force his joy 'in sad rimes to creepe' (l. 2). Astrophil willingly gives his Muse her head, rising to a climax in line 11:

> Come then my Muse, shew thou height of delight
> In well raisde notes, my pen the best it may
> Shall paint out joy, though but in blacke and white.
> Cease eager Muse, peace pen, for my sake stay,
>   I give you here my hand for truth of this,
>   Wise silence is best musicke unto blisse. (ll. 9–14)

Rather than creeping in 'sad rimes', his penis-like pen rises to the challenge, but at the moment of climax, the shortfall of 'blacke and white' from 'paint' seems to lead to a loss of faith in the pen, and to 'wise silence'. Unlike F.J.'s silence at his moment of bliss, which G.T. tells us was filled with a secret writing that expressed and renewed his sexual joys, Astrophil's attempt to embody his joys in words exposes for us and for him a discrepancy between idea and achievement. The inadequate agency of the poet-lover's writing 'hand' produces the final deflation and silence of his pen.[48] The metaphorical conflation of the pen and the penis that offered such seductive possibilities to F.J., is inadequate for Astophil's joys, as the ministrations of his hand necessarily fall short of an imagined union with Stella. By focusing on writing's part in producing, but at the same time its inadequacy in expressing, the passionate self, sonnets 69 and 70 typify recurring concerns in *AS*.[49] At the same time as sonnet 70 dramatizes the shortcomings of author Astrophil's penmanship, however, it draws our attention to the skilful manipulations of Astrophil's alter ego, the witty and ironic Philip Sidney. We shall return to this typically double sense of the writer of the sequence later.

It has long been recognized that the story of Astrophil's desire is also a story of his struggles with language.[50] Astrophil aspires to a fresh language of the heart that will be unique to him, and scorns those who attempt, hopelessly, to express their passion in the second-hand language of others: '*Pindare's* Apes', he calls them in sonnet 3, or those whose 'denisend wit' merely translates 'poore *Petrarch's* long deceased woes' (15). Famously, in the first sonnet of the sequence, Astrophil confronts the question of how to write his desire. He casts around for 'an invention' which Gascoigne tells us is the 'first and most necessarie poynt...to be considered in making of a delectable poeme' and which he defines as 'some good and fine devise, shewing the quicke capacitie of a writer'.[51] Where Gascoigne's advice concerns the art of 'delectable poemes', Astrophil aspires to a poetics of artless self-expression, finding resolution only when his Muse offers him the possibility of the unmediated writing of what is within: ' "Foole," said my Muse to me, "looke in thy heart and write" ' (l. 14). Within his heart, the seat of the passions, desire and Stella seem united: his heart 'shrines in flesh so true a Deitie' (sonnet 4). In a fantasy of full expression of the inner self into the outer air, Astrophil, in sonnet 28 explains that he need do no more than breathe out of his mouth the spirits arising from this shrine of flesh:

> know that I in pure simplicitie,
> Breathe out the flames which burne within my heart,
> *Love* onely reading unto me this art. (28, ll. 12–14)

Such art is artless; in a poetics in which 'When I say *"Stella"*, I do meane the same' (28, l. 5), there is no mediation between the thing and its expression, signified and signifier.

Of course, Astrophil's hubris about his powers of expression, and, indeed, his faith in the capacity of his flesh to become word, are doomed to the same failure as his passion.[52] Astrophil's unequal struggles are dramatized in sonnet 50 in which his words, breathed out of his 'panting breast', emanate, ambiguously, from somewhere between his excited imagination and his enflamed heart:

> *STELLA*, the fulnesse of my thoughts of thee
> Cannot be staid within my panting breast,
> But they do swell and struggle forth of me,
> Till that in words thy figure be exprest. (ll. 1–4)

Here, the 'pure simplicitie' of sonnet 28 is replaced by complexity and obstruction. Astrophil's expression of his inner fullness is not an unmediated breathing out of his desire (which is also the naming of Stella), but a struggle to transform turbulent humoural spirits into words that prove a disappointing issue:

> With sad eyes I their weake proportion see,
> To portrait that which in this world is best.

> So that I cannot chuse but write my mind,
> And cannot chuse but put out what I write,
> While those poore babes their death in birth I find. (ll. 7–11)

As in the case of sonnet 70, what should have been painted in colour, is written only in black and white, but whereas in 70 this led to silence, in 50, the written words are figured as assuming a life of their own. Astrophil's dream, in sonnet 28, of an artless expression of what lies within is parodied in this poem as loss of control; he cannot 'chuse' what he writes, how it is written, nor even the act of writing at all. In the sonnet's final lines, the words themselves change their nature, transformed in the humoural chaos of Astrophil's body from surfeits of inflamed spirits to 'poore babes', a heterogenous progeny no longer subject to authorial control:

> And now my pen these lines had dashed quite,
> But that they stopt his furie from the same,
> Because their forefront bare sweet *Stella's* name. (ll. 12–14)

The lines, like sonnet 50 itself, bear the graph '*STELLA*' in their forefront, but unlike the union of sign and signifier fantasized in sonnet 28, 'When I say "*Stella*", I do meane the same', the lines he writes in sonnet 50 neither quite bear Astrophil's meaning, nor do they adequately 'portrait' Stella. Unlike Thomas Whythorne, who felt a certain pride that his songs 'shiuld bee, az my childern', furnishing them in the frontispiece with his arms and his picture, 'to reprezent vnto þoz who shiuld ywz þe childern, þe form and favor of þeir parent', Astrophil's relationship to his words is tenuous and uncertain; spawned by him they are nevertheless strange, unpredictable, despised and ingratiating.[53] The 'pure simplicitie' of Love's art proves elusive.

Astrophil's dream of language as the unmediated expression of his heart, transforming words into real presence, is repeatedly thwarted and mocked through the sequence. Astrophil's 'breath of my complaints' (44, l. 10), and even the non-verbal bodily signs, 'the verie face of wo' (45, l. 1) with which he attempts to express his passion, are misinterpreted, most notably by Stella herself in whose divine mind and hearing 'the sobs of mine annoyes I Are metamorphosd straight to tunes of joyes' (44, ll. 13–14). Not that Astrophil's mortal mind and hearing prove any surer instruments for discerning truth in the signs of others. In sonnet 67 he labours to interpret or perhaps misinterpret the 'faire text' of Stella, translating 'Her eye's-speech' and the 'blushing notes' in her margins.

The body embodied in signs proves ever elusive, and indeed ever unfixed. The Astrophil who boasted that his only art was Love's art that taught him to 'Breathe out the flames which burne within my heart' (sonnet 28), finds increasingly that he is usurped by less welcome voices beyond his control: 'Wo' speaks through him in sonnet 57, and 'Griefe' in sonnet 94 'find[s] the words' to 'waile thy selfe' in his writing.

As in the case of 'Master F.J.', *AS* is concerned with both the expressive effects and the sense of moral danger in writing about amorous desire. The sequence of sonnets unfold the implied narrative of Astrophil's hopeful courting, his disappointment and his final despair. Thomas Nashe in his preface to the first edition of the sequence, described its narrative in terms of a theatrical plot: 'Here you shal find a paper stage ... The chiefe actor here is *Melpomene*, whose dusky robes, dipt in the ynke of teares, as yet seeme to drop when I view them neere. The argument cruell chastitie, the Prologue hope, the Epilogue dispaire.'[54] But while the predictable plot of the amorous lover unfolds, not without humour, on the paper stage, the 'chiefe actor' of the sequence is not a histrionic Melpomene, muse of tragedy, but a complex figure who is both Astrophil and a version of Sidney.

The sequence playfully alludes to and veils an identity between Astrophil and an authorial Sidney. Astrophil carries the Sidney heraldic sign of the arrowhead in his arms (sonnet 65), he shares the same father (30) and at one point, through 'sir *Phip*' the sparrow, the same name (83). The Stella he woos is ostentatiously associated with the married name Rich (sonnets 24, 35, 37), alluding to Penelope Devereux/Rich to whom Sidney had once nearly been betrothed (sonnet 33). On the other hand, the differences of names, Philip Sidney/Astrophil, signals that the two are not identical. No doubt the play of differences and similarities in identities would have contributed considerably to the pleasure with which the sequence was read in manuscript by the privileged coterie for whom it was written.[55]

'Master F.J.' tantalizes readers with veiled suggestions that F.J.'s adventures function as a *roman à clef* hiding historical identities and incidents behind fictional pseudonyms. *AS* similarly produces a sense of veiled allusions and constructs the privileged world in which it is set as one of secrets and private affairs, both glamorously exclusive and shameful. The social world it implies is one of adulterous wooings, of the innuendo of songs and tales used in courtly pastime (sonnets 44, 45, 57, 58), of intimate tête-à-têtes in bedchambers at night, and in private groves (4th and 8th songs). *AS* represents that courtly world as both highly desirable and vain. It is inhabited by the idealized Stella, but it is also a place of competition, backbiting, and moral danger. At a time when Sidney's political career at court was stagnating, the sequence figures this coded and allusive world as fascinating and morally dangerous, with an Astrophil/Sidney who is both participant and commentator, an accomplished performer of courtly skills, and an ironic author, morally detached from the follies he displays.[56]

The authorial Sidney remains, however, a shadowy figure, only knowable through his own playfully ironic text. If *AS* thematizes the impossibility of ever embodying in language what lies within the heart, that is, the meaning of Stella, then where does that leave the poetic desires and programmes of the authorial Sidney? Can the two authorial voices be kept securely distinct?

The complex relationship of the two voices is evident in, for example, sonnet 47, in which Astrophil undergoes a sudden change of mind:

> What, have I thus betrayed my libertie?
>   Can those blacke beames such burning markes engrave
>   In my free side? Or am I borne a slave,
> Whose necke becomes such yoke of tyranny?
> Or want I sense to feele my miserie?
>   Or sprite, disdaine of such disdaine to have?
>   Who for long faith, tho dayly helpe I crave,
> May get no almes but scorne of beggerie.
>   Vertue awake, Beautie but beautie is,
> I may, I must, I can, I will, I do
> Leave following that, which it is gaine to misse.
> Let her go. Soft, but here she comes. Go to,
>   Unkind, I love you not: O me, that eye
> Doth make my heart give to my tongue the lie.

The verse produces contesting authorial voices. There is the voice of the poet-lover Astrophil who seems to ejaculate his contradictory reactions even as he experiences them. We may also detect the implied voice of an ironic and detached Sidney who artfully dramatizes (and mocks) the dilemma of his creation, Astrophil. Alternatively, we may hear the voice of a self-reflexive Astrophil (who includes the ironic perspective of the implied Sidney) artfully dramatizing (both mocking and lamenting) his own dilemma. It may be that most readers shift irresolutely between these possibilities, not only in this sonnet but also throughout the sequence. The sense of a speaking voice given us by sonnet 47 is far more complex than the clear split between passionate and narrative/editorial

perspectives in 'Master F.J.'. One effect is to produce a far more sophisticated and flexible model of the self and of self-expression than we met
in Gascoigne: a self-reflexive Astrophil who sees and comments on his
own behaviour, dramatizing his own dilemmas perhaps with ironic self-
mockery, or perhaps, as part of the kind of looking within the heart as a
prerequisite for self-knowledge, recommended by humanist moralists.

This self-knowing, self-critical Astrophil, caught between his experience of his passion, and his knowledge of his own moral failures, offers
a new kind of self-expressive voice in English, closer to the voice of the
Petrarchan lover, constructed out of the tropes of self-division and
oxymora. In Petrarch's case, the striving to possess the object of desire,
signalled by tropes of fragmentation, suggested 'a lack generated by
man's fallen state' which is finally resolved after Laura's death as the
poet turns to the heavenly idea of Laura. In Astrophil's case, the dilemmas are less idealized, more immediate, and their solution less easily
determined.[57] The sequence focuses not on the painful elevation of the
lover/Petrarch to that of a worthy, though mortal, acolyte of the divine,
but on the tragic/absurd dilemma of Astrophil whose desire always
measures his irreducible distance from possession of that which he
desires, or even of its expression; the whole sequence constitutes a
lengthy inexpressibility topos.

In the final lines of sonnet 47 Stella's 'eye' measures the difference
between Astrophil's heart and his tongue: 'O me, that eye I Doth make my
heart give to my tongue the lie.' Astrophil's desire betrays his manly
determination to regain a virtuous mastery of the self, but the line also
focuses our attention on Astrophil's incapacity to ever express what is in
his heart, to find and utter (outer) the meaning of Stella. What is her
meaning for Astrophil/Sidney? Is she a figure for divine beauty (song 70),
or a courtly lady implicated in the risqué pastime of the court? Astrophil's
dilemma is not only one of expression and desire, but also of judgements:
between competing ideas of manliness and of courtly behaviours, and
between competing models of aristocratic self-assertion and Protestant
submission of the self. Caught within these dilemmas, Astrophil, and,
implicated in him, Sidney, articulates a complex and sophisticated experience of the kinds of self-division represented by the competing discourses of courtliness and morality in the late sixteenth century.

The extraordinary rhetorical artistry of sonnet 47, like that of all the
AS sonnets, foregrounds the difficulty of keeping the voices of Astrophil
and Sidney distinct. The ostentatious spontaneity dramatized in this
sonnet is entirely the product of virtuoso art. Astrophil's ejaculatory
speech is fitted into the highly regulated rhyming, rhythmical, and

logical sub-divisions of the exacting sonnet form. The questions of the first eight lines (the octave) accumulate in speed and thus in urgency from the relatively leisurely first quatrain until they reach a climax of resentment in the final two lines of the second quatrain. The 'turn' or change of direction comes, as it should, at the beginning of a third quatrain that in terms of sense runs into the final couplet to make a sestet. The couplet, however, marks the final capitulation. Even while the drama of the sonnet is contained within such formal divisions, the apparently unpremeditated and confused speech of the lover, with its inelegant monosyllables and constant run-over lines, fits perfectly into the rhythmic and rhyming units of the lines.

Perhaps appropriately, dealing as it does with Astrophil's attempt to submit himself to moral humanist ideas of virtue, the sonnet deploys a plain-speaking style, associated with truth-telling in the mid-sixteenth century, and characterized by a monosyllabic vocabulary and the use of aphoristic phrases ('get no almes but scorne of beggerie', 'gaine to misse').[58] Ironically the moral plain style is used to express Astrophil's frank confession of his capitulation to Stella's beauty: 'that eye I Doth make my heart give to my tongue the lie.' The exhortations of the humanist moralists with which Astrophil tries to stiffen his resistance to Stella become stylistic techniques in the service of a new kind of true-seeming rhetoric of passionate self-expression. Even while Astrophil is constructed as confused and as wasting his ink and marring his mind (sonnet 34), the virtuoso art of the sonnet points to more accomplished authorial selves, but those too are produced by the rhetoric. Whether we imagine the writer of this sonnet as an ironically self-conscious and skilled courtier Astrophil, or as a detached masterly Sidney, or oscillate between the two, the mediation of art and rhetoric in the construction of the self-expressive self is brought forcefully to our attention. Whatever is produced in *AS* is produced in language and is subject to the veiled mediations of rhetoric.

Sonnet 34 enacts a debate about the purposes of writing. Competing voices make various claims:

> Come let me write, 'And to what end?' To ease
>   A burthned hart. 'How can words ease, which are
>   The glasses of thy dayly vexing care?'
> Oft cruell fights well pictured forth do please.
> 'Art not asham'd to publish thy disease?'
>   Nay, that may breed my fame, it is so rare:
>   'But will not wise men thinke thy words fond ware?'

Then be they close, and so none shall displease.
'What idler thing, then speake and not be hard?' (ll. 1–9)[59]

Writing as well as a vain disburdening of the heart, may move others (including the writer himself as reader), may 'please', may invite judgement, and may 'breed ... fame'. The effects of verse are difficult, if not impossible, to control, it seems. The conclusion may be extended to *AS* itself. The verse may be autobiographical and also a mirror to the poet-lover (Astrophil or Sidney) of his own follies; it may be a courtly game written to amuse an intimate circle; it may be designed to teach a delightful lesson about the dangers of courtly amorousness or it may produce a version of the court that is as desirable as it is frustrating; it may be a warning about indulging too freely in the composition of amorous verse, or a hubristic display of how to write a new kind of true-seeming passionate rhetoric, in which, of course, the display will always undermine the truth.[60]

Sonnet 34 represents writing in terms of alternatives that Sidney's writing elsewhere confuses: that verse is transparently self-expressive, or that verse may be manipulated to move others. The idea that poetry should move others is central to Sidney's defence of poetry in *An Apology*, although he acknowledges that in the wrong hands the rhetorical arts of verse can produce dangerous effects: 'Poesy may not only be abused, but that being abused, by the reason of his sweet charming force, it can do more hurt than any other army of words.'[61] The 'forcible-ness or *energia*' (p. 138) of poesy, that true-seeming rhetorical skill of the poet, should instead be used 'to teach and delight' (p. 102). What differentiates the titillating rhymer or verser from the true instructive poet, lies in the '*Idea* or fore-conceit, and not in the work itself', that is, it lies in the mind and purposes of the writer. But, in a circular piece of reasoning, the '*Idea* or fore-conceit' can only be known through the work: 'And that the poet hath that *Idea* is manifest, by delivering them forth in such excellency as he hath imagined them' (p. 101). The authorial '*Idea*', that which controls the rhetoric and brings the truth the poet wishes to express irresistibly before the reader, may only be known from the language itself. Sidney's '*Idea*' it seems is not unlike Astrophil's heart, or the meaning of Stella, something that is never able to escape the ever-lasting play and displacements of language.

In the final lines of sonnet 47, Astrophil complained that Stella's 'eye | Doth make my heart give to my tongue the lie.' Stella's 'eye' is both the object of Astrophil's desiring gaze, and, by returning his gaze, the measure of Astrophil's shortfall, his distance from the object of his desire. If 'eye' is read as a pun on 'I', then again, in asserting her selfhood, Stella establishes her difference from Astrophil; she is that which his heart and tongue can never possess. That distance/difference defines Astrophil as the subject of a desire that is, in Mazzotta's terms 'a pure privation, a lack'.[62] Stella's eye/I thus measures the shortfall between Astrophil's heart and his tongue; his inability ever to mean what he says or to make either his heart or Stella fully present to us or to himself. The gap between Astrophil's heart and his tongue, between what is meant and what is written, produces the proliferating sonnets of the sequence. Interestingly one of the manuscript versions of the sequence and the first printed version, alter the final two lines of sonnet 47, substituting 'I' for 'eye': '(woe me) that I I must make my heart thus give to my tongue the lie.'[63] Scholars regard this version as corrupt, but it brings into focus the poet's 'I' whose heart is never expressed in his tongue. That endlessly discursive 'I' might figure for us the authorial presence of Sidney in *AS*.

6
'My name is Will': *Shakespeare's Sonnets*

The first-person speaker of Shakespeare's sonnets is, as with his illustrious predecessors, Petrarch and Sidney, both lover and poet. His sonnet sequence, like theirs, masquerades, if only at the moment in sonnet 136 when the lover-poet names himself as Will, as a version of the author's own story. In this chapter I shall explore the first-person subject constructed through Shakespeare's sequence and consider ways in which its presentation of the 'I' as authorial, and in some sense autobiographical, develops themes and ideas apparent in earlier texts but takes them in unprecedented directions. It is often said that modern subjectivity is first given expression in Shakespeare's work, particularly in the character of Hamlet. Francis Barker, for example, writes that 'Hamlet utters...a first demand for the modern subject. In the name...of the secular soul, an interior subjectivity begins to speak here.'[1] Anne Ferry in her detailed study of the language of 'inwardness' in sixteenth-century verse, associates what she sees as the innovation of Hamlet's inwardness with the writing of the *Sonnets*: 'both the nature of poetry about inward experience and the notion of what is in the heart rendered by it changed radically between Wyatt's lifetime and about 1600, when Shakespeare was writing *Hamlet* and shortly after he is thought to have written his sonnets.'[2] Joel Fineman, in his study of subjectivity in the *Sonnets*, describes the sonnets particularly those that come late in the sequence as 'something new...developing...a new poetic persona at odds with its self'.[3] As I have tried to show throughout this book, secular autobiographical selves, constructed in conflict with the social and emotional givens of the worlds in which they place themselves, and thus voicing divided and conflicted consciousnesses, had already been developed by a number of Shakespeare's Elizabethan predecessors, often with sophistication and subtlety. In this chapter I want to explore how themes and discourses, already apparent in earlier Elizabethan verse, produce a voice of new and shocking power in *Shakespeare's Sonnets*.

Characteristically, as we have seen, particularly in Chapters 2, 3 and 4, early Elizabethan writers situate their autobiographical personae on the margins of social success, and often, specifically, on the margins of the court. Even in the case of the privileged and courtly Sidney, Marotti has plausibly argued that his exclusion from the court, and uncertainty about his future role, play a significant part in his self-representation as the accomplished but unsuccessful courtier Astrophil.[4] Representing themselves as skilled in elite cultural forms such as verse writing or musicianship, and often identifying themselves as of gentle birth, the writers studied in this book nevertheless also figure themselves as excluded from the social rewards and prestige to which they aspire. At the same time, their exclusion is often represented as a sign of virtue and, paradoxically, an opportunity for self-assertion; they define themselves as dependent on, but different from, a social and particularly a courtly elite who lack the inner worth and abilities of those excluded by the accidents of birth or fortune. Like the poetic self-figurations of Thomas Howell, George Gascoigne, Isabella Whitney, or Thomas Whythorne, Shakespeare's poet-lover, while participating in elite forms of verse, situates himself on the margins of courtly society, his pen a sign of social dependency, the mark of the client, but also the means of social self-promotion and self-assertion. *Shakespeare's Sonnets* evokes a social milieu in which success is measured in terms of access to, and the favour of, privileged inhabitants of a courtly world that is both highly desirable and deeply tainted. Far more intensely than his early Elizabethan predecessors, *Shakespeare's Sonnets* articulates the ambivalence and abjection of a self on the margins.

It is evident that the sonnets collected together in the 1609 edition were written over a protracted period, possibly from as early as 1582 through to the publication date. On the basis of two sonnets about the 'dark lady' published in 1599 (138 and 144), it is very possible that many of the 'dark lady' sonnets (127–54), which appear at the end of the 1609 sequence, were in fact among the earliest to be written.[5] In her recent edition of the sonnets, Katherine Duncan-Jones has made a strong case for the 1609 printing as approved, if not press-corrected, by Shakespeare before he left London for Stratford at the onset of yet another outbreak of the plague.[6] While accepting that the published sequence incorporates some work going back to the 1590s at least, she argues that it was arranged and at least partly written and rewritten in the years between 1604 and 1609. However retrospective and at times even arbitrary the 1609 sequencing may appear to be, no doubt bringing together groups of sonnets written for other occasions and specific readers, my own reading finds in the printed sequence, in spite of its unusual gendering of the object of love in many of the sonnets, a familiar and coherent narrative trajectory from idealism to disillusion, reiterated in so many early Elizabethan amorous narratives for which Chaucer's *Troilus and Criseyde* was the paradigm.

Shakespeare's sequence, like Spenser's *Amoretti and Epithalamion*, Gascoigne's 'Adventures of Master F.J.' and Sidney's *Astrophil and Stella*, extends, as diachronic narrative, conflicts and contradictions synchronically present in early modern discourses of passionate love. Shakespeare's sequence follows a less clear chronological sequence and foregrounds, to a far greater extent than the other amorous narratives we have examined, the reversals, contradictions, and inconsistencies associated with the unreason of passion. To give just one example, sonnet 105, with its claim that the idealized youth is 'fair, kind and true' follows just ten sonnets after 95 in which the young man's vice veiled by his beautiful form, is compared to 'a canker in the fragrant rose'. As Janette Dillon has remarked, 'the closed inwardness and self-contained quality of each sonnet, the refusal of one sonnet to be bound by the self-images offered by other sonnets, [and] the fluidity of the sequence, in which each sonnet seems to embody a truth which holds true only for the moment in which it is stated' are all appropriate characteristics of a sequence centrally concerned with 'the transformations of subjectivity'.[7]

Subjectivity, as Emile Benveniste points out, in a passage that I quote in my Introduction, is a function of discourse and intimately associated with direct address to another:

> language puts forth 'empty' forms which each speaker, in the exercise of discourse, appropriates to himself and which he relates to his 'person', at the same time defining himself as *I* and a partner as *you*.[8]

Summarizing Benveniste's account, Kaja Silverman writes: 'the individual finds his or her own cultural identity only within discourse, by means of the pronouns "I" and "you". He or she identifies with the first of these, and is defined in opposition to the second.' She goes on:

> Like the linguistic sign, the subject relies upon another term within the same paradigm – here the personal pronoun 'you' – for its meaning and value. And that paradigm can only be activated through discourse. In the space between two discursive events, subjectivity,

like the pronouns which sustain it, falls into abeyance. Benveniste emphasizes the radical discontinuity which characterizes the condition of subjectivity, its constant stops and starts.[9]

Within *Shakespeare's Sonnets*, the subjective 'I' of the poet-lover is shaped and defined by the relationships with others, the young man and the dark lady, dramatized in each sonnet and in groups of sonnets. The self is redefined from sonnet to sonnet as the relationships between 'I' and 'you' change. Even when the other is not directly addressed, he or she, as the object of desire or repulsion, or both at once, shapes the desiring 'I'. This symbiotic relationship also points to a threatening absence that increasingly becomes a focus of the sequence: if the defining differences of the 'I' and 'you' are lost, the first-person speaker and the object of desire are in danger of losing distinctiveness in a general identity. Ironically, it is in those sonnets that name the poet-lover as 'Will' (sonnets 135 and 136) that the threatening absence of individual difference is most fully explored.

The poet's role in the first group of seventeen sonnets is a relatively detached and self-effacing one. In these sonnets, an aristocratic young man is urged to marry in order to preserve his beauty and name by reproducing himself in a child. The first-person voice shifts between the roles of wise adviser, poet-client, and loving friend. As client and adviser, he voices the established commonplaces of his culture and the dynastic concerns of the young man's family: 'You had a father, let your son say so' (13).[10] As a loving friend, the tone is passionate but apparently disinterested:

> But, love, you are
> No longer yours, than you yourself here live;
> Against this coming end you should prepare,
> And your sweet semblance to some other give. (ll. 1–4)

The young man, the recipient of the poet's advice and concern, is a beautiful and rare object, the silent, and indeed threateningly self-contained focus of the concern of his family and friend. His fault is that of the self-loving Narcissus, an unwillingness to share the perfect singularity of his body, thus threatening the dynastic economies of inheritance:

> Look in thy glass, and tell the face thou viewest
> Now is the time that face should form another,
> Whose fresh repair if now thou not renewest
> Thou dost beguile the world, unbless some mother. (3. 1–4)

The terms in which the poet celebrates the young man formulate a conundrum that will in various guises reappear throughout the sequence. The young man's value depends on his rare beauty and elite singularity, but in order to preserve that singularity, he must double or copy himself. The exceptional young man must traffic with that which is less perfect, tilling the 'uneared womb', the unseeded soil, of 'some mother' (3. 1.5), in order to produce a simulacrum of himself. The poet's images of reproduction attempt to efface the carnality of this transaction; to imagine the process as one of mirroring, or distillation, self-produced without the agency of any other, or any essential loss of self: 'To give away yourself keeps yourself still, | And you must live drawn by your own sweet skill' (16. 13–14). Like the naïve Astrophil, the poet at this stage dreams of an unmediated 'Copying... what...Nature writes' (*AS*, 3), but, unlike Astrophil's fantasy, such copying is not to be through the agency of 'barren rhyme' (16. 4), but rather a magical process of aristocratic self-production.

The material, and transformative, medium through which even self-production must be effected, cannot however be wholly effaced. In sonnet 6, the poet imagines the young man's self-copying in terms of a distilled essence:

> Then let not winter's ragged hand deface
> In thee thy summer, ere thou be distilled:
> Make sweet some vial, treasure thou some place
> With beauty's treasure, ere it be self-killed. (6. 1–4)

The pure, uncontaminated, transparent glass vial that will preserve the distillation of the young man like a rose figures the female womb. This legitimate receptacle is dramatically different, in class and social purpose, from the illegitimate and promiscuous container of the black lady's 'treasure' to be described later in sonnet 136, filled 'full with wills, and my will one'. Exclusive and legitimate as the womb of sonnet 6 may be, the image's erasure of the bloody *prima materia* of female sexuality, betrays, in its own fastidiousness, its fears of contamination. The fantasy of a pure distillation of the young man's perfection is only possible in the carefully selected idealist images of the poet-client.

The precarious idealism of the representation of the young man in the first seventeen sonnets becomes increasingly apparent as the sequence of sonnets to the young man proceeds beyond the first seventeen. The implied relationship between the poet and his addressee alters significantly at sonnet 18 when the poet ceases to urge the young man to immortalize himself through aristocratic procreation, but instead makes himself and his pen the means of the young man's immortality: 'So long as men can breathe or eyes can see, I So long lives this, and this gives life to thee' (18). The poet ceases to be the implied client and spokesman of established aristocratic interests, and instead becomes a client-lover of the young man himself addressing him in a context of secret intimacy.

As the relationship between poet and beloved shifts, so do the roles assigned to each. Having proved himself a 'tender churl' (1) in the first seventeen sonnets for refusing to play his part in the aristocratic trafficking of dynastic self-perpetuation, the young man now enters an economy of clientage and the crossing of social borders, spilling his refined essence in a demotic world of writers, actors and the dark mistress. Within this world the circulation of the young man's favours produces copies, and indeed, a copia that, far more explicitly than in the first seventeen sonnets, compromises the young man's integrity, the rarity and excellence of his beauty and worth. The rival poets flatter him with their 'rich praises', the lover-poet copies his betrayals in black ink, and the dark lady transforms him into one Will among many.

The poet's role also changes from authorized adviser and loving friend, to social inferior and dependent wooer. By addressing his first 126 sonnets to an aristocratic young man, Shakespeare at first seems to alter radically the relationship of power between the male lover-poet and the female object of Petrarchan verse. Where in the Petrarchan sequence the female beloved is the fragmented, silent, and often absent object of male desire, the 'master mistress' of Shakespeare's sequence is represented as the source of the controlling gaze. Sonnet 20 contrasts the confident selfhood of the male with the indefiniteness of the female:

> An eye more bright than theirs, less false in rolling,
> Gilding the object whereupon it gazeth;
> A man in hue, all hues in his controlling,
> Which steals men's eyes, and women's souls amazeth. (20. 5–8)

In relation to this perfect and controlling figure, the poet-lover represents himself as abject and powerless. He is barred by fortune from 'public honour and proud titles' (25); his relationship to the young man is a kind of 'vassalage' in which he is as though bare and naked, looking to the young man's graciousness to 'put apparel on my tattered loving' (26). His service to the young man entails slavish dependence, with 'no services to do, till you require', and enforced patience, 'Whilst I, my sovereign, watch the clock for you' (57 and cf. 58). He is 'in disgrace with fortune and men's eyes' and 'outcast' (29), 'made lame by fortune's dearest spite' (37); he is marked not only by social exclusion, but also by scandal and disgrace, with 'vulgar scandal stamped upon my brow' (112). He is a figure of ridicule, making himself 'a motley to the view' (110), and behaving like an 'unperfect actor' (23). Where in the first seventeen sonnets he spoke as a wise adviser, he is in sonnet 73, simply old, his limbs like bare 'boughs which shake against the cold'; 'a decrepit father' (37, and cf. 22, 126), 'chopped and stained' (62).

Inferior due to social misfortunes and low birth, the poet nevertheless feels his worth is greater than his condition and appeals to the young man as a discerning patron:

> O, for my sake do you with Fortune chide,
> The guilty goddess of my harmful deeds,
> That did not better for my life provide
> Than public means, which public manners breeds;
> Thence comes it that my name receives a brand,
> And almost thence my nature is subdued
> To what it works in, like a dyer's hand;
> Pity me, then, and wish I were renewed (ll. 1–8)

The poet-lover is almost indelibly, but unjustly, marked by the public, staining, and compromised social world he inhabits. The fault is not in his nature but due to the 'guilty goddess ... That did not better for my life provide'. He is stained, as a dyer, through labouring in the only way he can to earn his living so that his nature is 'almost' but not quite subdued; there is still time to rescue him. Like so many other poets, Gascoigne, Howell, Churchyard, Whythorne, who used verse to demonstrate their personal gentility, the poet-lover appeals to the generous discernment of a patron. The potential patron becomes not merely the purchaser of a piece of work or a service, but one who recognizes the innate, if obscured, worth of the client-poet, offering him access to the privileged world to which his 'nature' in some way belongs.

At the same time as Shakespeare's lover-poet aspires to escape the public market place and gain privileged access to the young man's favour, he repeatedly emphasizes irreducible differences of class and kind. In sonnet 37, the lover-poet likens himself to a 'decrepit father' who finds a new self in the youth and beauty of his privileged child:

> So I, made lame by fortune's dearest spite,
> Take all my comfort of thy worth and truth:
> For whether beauty, birth, or wealth, or wit,

> Or any of these all, or all, or more,
> Entitled in thy parts do crowned sit,
> I make my love engrafted to this store:
> So then I am not lame, poor, nor despised,
> Whilst that this shadow doth such substance give. (ll. 3–10)

The paradox of a fortuneless 'father' engrafting himself on the young man's privileged 'birth' (l. 5), and the impossibility of a shadow giving substance (l. 10), expose the fictiveness of this fantasy of transformation. Bounty from above seems unable to bridge the gap between the privileged young man and the 'despised' poet-lover.

Not only is the young man's 'store' unable to transform the demotic poet, the latter's 'blots' may contaminate the young man. Sonnet 36, envisages this scenario:

> I may not evermore acknowledge thee,
> Lest my bewailed guilt should do thee shame,
> Nor thou with public kindness honour me,
> Unless thou take that honour from thy name. (ll. 9–12)

The young man's privileged difference seems to depend precisely on exclusion of the lover-poet and his world of 'public manners'. On the one hand, in sonnets 111 and 37, the poet-lover represents himself as a worthy object of the young man's love and patronage, and even, as a father's interest in his son, entitled to a share in the young man's beauty and wealth, while on the other his exclusion seems central to maintaining the young man's precious difference. The poet-lover's idealization of the young man is predicated on his purity, his absolute difference from the time- and vice-ridden world of the poet.

Intruding into the sequence to the young man, however, a small group of sonnets (40–2) anticipate the sequence to the dark lady. In these sonnets a triangular relationship between the young man, the poet-lover, and the poet-lover's mistress, is constructed. In this relationship differences are contaminated: the young man substitutes a sexual relationship with the mistress for his friendship to the poet, and the mistress substitutes the patron for the poet-client. While the poet-lover cannot so easily substitute one for the other in his bed, the difference and exclusiveness of the idealized young man is threatened by this union with the promiscuous mistress. With savage irony, the poet describes the young man's loss of his elite distinction in terms of the gestures of elite courtliness:

> Gentle thou art, and therefore to be won;
> Beauteous thou art, therefore to be assailed;
> And when a woman woos, what woman's son
> Will sourly leave her till he have prevailed?
> Ay me, but yet thou mightst my seat forbear. (41. 5–9)

The marks of aristocratic gentleness are eroded by the young man's response to temptation like any 'woman's son'. While the young man compromises his aristocratic distinction, the poet-client whose 'seat' has been occupied, behaves in sonnet 40 with a largess that foully parodies a fantastic aristocratic bounty: 'Take all my loves, my love; yea, take them all ... Although thou steal thee all my poverty' (ll. 1 and 10). The young man does, indeed, steal the poet's poverty, and in doing so demonstrates 'public manners' (111) as foul, or fouler than those of the demotic poet.

Fears of contamination and questions of guilt also lurk in the sequence of sonnets that deal with the lover-poet's rivalry with other client poets for the young man's patronage (78–86). Shakespeare's lover-poet represents himself as humbly submissive to the young man's trans-ferred favour to one or more rival poets. At the same time, he self-assertively claims for himself a morally superior language of truth and plainness:

> Thou art as fair in knowledge as in hue,
> Finding thy worth a limit past my praise,
> And therefore art enforced to seek anew
> Some fresher stamp of the time-bettering days,
> And do so love; yet when they have devised
> What strained touches rhetoric can lend,
> Thou, truly fair, wert truly sympathized
> In true plain words, by thy true-telling friend. (82. 5–12)

The poet's language is true and plain, he is a 'true-telling friend', imply-ing falsehood in the 'strained touches of rhetoric' used by his rivals. The 'rhetoric' of the rivals implies an inflated flattery. The rival's verse is 'of proudest sail' (80), 'the proud sail of his great verse' (86), unlike the poet's own 'saucy bark' (80). However, it seems that both kinds of verse find their source in the young man himself: 'what of thee thy poet doth invent | He robs thee of, and pays it thee again' (79. 7–8).

The poet-lover, echoing Astrophil's artless art of 'But Copying ... what in her Nature writes' (*AS*, 3) also claims to 'but copy what in you is writ':

> Who is it that says most? Which can say more,
> Than this rich praise: that you alone are you,
> In whose confine immured is the store
> Which should example where your equal grew?
> Lean penury within that pen doth dwell
> That to his subject lends not some small glory;
> But he that writes of you, if he can tell
> That you are you, so dignifies his story.
> Let him but copy what in you is writ,
> Not making worse what nature made so clear,
> And such a counterpart shall fame his wit,
> Making his style admired everywhere.
> > You to your beauteous blessings add a curse,
> > Being fond on praise, which makes your praises worse. (84)[11]

The implicit allusions to Astrophil's vain attempts to express the Stella that lies within his heart, provide one among a number of ironic perspectives on the poet-lover's claim that telling 'that you are you' is enough to make 'his style admired everywhere'. Telling that 'you alone are you' involves, at the very least, adding a curse to the young man's beauty by revealing the ease with which he compromises his integrity 'being fond on praise'. Thus, copying what in you is writ', the lover-poet's copy produces something different from the 'rich praises' of 'you alone are you'. He makes 'worse what nature made so clear'. Is the poet-lover supplementing and corrupting as he accused the rival poets of doing, or is he but copying what is already corrupted? Copies, it seems, are inextricably associated with the corruption of that ideal pristine 'example' immured, and thus inaccessible, within the confined store of the young man's undoubled self.

The 'true plain words' of 'true-telling' friendship lead the poet-lover to some blunt truths. The rival poets do not merely flatter, but in flattering corrupt the young man, or is it that the young man's desire for praise rather than plain truth-telling corrupts the client poets? Has the poet-lover lost his patron-beloved's favour because he tells the 'saucy' truth? In sonnet 86, it is not the rival poet's inspiration inflating his 'great verse' that daunts the poet-lover, but 'your countenance [that] filled up his line.' The possibility that the young man's favour to the flattering rival poets is but a symptom of his own inner corruption seems confirmed by the way in which the series of sonnets on rival poets leads to another series (92–6) in which what threatens the poet-lover's relationship with the young man is not, or not simply, a rival poet, but the young man's own treachery.

With the possibility of the young man's failure to foster the honest 'true-telling' worth that lies beneath the stains of 'public manners' in his true poet, comes doubt of the young man's integrity: 'Thou mayst be false, and yet I know it not' (92). Whether the young man's suspected treachery is sexual, recalling the triangular relationship with the dark lady of sonnets 40–2, or whether it is figured in terms of corrupted patronage, the suspected hidden fault of the young man implicates him in the grubby compromised world of client poets and client mistresses. The aristocratic young man's difference, his world of exclusive privilege and grace, loses its distinction before the mercenary, commonplace transactions of lust and deception. In sonnet 93, covert betrayal, traditionally figured by the treacherous female, closely allies the young man with the poet's betraying mistress:

> So shall I live, supposing thou art true,
> Like a deceived husband; so love's face
> May still seem love to me, though altered new,
> Thy looks with me, thy heart in other place;
> For there can live no hatred in thine eye,
> Therefore in that I cannot know thy change.
> In many's looks, the false heart's history
> Is writ in moods and frowns and wrinkles strange;
> But heaven in thy creation did decree
> That in thy face sweet love should ever dwell;
> Whate'er thy thoughts or thy heart's workings be,
> Thy looks should nothing thence but sweetness tell.
>   How like Eve's apple doth thy beauty grow,
>   If thy sweet virtue answer not thy show.

This sonnet recalls 40 in which the young man occupied the part of the deceiving mistress leaving the poet to play the cuckolded husband. It also anticipates the dark lady sequence with its themes of deception and corruption. The contrast between the clear gaze of the 'master mistress' of sonnet 20 and the 'shifting change' there characterized as female, is no longer tenable by sonnet 93. The distinctions of birth, beauty, age, and behaviour on which the poet's idealization of the young man, his celebration of his unique perfection, were based are rendered increasingly uncertain. Is it that the young man has grown common through trafficking with a demotic world of dark mistresses and flattering client poets, or is he rather the tempter, corrupting with luxurious vices those with whom he comes into contact, hiding Eve's tempting but Satanic apple beneath refinement and glamour?

The poet-lover's relationship to the young man, and thus his own identity, shift over the course of the first 126 sonnets. In the first seventeen sonnets, the young man is remote and privileged, representing an aristocratic perfection and economy in relation to which the poet-friend-client fulfils a formal and idealizing role. With the increasing intimacy of the poet's relationship with the young man after sonnet 18, the clear distinctions of class and nature that seemed to separate the two become confused and uncertain. The poet-lover's sense of inferiority and abjection before the young man's aristocratic masculine entitlement to power and privilege, give way to disillusion, and even to a sense of moral superiority to the young man. In sonnet 36, the poet-lover urged the young man to protect his reputation by keeping his distance from the compromised poet-lover: 'I love thee in such sort, | As thou being mine, mine is thy good report' (36. 13–14). In sonnet 96, Shakespeare exactly repeats this final couplet from 36, but this time the fear of contamination is that of the poet and derives from the young man's deeds. The clear differentiations between young man and poet-lover on which distinct identities and ideals of class and nature were built are being increasingly eroded.

Sonnet 93, in which the double and deceitful young man is gendered feminine, anticipates the final sequence of dark lady sonnets in which all idealist distinctions and differences are confounded in a general identity. The depiction of the desired lady as erotically fascinating but treacherous is, as we have seen, almost ubiquitous in amorous verse of the 1560s and 1570s in which she frequently figures as a second Cressida. In that verse, female sexuality functions at least in part to figure the perceived duplicity of courtliness, its glamorous attractions as well as its meretricious deceptions. Typical is a verse by Lord Vaux printed in the 1576 edition of *The Paradise of Dainty Devices* in which the lover 'renounceth all the affectes of loue':

> And I also must lothe those learying looks,
> Where loue doeth lurke still with a subtill slaight:
> With painted mocks, and inward hidden hooks,
> To trapp by trust, that lieth not in waite.
> The ende whereof, assaie it who so shall,
> Is sugred smart, and inward bitter gall.[12]

Joel Fineman describes as a 'thematic innovation', the association of love with suspicion and deception: 'it is only when the poet *literally* puts his suspicion of true vision into words, that lust can be a powerful theme in the Renaissance sonnet.'[13] Such a statement ignores the misogynist tradition of Wyatt and his early Elizabethan successors, even if most of their songs and sonnets are not of the strictly fourteen-line Petrarchan form. Lust and its divisive effects on the self already existed as a powerful theme in Elizabethan verse.

Shakespeare's 'dark lady' shares many of the characteristics such as the 'learyng looks' and 'painted mocks' of her Cressida-like cousins in earlier Tudor verse, but she exists more ambiguously on the margins of courtliness. On the one hand, she plays the virginals, and associates with the aristocratic young man of the first 126 sonnets of Shakespeare's sequence, on the other she is sexually accessible to an ageing client-poet, as well as to many others, suggesting a more demotic social positioning. She is, as sonnet 137 puts it, 'the wide world's commonplace', her access to all defining her as that which is not exclusive or privileged, while her courtly skills and aristocratic lover position her as at least intimately related to courtly behaviours. Her social position, in fact, is very like that of the lover-poet himself, a performer of skills in demand by the courtly, a wearer of 'costly gay' garments (sonnet 146), and the client of the same aristocratic young man. Unlike so much early Elizabethan verse in which a masculine anxiety to differentiate male behaviours and attributes from a dangerous femininity is evident, Shakespeare's sonnets to the dark lady emphasise to a remarkable degree the lack of difference, the likenesses between the speaking subject and the female sexual object.

The peverse mirroring of the poet-lover and the dark lady structures sonnet 142:

> Love is my sin, and thy dear virtue hate,
> Hate of my sin, grounded on sinful loving;
> O but with mine compare thou thine own state,
> And thou shalt find it merits not reproving;
> Or if it do, not from those lips of thine,
> That have profaned their scarlet ornaments,
> And sealed false bonds of love as oft as mine,
> Robbed others' beds' revenues of their rents.
> Be it lawful I love thee as thou lov'st those
> Whom thine eyes woo, as mine importune thee,
> Root pity in thy heart, that when it grows,

> Thy pity may deserve to pitied be.
> If thou dost seek to have what thou dost hide,
> By self-example mayst thou be denied.

Through careful rhetorical patterning, the likeness of 'I' and 'thou' is repeatedly emphasised.[14] While the first two lines seem to establish a difference between the two – he is sinful and loving, she is virtuous and hates (my sinful loving) – the fluid significance of words and syntax invite readings based on similarities – her hatred of my sinful loving is grounded on her own sinful loving (promiscuity) which my jealousy impedes, or her hatred of my sinful loving (promiscuity) is a result of her jealousy (a kind of love) of me. The similarities become more overt in the second quatrain in which both lady and lover are implicated in similar sexual sins, sealing 'false bonds of love' and robbing 'other's beds'; both are adulterers, sexual cheaters and thieves. On the basis of the identity between the two, the lover pleads for 'pity', which Duncan-Jones notes is 'here equated with sexual compliance'.[15]

One detail does differentiate these two adulterous, betraying lovers. The dark lady profanes with her scarlet lips, an allusion to the female genitalia as well as to her words.[16] Where the lover admits his all too evident desires, that 'rising at thy name doth point out thee' (151), the lady's lusts are hidden away, not apparent to the sight, and unconfessed. However similar, socially and morally, the lover and his mistress may be, the lady's anatomy and her unheard words nevertheless function in this discourse of misogyny as permanent signs of deception which differentiate her from the lover. Her sexual relationships with others are, for the lover-poet, acts of betrayal, by their very nature, hidden and unknown, sites of feverish speculation and suspicion. It is ironic that one of the few characteristics that Shakespeare's dark lady shares with the Petrarchan lady is that we do not hear her speak.[17] She is spoken by a male discourse and through the words of a male writer. But the dark lady's silence is not, as is Laura's, a sign of female modesty and virtue. On the contrary, the verse often reports that she speaks disdainfully (140), with hatred (149, 152) and lies (138), although her words are on only one occasion reported (145). Her silence in sonnet 142 is as duplicitous as her words, a sign of the absence of truth. The dark lady's scarlet lips are a sign of 'feminine' duplicity and faithlessness, whether her words are heard or unheard.[18]

In this respect, she is close kin to the young man of sonnet 93. Both represent for the poet-lover a betrayal that is gendered feminine, and is uncontrollable. In the sequence of dark lady sonnets, the sexual relationship of the mistress and the young man reappears as a motif with the separate identities of lover, mistress and young man increasingly confused. In sonnet 144, clear distinctions become confounded in the unknowable loss of distinctions that is female sexuality:

> Two loves I have, of comfort and despair,
> Which, like two spirits, do suggest me still:
> The better angel is a man right fair,
> The worser spirit a woman coloured ill.
> To win me soon to hell my female evil
> Tempteth my better angel from my side,
> And would corrupt my saint to be a devil,
> Wooing his purity with her foul pride;
> And whether that my angel be turned fiend
> Suspect I may, yet not directly tell;
> But being both from me both to each friend,
> I guess one angel in another's hell. (ll. 1–12)

Here angels turn into each other, and friends turn fiends in a female hell in which 'I' joins his alter egos.

As we have already noted, the sonnets in which the poet-lover names himself as Will (135 and 136), the name of the author-poet of the sequence Will Shakespeare, are those within which any difference or distinctiveness attaching to 'I' and 'you' are confounded in an all consuming identity of wills:

> Whoever hath her wish, thou hast thy Will,
> And Will to boot, and Will in overplus;
> More than enough am I, that vex thee still,
> To thy sweet will making addition thus. (135. 1–4)

The 'I' who is Will becomes merely supplemental to the other 'Wills' who serve the lady's appetite, that is, her 'will' which is 'large and spacious' enough 'to hide my will in thine' (135. 5–6).[19] Among these Wills may be Mr W.H., the cipher that hints at but hides the identity of the young man.

In sonnet 136, among a multiplicity of 'wills', the poet himself becomes a cipher, a one that is the equivalent of nothing:

> If thy soul check thee that I come so near,
> Swear to thy blind soul that I was thy Will,
> And will, thy soul knows, is admitted there;

> Thus far for love, my love-suit sweet fulfil.
> Will will fulfil the treasure of thy love,
> Ay, fill it full with wills, and my will one;
> In things of great receipt with ease we prove
> Among a number one is reckoned none.
> Then in the number let me pass untold,
> Though in thy store's account I one must be.
> For nothing hold me, so it please thee hold
> That nothing, me, a something sweet to thee.
>   Make but my name thy love, and love that still;
>   And then thou lov'st me, for my name is Will.

As Eve Kosofsky Sedgwick comments, the lover's ploy is to court the lady 'on the basis simply that she will not know you are there'.[20] Her suggestion that the voice of the poet-lover is here that of a 'cutely boyish speaker' ignores, however, the savagery of the sonnet's reduction of the relationship of 'I' and 'thou' to an exchange of appetite. The 'I one' (l. 10) is indistinguishable from other wills in the 'store' of female 'treasure', absorbed by her 'nothing' (ll. 11–12), the round O that denotes the female vagina.[21] The first person 'I' is a digit 1 that is absorbed into the female sexual 0. The lady's 'blind soul' that recognizes 'will's' right of admittance 'there', is, surely, the vegetal soul, whose function was merely nourishment and generation.[22] Will's relation to the lady, at the level of appetite and copulation, renders the phrase 'love-suit sweet' mockingly inappropriate. The word 'sweet' echoes back to its repeated use in the first seventeen sonnets where it described the young man's exquisite beauty: 'Make sweet some vial, treasure thou some place'. That sweetness and treasure finds its nemesis in the store of the dark lady's womb. The sonnet takes to nightmarish lengths the loss of the ordered masculine self feared as the corollary of amorousness in so much mid-century writing, whether in the wary negotiation of a Cressida-like mistress in the verse, or in the warnings against passion in the writings of moralists: 'The flesh molesteth vs … with an armie of vnruly passions, for the most parte, withdrawing from goodnesse, and haling to ilnesse, they tosse and turmoyle our miserable soules, as tempests & waues the Ocean sea'.[23] In the commonplace of sexual appetite there are no distinctions, only an endless iteration of 'wills'.

Such endless inscription of 'I' by the male penis in the female 'nothing' figures in its bleakest form the themes of copying and reproduction that recur through the volume. The idealist persuasion of the first seventeen sonnets, in which the young man was urged to reproduce his singular perfection in the glass vial of a wedded wife (6), here meets its nemesis in the adulterate womb of the dark lady. The careful preservation of hierarchical difference and pure essences envisaged in sonnet 6 is juxtaposed to images of indistinguishable repetitions in sonnet 136 in which 'among a number one is reckoned none' (l. 8). The loss of individual difference in the democratic commonplace of sexual lust destroys the sequence's strenuous investment in the aristocratic young man as guarantor of idealized values and hierarchy, an investment that located the client-lover-writer of the sonnets as inferior, contaminated and excluded. But as writer and copyist, the lover-poet is also the producer of the sequence. Copies are never the same, they always produce difference, corrupting singularity, and out of the endless play of differences, through the poet's inscribing pen, proceeds the cornucopia of the sonnet sequence; and its subject, the authorial hero Will.

The sonnet sequence gradually destroys the illusory 'other' of the idealized male object, identifying him as identical with the desiring male subject, merely another 'will'. The dark lady sequence nevertheless seem to assert a precarious difference at least between the phallic 'Wills' and the lady's dark embrace. The word 'will' implies volition, the active agency of the subject 'I'. The *OED* gives, amongst other definitions of 'will', 'carnal desire or appetite' ('Will' n.1. 2), and 'the action of willing or choosing... some action, physical or mental' ('Will' n.1. 5). The dark lady, by contrast, is represented by images of passivity; it is in her 'hell' (144), the undifferentiating 'bay where all men ride' (137), the 'wide world's commonplace', that the active male 'I one' is received and lost. If the desirable male object of the sonnets collapses into a version of the desiring subject, then the distinctive identity of the male subject, the assertive 'will', seems to gain definition at the very moment at which it is threatened with extinction in the female nothing. But this self-definition is also deconstructed within the language of the sonnets. The dark lady of the sonnets is also a desiring subject with a 'will' of her own: 'So thou, being rich in Will, add to thy Will | One will of mine, to make thy large Will more' (135). The 'will' of the male subject may become the object 'nothing' of the desiring woman: 'For nothing hold me, so it please thee hold | That nothing, me, a something sweet to thee' (136).[24] The male assertion of 'will' is added to the 'treasure' or 'store' of undifferentiating female appetite out of which is produced not only the copies of a new generation, but also a new copia of desire and the writing of desire.

At the very moment of the authorial naming of Will, Shakespeare's sonnets enmesh the speaking subject in a web of identities that dissolve all distinctions of hierarchy, gender, and value. Authorial identity is rendered radically unstable, but it still persists as an effect of the discourse, the 'I' whose voice is heard. Shakespeare's Will, naming himself as desiring subject, luckless client, and demotic writer, is constructed out of identities already existing in discourse that in turn produce a new phenomenon, a self-assertive, dispossessed, and shocking voice that speaks with deeply seductive invitation to future writers.

*   *   *

Shakespeare's Will may be seen as emblematic of the bold but deeply contradictory enterprise of writing the authorial self in which all the texts studied in this book are engaged. As we have seen, 'will' implies volition, the assertion of purpose or intention, a sign of human power and selfhood. At the same time, it means desire and appetite, those aspects of human behaviour that in the sixteenth century were understood as deeply threatening to human selfhood and control. The writing of a 'will' or final testament (*OED* 'Will' n.1. 23) is at the same time a recognition of the final dissolution of the self in death, and a written trace of self-assertion. It is therefore appropriate that the genre of the last will and testament, in which nothing more than words and fictions are left as traces of the absent writer, recurs among the texts we have studied: Isabella Whitney, playfully making a demotic and indifferent London her legacy, Thomas Churchyard, using his last 'will' to attack a court he repeatedly sought and failed to penetrate, or George Gascoigne bequeathing nothing but chameleon identities as the Green Knight or Dan Bartholmew of Bathe. The stories of authorial selves that get told in the texts considered in this book never claim the status of truth or confession. They always, in some way, signal their contingency, their participation in conventions and fashionable fictions. Self-assertion in these texts is always fragile and self-effacing, hovering on the verge of denial and evasion, but nevertheless bound up with the telling of new kinds of story. Authorized by their possession of the pen, however imperfect and contingent, the subjects of these texts name themselves as authors, constructing identity out of the writing of others.

Notes

Introduction

1 George Gascoigne, *A Hundreth Sundrie Flowres*, ed. G.W. Pigman III (Oxford: Clarendon Press, 2000) no. 77, p. 319. All future quotations from Gascoigne's work will be from this text, with page references given in parentheses.

2 Charles Taylor, *Sources of the Self: The Making of the Modern Identity* (Cambridge: Cambridge University Press, 1989), pp. 181–2. On the coinage of the term see Paul Delaney, *British Autobiography in the Seventeenth Century* (London: Routledge & Kegan Paul, 1969), p. 1, and Michael Sprinker, 'Fictions of the Self: The End of Autobiography' in *Autobiography: Essays Theoretical and Critical*, ed. James Olney (Princeton: Princeton University Press, 1980), pp. 321–42 (p. 325).

3 For particularly helpful discussions of some of the difficulties attending modern discussions of 'self-writing' in the early modern period, see Elspeth Graham, 'Women's Writing and the Self' in *Women and Literature in Britain, 1500–1700*, ed. Helen Wilcox (Cambridge: Cambridge University Press, 1996), pp. 209–33, and for early modern subjectivity, see Elizabeth Hanson, *Discovering the Subject in Renaissance England* (Cambridge: Cambridge University Press, 1998). For a helpful overview of ideas about autobiography in the Renaissance, see Peter Burke, 'Representations of the Self from Petrarch to Descartes' in *Rewriting the Self: Histories from the Renaissance to the Present*, ed. Roy Porter (London and New York: Routledge, 1997), pp. 17–28.

4 For details of printing, see Gascoigne, *A Hundreth*, pp. lvii–lix.

5 For Arthur Grey, fourteenth Baron Grey de Wilton, see *DNB*. Gascoigne addressed other poems to him, discussed in Ch. 3 below.

6 For Gascoigne's biography, see C.T. Prouty, *George Gascoigne: Elizabethan Courtier, Soldier, and Poet* (New York: Columbia University Press, 1942). On the representation of the writer as prodigal, especially Gascoigne, see Richard Helgerson, *The Elizabethan Prodigals* (Berkeley: University of California Press, 1977).

7 Emile Benveniste, *Problems in General Linguistics*, trans. Mary Elizabeth Meek (Coral Gables, Florida: University of Miami Press, 1971), p. 227.

8 Quoted by Sprinker, 'Fictions of the Self', p. 324, from Jacques Lacan, *The Language of the Self: The Function of Language in Psychoanalysis*, trans. Anthony Wilden (Baltimore and London: 1968). See the useful discussions of Benveniste's and Lacan's ideas in Kaja Silverman, *The Subject of Semiotics* (New York: Oxford University Press, 1983), pp. 43–53, and 157–84.

9 Silverman, *The Subject of Semiotics*, p. 199. See also Sprinker, 'Fictions of the Self', p. 325.

10 Michel Foucault, 'What Is an Author?' in *Modern Criticism and Theory: A Reader*, ed. David Lodge (London and New York: Longman, 1988), pp. 197–210 (p. 202). See also Roland Barthes's essay 'The death of the author', reprinted in the same collection pp. 167–72.

11 Jacob Burckhardt, *The Civilization of the Renaissance* (Oxford: Phaidon Press, 1944), p. 81. Burckhardt's italics. For a systematic refutation of such generalizations, see David Aers, 'A Whisper in the Ear of Early Modernists; or, Reflections on Literary Critics Writing the "History of the Subject" ' in *Culture and History 1350–1600: Essays on English Communities, Identities and Writing*, ed. David Aers (New York and London: Harvester Wheatsheaf, 1992), pp. 177–202.

12 See the essay by J. A. Burrow, 'Hoccleve's *Series*: Experience and Books' in *Fifteenth-Century Studies: Recent Essays*, ed. R.F. Yeager (Hamden, CT: Archon, 1984), pp. 259–73.

13 Thomas Hoccleve, *Thomas Hoccleve's Complaint and Dialogue*, ed. J. A. Burrow (Oxford: Oxford University Press for The Early English Text Society, 1999), pp. lvii–lxii. Quotations will be from this edition with line numbers given in parentheses.

14 Delaney, *British Autobiography in the Seventeenth Century*, p. 12, suggests the development of high-quality mirrors in the late fifteenth century may be related to what he calls the 'discovery of self'.

15 Lee Patterson, 'On the Margin: Postmodernism, Ironic History, and Medieval Studies', *Speculum* 65 (1990): 87–108 (p. 99). See also Sarah Kay, *Subjectivity in Troubadour Poetry* (Cambridge: Cambridge University Press, 1990), esp. p. 213.

16 J. A. Burrow, 'Autobiographical Poetry in the Middle Ages: The Case of Thomas Hoccleve', *Proceedings of the British Academy* 68 (1982): 389–412 (p. 402).

17 James M. Osborn, ed., *The Autobiography of Thomas Whythorne* (Oxford: Clarendon Press, 1961), p. 134. This edition of Whythorne's manuscript uses the original idiosyncratic orthography.

18 For seminal discussions on flexible Renaissance selves, see Thomas Greene, 'The Flexibility of the Self in Renaissance Literature' in *The Disciplines of Criticism*, ed. P. Demetz (New Haven: Yale University Press, 1968), pp. 241–64, and Stephen Greenblatt, *Renaissance Self-Fashioning* (Chicago and London: University of Chicago Press, 1980).

19 James M. Osborn, ed., *The Autobiography of Thomas Whythorne (Modern-Spelling Edition)* (Oxford: Oxford University Press, 1962), p. xii. This edition is abbreviated as well as in modern spelling.

20 David R. Shore, 'Whythorne's *Autobiography* and the Genesis of Gascoigne's *Master F.J.*', *Journal of Medieval and Renaissance Studies* 12 (1982): 159–78.

1 'To mak my self to be known of many': miscellanies and the well-formed gentleman

1 The quotation is from James M. Osborn, ed., *The Autobiography of Thomas Whythorne* (Oxford: Clarendon Press, 1961), p. 173. An early version of the argument of this chapter appeared as Elizabeth Heale, 'Songs, Sonnets and Autobiography: Self-Representation in Sixteenth-Century Verse Miscellanies' in *Betraying Our Selves Forms of Self-Representation in Early Modern English Texts*, ed. Henk Dragstra, Sheila Ottway and Helen Wilcox (Basingstoke: Macmillan Press, 2000), pp. 59–75.

2 For a history of the Elizabethan miscellanies, see Elizabeth W. Pomeroy, *The Elizabethan Miscellanies: Their Development and Conventions* (Berkeley, Los

Angeles, London: University of California Press, 1973). I am particularly indebted, throughout this chapter, to three discussions of the miscellanies and early Elizabethan printed verse: those by Wendy Wall, *The Imprint of Gender: Authorship and Publication in the English Renaissance* (Ithaca and London: Cornell University Press, 1993), Arthur F. Marotti, *Manuscript, Print, and the English Renaissance Lyric* (Ithaca and London: Cornell University Press, 1995), Chs 4 and 5, and Mary Thomas Crane, *Framing Authority: Sayings, Self and Society in Sixteenth-Century England* (Princeton: Princeton University Press, 1993), Ch. 8.

3 For the phrase 'autobiographical assumpton' see Sarah Kay, *Subjectivity in Troubadour Poetry* (Cambridge: Cambridge University Press, 1990), p. 2. It will be evident that my argument throughout this chapter challenges the view that single-author miscellanies can be differentiated from sonnet sequences by authorial absence, stated in the otherwise excellent essay of Richard C. Newton, 'Making Books from Leaves: Poets Become Editors' in *Print and Culture in the Renaissance*, ed. Gerald P. Tyson and Sylvia S. Wagonheim (Newark: University of Delaware Press, 1986), pp. 246–64.

4 Biographical information on Barnabe Googe, the first of the single-author miscellanists can be found in the biographical introduction to Barnabe Googe, *Eclogues, Epitaphs, and Sonnets*, ed. Judith M. Kennedy (Toronto, Buffalo, London: University of Toronto Press, 1989), and on Gascoigne, in C.T. Prouty, *George Gascoigne: Elizabethan Courtier, Soldier, and Poet* (New York: Columbia University Press, 1942), and the 'Biographical Introduction' to George Gascoigne, *A Hundreth Sundrie Flowres*, ed. G.W. Pigman III (Oxford: Clarendon Press, 2000), pp. xxiii–xliii. For other miscellanists, see Thomas C. Izard, *George Whetstone: Mid-Elizabethan Gentleman of Letters* (New York: AMS Press, 1966), pp. 1–34, and John Erskine Hankins, *The Life and Works of George Turbervile* (Lawrence, Kansas: University of Kansas, 1940), pp. 3–28. What little is known of the life of Isabella Whitney, can be found in Randall Martin, ed., *Women Writers in Renaissance England* (London and New York: Longman, 1997), p. 280.

5 Daniel Javitch, 'The Impure Motives of Elizabethan Poetry', *Genre* 15 (1982): 225–38 (p. 225). For discussions of the relationships between writing, courtly behaviours and employment as a secretary, see Jonathan Goldberg, *Writing Matter: From the Hands of the English Renaissance* (Stanford, CA.: Stanford University Press, 1990), esp. Ch. 5; Richard Rambuss, *Spenser's Secret Career* (Cambridge: Cambridge University Press, 1993), and Richard Rambuss, 'Spenser's Lives, Spenser's Careers' in *Spenser's Life and the Subject of Biography*, ed. Donald Cheney, Judith H. Anderson, Davis A. Richardson (Amherst, MA.: University of Massachusetts Press, 1996), pp. 1–17.

6 For a discussion of constructions of masculinity in this period, see Mark Breitenberg, *Anxious Masculinity in Early Modern England* (Cambridge: Cambridge University Press, 1996), esp. Introduction.

7 Crane, *Framing Authority*, p. 4.

8 For a famous discussion of the formation of masculinity via humanist education, see 'Latin Language Study as a Renaissance Puberty Rite' in Walter J. Ong, *Rhetoric, Romance, and Technology: Studies in the Interaction of Expression and Culture* (Ithaca and London: Cornell University Press, 1971), pp. 113–41.

9 Crane, *Framing Authority*, p. 6.

10 Ibid., p. 53, quoted from William Kempe, *The Education of Children in Learning* (1588). See also Ann Moss, *Printed Commonplace-Books and the Structuring of Renaissance Thought* (Oxford: Clarendon Press, 1996), esp. Ch. 6.

11 Gascoigne, *A Hundreth*, nos 58–62.

12 For discussions of courtly behaviours, and the influence of Castiglione, see Frank Whigham, *Ambition and Privilege: The Social Tropes of Elizabethan Courtesy Theory* (Berkeley, Los Angeles, London: University of California Press, 1984), and Daniel Javitch, *Poetry and Courtliness in Renaissance England* (Princeton: Princeton University Press, 1978). For the conflict between courtly and humanist codes, see Crane, *Framing Authority*, Ch. 5.

13 Catherine Bates, *The Rhetoric of Courtship in Elizabethan Language and Literature* (Cambridge: Cambridge University Press, 1992), Ch. 2 on the semantics of 'courting'.

14 Osborn, ed., *Whythorne's Autobiography* (1961), p. 33.

15 Roger Ascham, *The Scholemaster (1570)*, ed. Edward Arber (Birmingham: English Reprints, 1870), p. 50.

16 An earlier very popular collection of verse, including poems by Wyatt, whose influence is now hard to judge is *The Court of Venus*, which went through at least three editions before 1564; see Russell A. Fraser, ed., *The Court of Venus* (Durham, NC: Duke University Press, 1955), Introduction. Thynne's 1532 edition of Chaucer's *Workes* also provided a courtly and highly prestigious model of a single-author miscellany. For a discussion of the sixteenth-century tendency to interpret autobiographically much of the material in Thynne's edition, not all of it by Chaucer, see Alice S. Miskimin, *The Renaissance Chaucer* (New Haven and London: Yale University Press, 1975), pp. 81–95.

17 Hyder Edward Rollins, ed., *Tottel's Miscellany (1557–1587)*, 2 vols (Cambridge, MA: Harvard University Press, 1928–9), II. 7–36. Quotations in my text will be followed in parentheses by volume and page references to this edition.

18 See ibid., II. 99–100, and Marotti, *Manuscript, Print, and the English Renaissance Lyric*, p. 144.

19 Wall, *Imprint of Gender*, p. 97. See also Marotti, *Manuscript, Print, and the English Renaissance Lyric* pp. 215–17.

20 See Rollins, ed., *Tottel's Miscellany*, II. 67.

21 See, for example, I. nos 2, 12, 26, 265.

22 Crane, *Framing Authority*, p. 150.

23 Rollins, ed., *Tottel's Miscellany*, I. nos 27, 28, 118, 124, 170, 191,194, 200, 295.

24 Crane, *Framing Authority*, p. 170, and Germaine Warkentin, 'The Meeting of the Muses: Sidney and the Mid-Tudor Poets' in *Sir Philip Sidney and the Interpretation of Renaissance Culture: The Poet in His Time and in Ours*, ed. Gary F. Waller and Michael D. Moore (London and Sydney: Croom Helm, 1984), pp. 17–33 (p. 25), notes of the 'civic' voice of mid-Tudor miscellanies, that the poet 'himself stands as a historical reference point behind the experience he relates'.

25 For example, ll. 86 and 100.

26 Crane, *Framing Authority*, p. 150. Wall, *Imprint of Gender*, p. 26, suggests Tottel authorizes his verse as a form of 'personal utterance'. For discussions of the effects of Tottel's titles, see Anne Ferry, *The 'Inward' Language: Sonnets of Wyatt, Sidney, Shakespeare, Donne* (Chicago and London: University of Chicago Press, 1983) pp. 18–19, and Marotti, *Manuscript, Print, and the English Renaissance Lyric*, pp. 218–20.

27 See Rollins, ed., *Tottel's Miscellany*, II. p. 74 and discussion on pp. 70–5.

28 Ibid., I. no. 14, and II.141.

29 Thomas Nashe, *The Unfortunate Traveller and Other Works*, ed. J.B. Steane (Harmondsworth: Penguin, 1972), for example, pp. 299, 307, 315.

30 Michael Drayton, *The Works*, ed. Kathleen Tillotson William Hebel, and Bernard H. Newdigate, 5 vols (Oxford: Oxford University Press, 1931–41), II. 283.

31 Rollins, ed., *Tottel's Miscellany*, II. 287 ('Tagus, farewell' was 'done by the said Earle, or Sir Francis Brian').

32 Quotation from Osborn, ed., *Whythorne's Autobiography* (1961), p. 173.

33 Thomas Howell, *The Poems of Thomas Howell (1568–1581)*, ed. A.B. Grosart ([n.p.]: printed for subscribers, 1879), pp. 108–9. References in parentheses after quotations from Howell will be to Grosart's page numbers in this edition.

34 A third volume appeared in 1581, *H. His Devises for his owne exercise and his Friends pleasure*, dedicated to Mary, Countess of Pembroke.

35 For the idea of the poet as editor, see Newton, 'Making Books from Leaves: Poets Become Editors'. For printed collections that present themselves as manuscript collections, see Wall, *Imprint of Gender*, Ch. 4.

36 For example, Rollins, ed., *Tottel's Miscellany*, I. nos 4 or 18 (by Surrey) or 104 (by Wyatt).

37 Michael Brennan, *Literary Patronage in the English Renaissance: The Pembroke Family* (London: 1988), p. 74.

38 For a review of Renaissance thought on women, see Ian MacLean, *The Renaissance Notion of Women: A Study in the Fortunes of Scholasticism and Medical Science in European Intellectual Life* (Cambridge: Cambridge University Press, 1980). See also the useful anthologies of contemporary views, Kate Aughterson, ed., *Renaissance Women: Constructions of Femininity in England* (London and New York: Routledge, 1995), and Katherine Usher Henderson and Barbara F. McManus, eds, *Half Humankind: Contexts and Texts of the Controversy about Women in England, 1540–1640* (Urbana and Chicago: University of Illinois Press, 1985).

39 Howell is here drawing on Henryson's continuation of the Cressida narrative beyond the account in Chaucer's *Troilus and Criseyde*. Henryson's poem was printed in all sixteenth-century editions of Chaucer's works after 1532, and apparently taken to be by Chaucer. See Hyder Edward Rollins, 'The Troilus–Cressida Story from Chaucer to Shakespeare', *Publications of the Modern Language Association* 32 (1917): 383–429 (especially pp. 404–5 for Howell's poem).

40 Googe, *Eclogues, Epitaphs, and Sonnets*, pp. 38–9. Page references in parentheses will accompany quotations from this text in the following discussion.

41 On Burleigh's disapproval of aristocratic courtly verse, see Richard Helgerson, *The Elizabethan Prodigals* (Berkeley: University of California Press, 1977), Ch. 1, and Crane, *Framing Authority*, p. 165.

42 Thomas Becon, *The Early Works*, ed. J. Ayre (Cambridge: Cambridge University Press for The Parker Society, 1843), p. 266.

43 Gascoigne, *A Hundreth*, pp. 360 and 367. Gascoigne echoes Tottel's preface, which condemns readers 'that maketh the swete majerome not to smell to their delight'.

44 George Whetstone, *The Rocke of Regard, Diuided into Foure Parts (1576)*, ed. J. Payne Collier (privately printed, 1870), p. 143. Another example is a poem by John Keeper in the only existing copy of Howell's *Newe Sonets*, that assures

the 'Vpright Reader of these pretie Pamphilets' that 'though in Howels soyle, ilwillers seeme to see, I at first nought els but thritlesse thornes' on closer inspection they will find 'frutes and frutfull Herbes', Howell, *Poems*, p. 115.

45 Fraser, ed., *The Court of Venus*, pp. 57–61, and John Hall, *The Court of Virtue (1565)*, ed. Russell A. Fraser (London: Routledge & Kegan Paul, 1961), p. xii.

46 Fraser, ed., *The Court of Venus*, p. 15 (ll. 20 and 8).

47 Ibid., p. 16, ll. 16–17.

48 Helgerson, *Elizabethan Prodigals*, esp. Ch. 1. Lorna Hutson, *The Usurer's Daughter: Male Friendship and Fictions of Women in Sixteenth-Century England* (London: Longman, 1994), p. 125, suggests that the representations of women as deceitful and of the male miscellanists as reformed prodigals point to the writers' anxiety about appearing in the marketplace of print. Crane, *Framing Authority*, p. 166, points out that the reformed prodigal narrative is only one of a number used by writers of the period to negotiate a perceived opposition between the courtly and humanist systems.

49 Wall, *Imprint of Gender*, p. 102, cites an example, given by Marotti, of a reader who 'formed his or her own "plot"' by joining together poems by various authors through the use of connecting titles.

50 Ibid., p. 243, and Marotti, *Manuscript, Print, and the English Renaissance Lyric* pp. 223–25, and 302–8, for valuable discussions of *A Hundreth* and its reissue as *The Posies* (1575).

51 On the sixteenth-century version of Chaucer's biography, see Miskimin, *The Renaissance Chaucer*, esp. p. 243.

52 Gascoigne, *A Hundreth*, p. 510, points out that Gascoigne is not translating directly from the Greek.

53 I shall look further at '*Gascoignes wodmanship*' in Chapter 3.

54 Gascoigne, *A Hundreth*, nos 53, 49, 50, 53, 54, 57.

55 George Gascoigne, *The Complete Works*, ed. John W. Cunliffe, 2 vols (Cambridge: Cambridge University Press, 1907–10), I. 41–2.

56 On Gascoigne's use of the pen/penis pun, see Richard C. McCoy, 'Gascoigne's "Poemata Castrata": The Wages of Courtly Success', *Criticism* 27 (1985): 29–55, and Susan C. Staub, '"A Poet with a Spear": Writing and Sexual Power in the Elizabethan Period', *Renaissance Papers* (1992): 1–15.

57 Gascoigne, *A Hundreth*, p. 518.

58 Compare, for example, *Amores*, I. iv.

59 For the common use of words such as 'trifles' and 'toys' to describe verse, especially courtly verse, in this period, see Gascoigne, *A Hundreth*, p. 557, note to pp. 142, ll. 23–4.

60 On dating of editions, see Hankins, *The Life and Works of George Turbervile*, pp. 31ff., and George Turbervile, *Epitaphes, Epigrams, Songs and Sonets (1567)* and *Epitaphes and Sonnettes (1576)*, ed. Richard J. Panofsky (Delmar, NY: Scholars' Facsimiles and Reprints, 1977), pp. vi–vii. Quotations from Turbervile's verse are taken from this edition with Panofsky's added page numbers given in parentheses.

61 Turbervile, *Epitaphes*, ed. Panofsky, pp. v–vi, and Googe, *Eclogues, Epitaphs, and Sonnets*, pp. 9–10.

62 Panofsky, in his edition of Turbervile, *Epitaphes*, p. viii, hails the Tymetes and Pyndara sequence as the first lyric sequence in English verse, but this is to overlook such narrative sequences as *Troilus and Criseyde* or Hawes' *Pastime of Pleasure*.

63 See my discussion of echo in Ch. 4, p. 114 below.

64 Crane, *Framing Authority*, p. 258 fn.41 The first phrase is quoted from Harry Berger Jr.

65 See especially Jacques Derrida, *Of Grammatology*, trans. Gayatri Chakravorty Spivak (Baltimore and London: John Hopkins University Press, 1976), Ch. 1, and Roland Barthes, 'The Death of the Author' in *Modern Criticism and Theory: A Reader*, ed. David Lodge (London and New York: Longman, 1988), pp. 167–72.

66 Howell's *The Arbor of Amitie* and Turbervile's *Epitaphes, Epigrams, Songs and Sonets* are both dedicated to women, although the former also has a dedicatory epistle to John Keeper.

67 For the attack and defence tradition, see especially Linda Woodbridge, *Women and the English Renaissance: Literature and the Nature of Womankind 1540–1620* (Brighton: Harvester, 1984).

68 The Chaucerian provenance of these stanzas was first identified by Ethel Seaton, ' "The Devonshire Manuscript" and its Medieval Fragments', *Review of English Studies* n.s.7 (1956): 55–6. Richard Harrier, 'A Printed Source for "the Devonshire Manuscript" ', *Review of English Studies* n.s.11 (1960): 54, first identified the source of the fragments as Thynne's edition.

69 Fol. 91^v, reprinted in Kenneth Muir, 'Unpublished Poems in the Devonshire Ms', *Proceedings of the Leeds Philosophical Society: Literary and Historical Section* 6, pt. 4 (1947): 253–82, no. 53. From *Troilus and Criseyde*, Bk.II, ll. 785–88.

70 Fol. 90^r; ibid., no. 45.

71 John V. Fleming, 'Hoccleve's "Letter of Cupid" and the "Quarrel" over the *Roman De La Rose*', *Medium Aevum* 40 (1971): 21–40.

72 Quotations from Whitney's texts are from Danielle Clarke, ed., *Isabella Whitney, Mary Sidney and Aemilia Lanyer: Renaissance Women Poets* (Harmondsworth: Penguin Books, 2000). Page references to this edition will be given in parentheses after quotations.

73 The male-voiced poems are not given in Clarke's text and are quoted from the facsimile edition by Richard J. Panofsky, ed., *The Floures of Philosophie (1572) by Hugh Plat and a Sweet Nosgay (1573) and the Copy of a Letter (1567) by Isabella Whitney* (Delmar, NY: Scholars' Facsimiles and Reprints, 1982).

74 Clarke, ed., *Isabella Whitney*, p. 295 and Paul Marquis, 'Oppositional Ideologies of Gender in Isabella Whitney's *Copy of a Letter*', *Modern Language Review* 90 (1995): 314–24 (315).

75 Turbervile, *Epitaphes*, p. vi.

76 Ilona Bell, *Elizabethan Women and the Poetry of Courtship* (Cambridge: Cambridge University Press, 1998), in her discussion of *The Copy*, pp. 113–25, quotes Ann Rosalind Jones's comment that 'even when [Whitney's] aim is to criticize the opposite sex, the ammunition that comes to hand is determined by a history of suspicious and condemnatory discourses about women' (p. 121).

77 Hutson, *The Usurer's Daughter* makes this point in her discussion of the context of Whitney's volume, pp. 116–28.

78 This is not in Clarke's edition. I quote from Panofsky, ed., *The Floures of Philosophie*, sig.C.v^r.

79 Wall, *Imprint of Gender*, pp. 296–310.

80 Danielle Clarke, *The Politics of Early Modern Woman's Writing* (London and New York: Longman, 2001), p. 202, makes this point.

81   Hutson, *The Usurer's Daughter*, p. 126, suggests the book 'advertises Whitney's readiness to serve in some virtuous employment'.

2   The 'outward marks' and the 'inward man': Thomas Whythorne's 'songs and sonetts'

1   James M. Osborn, ed., *The Autobiography of Thomas Whythorne* (Oxford: Clarendon Press, 1961), p. xlii and Appendix 1. He published another volume of *Duos* in 1590, again with his own settings for his own verse. David R. Shore, 'The *Autobiography* of Thomas Whythorne: An Early Elizabethan Context for Poetry', *Renaissance and Reformation* 17 (1981): 72–86 argues that the manuscript ought to be seen in the context of the mid-century miscellanies.

2   The manuscript was edited by Osborn in its original orthography in 1961, and, in the following year, in a shortened modern-spelling edition: James M. Osborn, ed., *The Autobiography of Thomas Whythorne (Modern-Spelling Edition)* (Oxford: Oxford University Press, 1962). Whythorne's personal orthography uses 'þ' for 'th', '3' for 'j' or 'ge', and indicates long vowels with a dot under the letter, except in the case of y. I have retained the original spelling which seems to me an integral part of the self-presentation of the writer. I thus use Osborn's 1961 edition for quotations, but for ease of reading I omit editorial marks indicating interlinear alterations and lacunae. Quotations in my text will be followed by page references to the 1961 edition.

3   For two recent accounts of the ages of man, see J. A. Burrow, *The Ages of Man: A Study of Medieval Writing and Thought* (Oxford: Clarendon Press, 1986), and Mary Dove, *The Perfect Age of Man's Life* (Cambridge: Cambridge University Press, 1986), who refers to Whythorne on p. 27.

4   Whythorne again addresses his friend on p. 206 after a lengthy description of a wooing, expressing the hope that it may prove useful 'if yee chauns to hav þe lẏk happen to yow'.

5   David R. Shore, 'Whythorne's *Autobiography* and the Genesis of Gascoigne's *Master F.J.*', *Journal of Medieval and Renaissance Studies* 12 (1982): 159–78 is inclined to think there is no direct influence.

6   George Gascoigne, *A Hundreth Sundrie Flowres*, ed. G.W. Pigman III (Oxford: Clarendon Press, 2000), pp. 364–9.

7   Ibid., p. 366.

8   Shore, '*Autobiography* of Thomas Whythorne', p. 83, makes this point.

9   Gascoigne, *A Hundreth*, p. 145.

10   Shore, '*Autobiography* of Thomas Whythorne', p. 74.

11   Burrow, *Ages of Man*, p. 177.

12   See Andrew Mousley, 'Renaissance Selves and Life Writing: The *Autobiography* of Thomas Whythorne', *Forum* 26 (1990): 222–30.

13   The exception is his service to Bromfield, as tutor to his son at Cambridge and subsequently as a caretaker for his affairs in London, Osborn, ed., *The Autobiography of Thomas Whythorne*, (1961), pp. 114–63.

14   For example by Philippa Berry, *Of Chastity and Power: Elizabethan Literature and the Unmarried Queen* (London and New York: Routledge, 1989) and Catherine Bates, *The Rhetoric of Courtship in Elizabethan Language and Literature* (Cambridge: Cambridge University Press, 1992).

15   For this point, see Shore, '*Autobiography* of Thomas Whythorne,' pp. 74–5.
16   Mousley, 'Renaissance Selves', p. 225, comments that Whythorne writes his manuscript 'to convert the unsettling sense of masterlessness into the confident sense of being or becoming "mȳn own man"'.
17   Thomas Howell, *The Poems of Thomas Howell (1568–1581)*, ed. A.B. Grosart ([n.p.]: printed for subscribers, 1879), p. 153, and I.M., *A Health to the Gentlemanly Profession of Serving-Men* (1598), ed. A.V. Judges (London: Oxford University Press for the Shakespeare Association, 1931), sig. H4ᵛ.
18   For examples of Tottel poems, including those by Wyatt and Surrey, see Hyder Edward Rollins, ed., *Tottel's Miscellany (1557–1587)*, 2 vols (Cambridge, MA: Harvard University Press, 1928–29), I. nos 118, 124, 295, 170, 191, 194, 200, 216. Mary Thomas Crane, *Framing Authority: Sayings, Self and Society in Sixteenth-Century England* (Princeton: Princeton University Press, 1993), p. 170, notes that it is 'one thing for Wyatt or another courtier to praise the mean and sure estate, and another thing altogether for a grocer to read about it.'
19   Baldassare Castiglione, *The Book of the Courtier*, trans. Sir Thomas Hoby, *Everyman's Library* (London: Dent, 1928), p. 46.
20   Shore, '*Autobiography* of Thomas Whythorne', p. 75, suggests the manuscript may have started life as this projected collection.
21   On early modern preparations for death, see Ralph Houlbrooke, *Death, Religion, and the Family in England 1480–1750* (Oxford: Clarendon Press, 1998).

3   Narratives of experience

1   See footnote 18 to Ch. 2 above.
2   Hyder Edward Rollins, ed., *Tottel's Miscellany (1557–1587)*, 2 vols (Cambridge, Mass.: Harvard University Press, 1928–9), I. no. 118. For an example of the use of the topic to teach quite blatantly a political quietism, see Sir Thomas Vaux's verses in Hyder Edward Rollins, ed., *The Paradise of Dainty Devices (1576–1606)* (Cambridge: Cambridge University Press, 1927) no. 88.
3   Thomas Howell, *The Poems of Thomas Howell (1568–1581)*, ed. A.B. Grosart ([n.p.]: printed for subscribers, 1879), pp. 118–19.
4   For instance, Surrey's 'So cruell prison' and Wyatt's 'Myne owne Iohn Poyns' in Rollins, ed., *Tottel's Miscellany*, I. nos 15 and 125.
5   I.M., *A Health to the Gentlemanly Profession of Serving-Men (1598)*, ed. A.V. Judges (London: Oxford University Press for the Shakespeare Association, 1931) sig. Hʳ⁻ᵛ.
6   Howell, *Poems*, pp. 153–9.
7   Thomas Churchyard, *A Generall Rehearsall of Warres, Wherein Is Fiue Hundred Seuerall Seruices of Land and Sea* (London: Edward White, [1579]), sig. M.iiiᵛ.
8   Thomas Tusser, *Five Hundred Points of Good Husbandry*, ed. Geoffrey Grigson (Oxford: Oxford University Press, 1984), p. xi. I quote from this modern edition of the 1580 edition, giving page references in parentheses.
9   Grigson, p. xvii, refers to the book becoming a 'miscellany'.
10   Grigson, p. xvii, tells us that he eventually died in debtor's prison on 8th May 1580.
11   The quotation is from Sidney's *Astrophil and Stella*, no. 45.

12 Cited by Thomas C. Izard, *George Whetstone: Mid-Elizabethan Gentleman of Letters* (New York: AMS Press, 1966), p. 11. 'Inventions of P. Plasmos' is in George Whetstone, *The Rocke of Regard, Diuided into Foure Parts (1576)*, ed. J. Payne Collier (privately printed, 1870) pp. 276–331. References to this edition will be given in parentheses in the text.

13 Izard, *George Whetstone: Mid-Elizabethan Gentleman of Letters*, p. 13.

14 Lorna Hutson, *The Usurer's Daughter: Male Friendship and Fictions of Women in Sixteenth-Century England* (London: Longman, 1994), p. 126. Hutson's comments preface a discussion of Whitney's 'Wyll and Testament'.

15 Danielle Clarke, ed., *Isabella Whitney, Mary Sidney and Aemilia Lanyer: Renaissance Women Poets* (Harmondsworth: Penguin Books, 2000), p. 18. Page references to this edition are given in parentheses.

16 The Dan Bartholmew sequence was first printed unfinished in *A Hundreth*, and subsequently appeared completed in *The Posies*. It is found on pp. 329–58 and 386–98 of George Gascoigne, *A Hundreth Sundrie Flowres*, ed. G.W. Pigman III (Oxford: Clarendon Press, 2000). '*The fruite of Fetters*' is on pp. 439–54. The quotation is from 'Continuation of *The reporters conclusion*', l. 399, p. 397. Page references, and where helpful, line references, to Pigman's edition will be given in parentheses in the text after quotations.

17 Stz. 129. See ibid., p. 725, for Pigman's patient disentangling of Gascoigne's disguised self-references and personae in relation to the green knight.

18 See Pigman's helpful note on p. 664.

19 Jonathan Crewe, *Trials of Authorship: Anterior Forms and Poetic Reconstruction from Wyatt to Shakespeare* (Berkeley, Los Angeles, Oxford: University of California Press, 1990), p. 130. Crewe's Chapter 5 provides an excellent discussion of the poem.

20 C.T. Prouty, *George Gascoigne: Elizabethan Courtier, Soldier, and Poet* (New York: Columbia University Press, 1942), pp. 293–304, and Pigman's introduction, p. xxvi. For examples of the sexual motif in hunting poems, see Elizabeth Heale, *Wyatt, Surrey and Early Tudor Poetry* (London: Longman, 1998), p. 46.

21 Oddly Pigman in his edition does not give madman as a possible meaning of 'wodman'.

22 Gascoigne's imitation in these lines of Wyatt's satire 'Myne owne John Poins' has been noted, e.g. by Pigman, p. 665.

23 From the Preface 'To the reverende Divines' in *Posies* 1575, Gascoigne, *A Hundreth*, p. 361.

24 Crewe, *Trials of Authorship*, p. 129.

25 Frank Tallett, *War and Society in Early Modern Europe, 1495–1715* (London and New York: Routledge, 1992), p. 114.

26 Izard, *George Whetstone: Mid-Elizabethan Gentleman of Letters*, pp. 28–9.

27 For the Netherlands, see Jan Albert Dop, *Eliza's Knights: Soldiers, Poets, and Puritans in the Netherlands, 1572–1586* (Alblasserdam: Remak, 1981), and David J.B. Trim, 'Ideology, Greed and Social Discontent in Early-Modern Europe: Mercenaries and Mutinies in the Rebellious Netherlands 1568–1609' in *Rebellion, Repression, Reinvention: Mutiny in Comparative Contexts*, ed. Jane Hathaway (Westport, Conn. and London: Praeger Press, 2001), pp. 47–61 (pp. 50–1). I am indebted to David Trim for guidance on this topic.

28 George Whetstone, *The Honorable Reputation of a Souldier* (London: Richard Jones, 1585), sig.Aiii^r.

29 Churchyard, *A Generall Rehearsall of Warres*, sig. M.ii^r.
30 Thomas Churchyard, *A Light Bondell of Liuely Discourses Called Churchyardes Charge, Presented as a Newe Yeres Gifte to the Right Honourable, the Erle of Surrie* (London: Jhon Kyngston, 1580), pp. 1–6^v.
31 Thomas Churchyard, *The First parte of Churchyardes Chippes, Containing Twelue Seuerall Labours* (London: Thomas Marshe, 1575), pp. 57^r–69^v.
32 Gascoigne, *A Hundreth*, pp. 398–439. References to stanza and line numbers from this poem are given in parentheses after quotations. Pigman's introduction, pp. xxviii–xxxviii, provides a very helpful summary of the events in the Netherlands to which the poem refers.
33 Pigman's edition has 'send our foes', but examination of the 1575 edition confirms that 'fend' is correct.
34 For a detailed discussion of these events and evidence concerning accusations of treachery against Gascoigne, see Gascoigne, *A Hundreth* pp. xxxv–xxxviii.
35 Thomas Churchyard, *A Discourse of the Queenes Maiesties Entertainment in Suffolk and Norfolk Whereunto Is Adjoyned a Comendation of Sir H. Gilberts Ventrous Journey*. (London: Henry Bynneman, [1578]), sig. Hii^r.
36 Quoted by Michael Nerlich, *Ideology of Adventure: Studies in Modern Consciousness, 1100–1750*, trans. Ruth Crowley, 2 vols (Minneapolis: University of Minnesota Press, 1987), I, p. 129.
37 George Turbervile, *Epitaphes, Epigrams, Songs and Sonets (1567) and Epitaphes and Sonnettes (1576)*, ed. Richard J. Panofsky (Delmar, NY: Scholars' Facsimiles and Reprints, 1977), p. 112. References to Panofsky's page numbers in this edition will follow quotations.
38 For brief comment on opposition to foreign travel in the context of suspicion of alien political systems, see Andrew Hadfield, *Literature, Travel, and Colonial Writing in the English Renaissance 1545–1625* (Oxford: Clarendon Press, 2001), pp. 3–4 and 18.
39 For evidence that the first edition may date to 1574, see John Erskine Hankins, *The Life and Works of George Turbervile* (Lawrence, KS: University of Kansas, 1940), pp. 36–7.
40 Rollins, ed., *Paradise*, no. 123.
41 David Beers Quinn and Raleigh Ashlin Skelton, eds, *The Principall Navigations, Voiages and Discoveries of the English Nation, by Richard Hakluyt, Imprinted at London, 1589* (Cambridge: published for the Hakluyt Society and the Peabody Museum of Salem by the Cambridge University Press, 1965). Page references to this edition are given in parentheses after quotations. Hakluyt also printed Turbervile's epistles from Moscow, albeit in a bowderlized form (no mention of 'bowgards') in *The Principall Navigations*, see Lloyd E. Berry, 'Richard Hakluyt and Turberville's Poems on Russia', *Papers of the Bibliographical Society of America* 61 (1967): 350–51.
42 For the poem and a translation, plus an invaluable introduction, and copious notes, see David Beers Quinn and Neil M. Cheshire, eds, *The New Found Land of Stephen Parmenius: The Life and Writings of a Hungarian Poet, Drowned on a Voyage from Newfoundland, 1583* (Toronto: University of Toronto Press, 1972).
43 Ibid., p. 171. See Mary B. Campbell, *The Witness and the Other World: Exotic European Travel Writing. 400–1600* (Ithaca and London: Cornell University Press, 1988), p. 222, for a similar observation.

44   For a detailed account of Hakluyt's life and intellectual milieu, see George Bruner Parks, *Richard Hakluyt and the English Voyages*, ed. James A. Williamson (New York: American Geographical Society, 1928).

45   I quote from Richard A. McCabe, ed., *Edmund Spenser: The Shorter Poems* (Harmondsworth: Penguin, 1999), pp. 28 and 346 (ll. 57, 59). Line references to this edition of Spenser's *Colin Clovt* will be given in parentheses in the text.

46   See especially, Julia Reinhard Lupton, 'Home-Making in Ireland: Virgil's Eclogue I and Book VI of *The Faerie Queene*', *Spenser Studies* 8 (1987): 119–45.

47   Gascoigne, *A Hundreth*, p. 280: 'Alexander Nevile *delivered him this theame*, Sat cito, si sat bene', ll. 67–8.

48   From 'A storie translated out of Frenche' in Churchyard, *A Light Bondell*, p. 3ʳ.

49   On the circumstances of Raleigh's marriage and disgrace, see Stephen Coote, *A Play of Passion: The Life of Sir Walter Ralegh* (London: Macmillan, 1993) pp. 196–201.

4   Spenser as Orpheus

1   Edmund Spenser, *The Shorter Poems*, ed. Richard A. McCabe (Harmondsworth: Penguin, 1999). Quotations from all Spenser's texts discussed in this chapter will be from this edition.

2   Alexander Dunlop, 'The Unity of Spenser's *Amoretti*' in *Silent Poetry: Essays in Numerological Analysis*, ed. Alastair Fowler (London: Routledge & Kegan Paul, 1970), pp. 153–69.

3   For a discussion of the evidence, see Edmund Spenser, *The Works: A Variorum Edition*, ed. Edwin Greenlaw *et al.*, 11 vols (Baltimore: John Hopkins University Press, 1932–57), *The Minor Poems*, vol. 2 (1947), pp. 647–52. See also Willy Maley, *A Spenser Chronology* (Basingstoke: Macmillan, 1994), pp. 61–2, 70, 85–6.

4   Sir Philip Sidney, *An Apology for Poetry*, ed. Geoffrey Shepherd (London: Nelson, 1965), p. 103.

5   Edmund Spenser, *A View of the State of Ireland: From the First Printed Edition (1633)*, ed. Andrew Hadfield and Willy Maley (Oxford: Blackwell, 1997), p. 11. This quotation is from the opening paragraph. The 1633 edition omits the word 'salvage' present in the Ellesmere MS 7041 version; see the list of 'Passages Omitted' in Hadfield and Maley's edition, p. 171.

6   Richard A. McCabe, *The Pillars of Eternity: Time and Providence in the Faerie Queene* (Dublin: Irish Academic Press, 1989), p. 226. Appendix A of this work investigates ideas of providence in *A Discourse*.

7   *A Discourse of Civill Life*, in Lodowick Bryskett, *Literary Works*, ed. J. H. P. Pafford (England: Gregg International Publishers Ltd., 1972) pp. 208–9. References to page numbers in this edition will be given in parentheses after quotations. *A Discourse* is largely a translation from the second part, *Discorsi della vita civile*, of Giambattista Giraldi (Cinthio)'s *Hecatommithi* (1565). For the probable period in which Bryskett sets *A Discourse*, see Henry R. Plomer and Tom Peate Cross, *The Life and Correspondence of Lodowick Bryskett* (Illinois: University of Chicago Press, 1927), pp. 77–84.

8   'A Discourse on Irish Affairs' in Sir Philip Sidney, *The Prose Works of Sir Philip Sidney*, ed. Albert Feuillerat, 4 vols (Cambridge: Cambridge University Press, 1962), vol. 3, pp. 46–50 (p. 49).

9   See Plomer and Cross, *Life and Correspondence of Lodowick Bryskett*, pp. 77–84.
10 See footnote 5. For recent scholarly discussions of Spenser's *View* in relation to 'New English' attitudes to Ireland, see especially: Nicholas Canny, 'Edmund Spenser and the Development of an Anglo-Irish Identity', *Yearbook of English Studies* 13 (1983): 1–19; Andrew Hadfield, *Edmund Spenser's Irish Experience: Wild Fruit and Salvage Soyl* (Oxford: Oxford University Press, 1997); Ciaran Brady, 'Spenser's Irish Crisis: Humanism and Experience in the 1590s', *Past and Present* 111 (1986): 17–49; and Willy Maley, *Salvaging Spenser: Colonialism, Culture and Identity* (Basingstoke: Macmillan, 1997), esp. Ch. 3.
11 In *Desiderata Curiosa Hibernica: A Selection of State Papers*, vol. 1 (Dublin: David Hay at the King's Arms, 1772), p. 33.
12 Richard A. McCabe, 'Edmund Spenser, Poet of Exile,' *Proceedings of the British Academy* 80 (1993): 73–103 (80). For the uneasy relation between force and civility in colonization schemes in relation to Ireland, discussed by Sir Thomas Smith and Gabriel Harvey, and possibly influencing Spenser, see Lisa Jardine, 'Encountering Ireland: Gabriel Harvey, Edmund Spenser, and English Colonial Ventures' in *Representing Ireland: Literature and the Origins of Conflict, 1534–1660*, ed. Brendan Bradshaw, Andrew Hadfield and Willy Maley (Cambridge: Cambridge University Press, 1993), pp. 60–75. See also F.J. Levy, 'Spenser and Court Humanism' in *Spenser's Life and the Subject of Biography*, ed. Judith H. Anderson, Donald Cheney and Davis A. Richardson (Amherst: University of Massachusetts Press, 1996), pp. 65–80 (p. 78).
13 Quoted by John N. King, *Spenser's Poetry and the Reformation Tradition* (Princeton: Princeton University Press, 1990), p. 160.
14 Heinrich Bullinger, *The Christen State of Matrimonye (1541)*, trans. Miles Coverdale (Amsterdam: Theatrum Orbis Terrarum, 1974) sig. Dv^r.
15 John Derricke, *The Image of Irelande* (London: Ihon Daie, 1581) sig. E.iii^r.
16 Cited by Thomas Cain, *Praise in the Faerie Queene* (Lincoln, NE: University of Nebraska Press, 1978), p. 13. Cain gives his own translation from the *Mythologiae sive explicationis fabularum libri decem*, Venice, 1568 edition, 7.14. See also Joseph Loewenstein, 'Echo's Ring: Orpheus and Spenser's Career', *English Literary Renaissance* 16 (1986): 287–302.
17 Charles Hughes, ed., *Shakespeare's Europe: Unpublished Chapters of Fynes Moryson's Itinerary* (London: Sherratt & Hughes, 1903), p. 199. Moryson was writing at the beginning of the seventeenth century.
18 For summaries of Spenser's use of the Orpheus myth throughout his verse and the sources he uses, see Henry Gibbons Lotspeich, *Classical Mythology in the Poetry of Edmund Spenser* (Princeton: Princeton University Press, 1932), p. 94, and the article on Orpheus by James Neil Brown in A.C. Hamilton *et al.*, ed., *The Spenser Encyclopedia* (Toronto, Buffalo, London: University of Toronto Press and Routledge, 1990), pp. 519–20. See also Cain, *Praise in the Faerie Queene*, esp. pp. 11–17, and, on the use of Orpheus in *Epithalamion*, Loewenstein, 'Echo's Ring: Orpheus and Spenser's Career', and Eileen Jorge Allman, 'Epithalamion's Bridegroom: Orpheus–Adam–Christ', *Renascence* 32 (1980): 240–7.
19 Loewenstein, 'Echo's Ring: Orpheus and Spenser's Career,' p. 289, and Douglas Anderson, '"Vnto My Selfe Alone": Spenser's Plenary Epithalamion', *Spenser Studies* 5 (1985): 149–66. Anderson interprets the poem as being as much about death as about marriage.

20 Comes interprets the serpent as the power of the unruly appetites, resistant to reason and law, who destroy the soul (Eurydice): Stephen Orgel, ed., *Mythologiae, Nathale Conti (1615 ed.) and Mythologia, M. Antonio Tritino (1616), The Philosophy of Images* (New York and London: Garland Publishing, 1979), p. 402. For Spenser's account of Orpheus' loss of his bride because of his desire, see his *Virgil's Gnat*, ll. 465–73.

21 See, for example, Alexander Dunlop, 'The Drama of *Amoretti*', *Spenser Studies* 1 (1980): 107–20, and Dunlop, 'Unity of Spenser's *Amoretti*'; also Carole V. Kaske, 'Spenser's *Amoretti* and *Epithalamion* of 1595: Structure, Genre, and Numerology', *English Literary Renaissance* 8 (1978): 271–95. William Kerrigan discusses Spenser's volume as just one example of a recognizably tri-partite structuring of volumes of sonnet sequences: William Shakespeare, *The Sonnets and a Lover's Complaint*, ed. John Kerrigan (London: Penguin Books, 1999), p. 13.

22 Dunlop, 'Unity of Spenser's *Amoretti*', pp. 158–9.

23 Ibid., p. 159.

24 Spenser, *The Shorter Poems*, p. 686 note.

25 Dunlop, 'Unity of Spenser's *Amoretti*'.

26 In Edmund Spenser, *The Yale Edition of the Shorter Poems*, ed. William A. Oram *et al.* (New Haven, Conn. and London: Yale University Press, 1989), p. 627.

27 This sonnet seems to imitate Sir Philip Sidney's *Astrophil and Stella* 81.

28 Kaske, 'Spenser's *Amoretti* and *Epithalamion* of 1595', pp. 275–6, and Dunlop, 'The Drama of Amoretti', p. 117, both argue that its repetition is pointedly significant. See also Spenser, *The Shorter Poems*, pp. xiv–xv.

29 See especially *Amoretti* 37, 42, 65, 71.

30 Thomas M. Greene, 'Spenser and the Epithalmic Convention', *Comparative Literature* 9 (1957): 215–28 notes that this conflation is unprecedented in the epithalmic tradition.

31 On the anacreontics as an integral part of the volume, see Kaske, 'Spenser's *Amoretti* and *Epithalamion* of 1595', pp. 276–80; Catherine Bates, *The Rhetoric of Courtship in Elizabethan Language and Literature* (Cambridge: Cambridge University Press, 1992), pp. 147–8, and Shakespeare, *The Sonnets*, ed. Kerrigan, p. 13. For a recent list of discussions of Spenser's anacreontic verses, see Bates, p. 207, fn 26.

32 Orgel, ed., *Mythologiae*, p. 402.

33 Loewenstein, 'Echo's Ring: Orpheus and Spenser's Career', p. 291.

34 Bates, *The Rhetoric of Courtship in Elizabethan Language and Literature*, p. 150.

35 Ovid, *Metamorphoses*, x. ll. 85–105 and 143–7.

36 Surprisingly the Irish dimension of the *Epithalamion* has not been much remarked, in spite of the recent burgeoning of criticism which stresses Spenser's involvement in 'New English' political attitudes to Ireland and their implications for his work. A notable exception is Judith Owens, 'The Poetics of Accommodation in Spenser's *Epithalamion*', *Studies in English Literature* 40 (2000): 41–62, whose argument is complementary to my own.

37 Ibid., pp. 47–8.

38 Hughes, ed., *Shakespeare's Europe*, p. 193.

39 R[ichard] V[enner], *Englands Ioy* (?London: ?1601), sig. Aii^v. The sole copy has no title page, and is sometimes attributed to Richard Verstegan. Compare

Spenser's association of Irish disorder with 'rauenous wolves' in *Colin Clovts Come Home Againe*, l. 318.

40   Spenser, *A View*, p. 59.

41   Derricke, *The Image of Irelande*, E.iii^r.

42   Bullinger, *The Christen State of Matrimonye (1541)*, sig. G.iv^{r-v}.

43   Owens, 'Poetics of Accommodation', p. 49.

44   'An Homily of the State of Matrimony' in *Sermons or Homilies Appointed to Be Read in Churches in the Time of Queen Elizabeth of Famous Memory* (London: For the Prayer Book and Homily Society, 1824), p. 522. For the political significance of husbandry depending on settled tilling and sowing rather than on the Irish custom of 'transhumance' in which herders followed their cattle to fresh pasturage, see Spenser, *A View*, pp. 149–50.

45   Sir John Davies, *A Discoverie of the State of Ireland: With the True Causes Why That Kingdom Was Neuer Entirely Subdued* (London: for A. Millar, 1747), p. 8. This is a reprint of the 1612 edition.

46   Spenser, *A View*, p. 70. The 1633 edition omits the phrase added in brackets from the Ellesmere MS. On the Statutes of Kilkenny (1366) that forbade intermarriage, see Hadfield, *Edmund Spenser's Irish Experience*, p. 21.

47   Quoted from *CSP Ireland 1588–92*, p. 565, by Christopher Highley, *Shakespeare, Spenser, and the Crisis in Ireland* (Cambridge: Cambridge University Press, 1997), p. 128.

48   On Elizabeth Boyle's background, see Spenser, *Variorum Works*, vol. 8, *Minor Poems*, vol. 2, pp. 648–52.

49   Michael MacCarthy-Morrogh, *The Munster Plantation: English Migration to Southern Ireland, 1583–1641* (Oxford: Clarendon Press, 1986), pp. 240–2; Anthony Sheehan, 'Irish Towns in a Period of Change, 1588–1625' in *Natives and Newcomers: Essays in the Making of Irish Colonial Society 1534–1641*, ed. Ciaran Brady and Raymond Gillespie (Dublin: Irish Academic Press, 1986), pp. 93–119 (pp. 99–104).

50   Alan Ford, *The Protestant Reformation in Ireland, 1590–1641* (Dublin: Four Courts Press, 1997), p. 37. Brendan Bradshaw, 'The Reformation in the Cities: Cork, Limerick and Galway, 1534–1603' in *Settlement and Society in Medieval Ireland: Studies Presented to F. X. Martin, O.S.A.*, ed. John Bradley (Kilkenny: Boethius Press, 1988), pp. 445–76.

51   Ford, *The Protestant Reformation in Ireland, 1590–1641* p. 40. Ford notes that Lyon's letter of 1604 is misplaced in the *C.S.P.* under 1607.

52   Sybil M. Jack, *Towns in Tudor and Stuart Britain* (Basingstoke: Macmillan, 1996). See also Sheehan, 'Irish Towns in a Period of Change, 1588–1625', p. 111.

53   Spenser, *A View*, pp. 156–7. References to this edition will be given in parentheses after quotations in the following discussion.

54   Sheehan, 'Irish Towns in a Period of Change, 1588–1625', p. 110.

55   The phrase is from Jack, *Towns in Tudor and Stuart Britain*, p. 12.

56   A. Kent Hieatt, *Short Time's Endless Monument* (New York: Columbia University Press, 1960).

57   Anderson, '"Vnto My Selfe Alone"', p. 164 sees these lines as being in part about death. Hieatt, *Short Time's Endless Monument*, p. 43, suggests the lines and the poem's numerological structure allude to a discrepancy between the 'perfect' daily rotation of the sphere of the fixed stars and the 'imperfect' daily movement of the sun, and thus to Spenser's favourite themes of mutability and mortality.

58 For example, the tales of Britomart, Amoret and Belphoebe in *The Faerie Queene*, Book 3, or of Radigund and Britomart in Book 5.
59 Bradshaw, 'The Reformation in the Cities', pp. 465–7, and Sheehan, 'Irish Towns in a Period of Change, 1588–1625', p. 111. See Owens, 'Poetics of Accommodation', pp. 53–4 on the political charge of this Protestant ceremony.
60 Spenser, *A View*, pp. 96 and 99. Pauline Henley, *Spenser in Ireland* (Dublin and Cork: Cork University Press, 1928), pp. 88–9, notes that the wood of Aherlow, close to the setting of Spenser's marriage was 'a plague spot...to the English at this period', constantly providing shelter for those attacking the colonists.
61 Compare the description of 'nightly bodrags' and 'hue and cries' in Colin's description of Ireland in *CCCHA*, l. 315.
62 Quoted in their excellent article by Ann Rosalind Jones and Peter Stallybrass, 'Dismantling Irena: The Sexualizing of Ireland in Early Modern England' in *Nationalisms & Sexualities*, ed. Andrew Parker *et al.* (New York and London: Routledge, 1992), pp. 157–71 (p. 164).

5 Gascoigne's 'The Adventures of Master F.J.' and Sidney's *Astrophil and Stella*

1 Mary Thomas Crane, *Framing Authority: Sayings, Self and Society in Sixteenth-Century England* (Princeton: Princeton University Press, 1993), p. 162, comments 'One of the elements missing from [the story of the transition from Wyatt to Sidney] is narrative itself.' As always, I am indebted to her discussions.
2 Anne Ferry, *The 'Inward' Language. Sonnets of Wyatt, Sidney, Shakespeare, Donne* (Chicago and London: University of Chicago Press, 1983), p. 29. Ferry's is a detailed and helpful examination of the changing rhetoric of inwardness through the sixteenth century, but differs from my analysis in seeming to assume an essential inner self that awaits a rhetoric sophisticated enough to render it articulate.
3 George Gascoigne, *A Hundreth Sundrie Flowres*, ed. G.W. Pigman III (Oxford: Clarendon Press, 2000), pp. 251–2. References to page numbers in this edition will be cited in parentheses in the text.
4 Sir Philip Sidney, *An Apology for Poetry*, ed. Geoffrey Shepherd (London: Nelson, 1965), pp. 137–8. The treatise, composed probably c. 1582–3, was first printed in 1595, after Sidney's death.
5 Baldassare Castiglione, *The Book of the Courtier*, trans. Sir Thomas Hoby, *Everyman's Library* (London: Dent, 1928), p. 46.
6 Gail Kern Paster, *The Body Embarrassed. Drama and the Disciplines of Shame in Early Modern England* (Ithaca and New York: Cornell University Press, 1993), p. 9.
7 Ibid., p. 10.
8 John Donne, *The Elegies and the Songs and Sonnets*, ed. Helen Gardener (Oxford: Clarendon Press, 1965), p. 214, for comment on the phrase in 'Farewell to Love'.
9 Timothy Bright, *A Treatise of Melancholie. Reproduced from the 1586 Edition*, ed. Hardin Craig (New York: Columbia University Press for the Facsimile Text Society, 1940), p. 92.
10 William Rossky, 'Imagination in the English Renaissance: Psychology and Poetic', *Studies in the Renaissance* 5 (1958): 49–73.

11 Sidney, *An Apology for Poetry*, p. 125.
12 Thomas Wright, *The Passions of the Minde (1601)*, Anglistica & Americana no. 126 (Hildesheim and New York: Georg Olms, 1973), p. 164. See also pp. 161–3 and 211–14.
13 For a discussion of the myth in terms of the Petrarchan lover's fear of dismemberment, see Nancy J. Vickers, 'Diana Described: Scattered Woman and Scattered Rhyme' in *Writing and Sexual Difference*, ed. Elizabeth Abel (Brighton, Sussex: Harvester Press, 1982), pp. 95–109.
14 I am indebted to Pigman's notes in his edition, p. 562.
15 Paster, *The Body Embarrassed*, p. 17, and Ian MacLean, *The Renaissance Notion of Women: A Study in the Fortunes of Scholasticism and Medical Science in European Intellectual Life* (Cambridge: Cambridge University Press, 1980) pp. 41–4.
16 Linda Woodbridge, *Women and the English Renaissance: Literature and the Nature of Womankind 1540–1620* (Brighton, Sussex: Harvester Press, 1984), pp. 185–9. For some suggestive remarks on the association of lyric with the feminine and effeminacy, see Patricia Parker, *Literary Fat Ladies Rhetoric, Gender, Property* (London and New York: Methuen, 1987), pp. 21–3, 64–6. For Jonson's well-known contempt for 'women's poets', see Ben Jonson, *The Complete Poems*, ed. George Parfitt (Harmondsworth: Penguin Books, 1975), 'Explorata: or Discoveries', p. 396.
17 Crane, *Framing Authority*, p. 181.
18 Holger M. Klein, ed., *English and Scottish Sonnet Sequences of the Renaissance*, 2 vols, vol. 1 (Hildesheim, Zurich and New York: Georg Olms, 1984), p. 45.
19 On the sixteenth-century reading of some of Chaucer's writing as autobiographical, see Alice S. Miskimin, *The Renaissance Chaucer* (New Haven and London: Yale University Press, 1975), pp. 81–95.
20 Ferry, *The 'Inward' Language*, Ch. 1. Ferry acknowledges that the language is already apparent in Chaucer's *Troilus and Criseyde*; Jonathan Goldberg, *Writing Matter: From the Hands of the English Renaissance* (Stanford, CA.: Stanford University Press, 1990), esp. pp. 267–8; Richard Rambuss, *Spenser's Secret Career* (Cambridge: Cambridge University Press, 1993), pp. 20–22, 48. Patricia Fumerton, *Cultural Aesthetics: Renaissance Literature and the Practice of Social Ornament* (Chicago and London: Chicago University Press, 1991), pp. 86–7, discusses the use by sonneteers of a language of secrets and privacy, and thus of exclusivity.
21 Ferry, *The 'Inward' Language*, p. 38.
22 Rambuss, *Spenser's Secret Career*, p. 41. See Ferry, *The 'Inward' Language*, p. 48.
23 Rambuss, *Spenser's Secret Career*, p. 48.
24 Pigman in his edition discusses the various permutations Gascoigne plays on the names Bartello and the ciphers Bartholmew and 'the Green Knight' on pp. 551–2.
25 For example, the naming of *Pergo*, p. 191.
26 Gordon Williams, *A Dictionary of Sexual Language and Imagery in Shakespearean and Stuart Literature*, 3 vols (London and Atlantic Highlands, NJ: Athlone Press, 1994), II, pp. 943–4.
27 Ibid., I, pp. 135–6.
28 Susan C. Staub, '"A Poet with a Spear": Writing and Sexual Power in the Elizabethan Period', *Renaissance Papers* (1992): 1–15, Richard C. McCoy,

'Gascoigne's "Poemata Castrata": The Wages of Courtly Success', *Criticism* 27 (1985): 29–55 (34, 47).

29 I adapt a comment by Jane Hedley, 'Allegoria: Gascoigne's Master Trope', *English Literary Renaissance* 11 (1981): 148–64 (p. 159).

30 Wright, *The Passions of the Minde*, p. 268.

31 For purse = scrotum, see Williams, *A Dictionary of Sexual Language*, II, p. 1118.

32 Prick song, demanding some skill on the part of the singer, was the singing of music from written notes, see James M. Osborn, ed., *The Autobiography of Thomas Whythorne (Modern-Spelling Edition)* (Oxford: Oxford University Press, 1962), p. 206. It was fairly commonly used to allude to copulation in sixteenth-century texts, see Williams, *A Dictionary of Sexual Language*, II, p. 1098. Pigman suggests 'plain song was the singing of a simple melody', p. 764.

33 Robert Burton, *The Anatomy of Melancholy* (London: Chatto & Windus, 1907), p. 553: Pt 3, Sec.2, mem.3.

34 Ferry, *The 'Inward' Language*, p. 69 cites a sixteenth-century definition of 'expression' as 'a wringing or squeezing out'. *OED* gives 'pressing out'.

35 Wright, *The Passions of the Minde*, p. 115.

36 Mark Breitenberg, *Anxious Masculinity in Early Modern England* (Cambridge: Cambridge University Press, 1996), p. 132.

37 Staub, ' "A Poet with a Spear" ', pp. 12–13.

38 M.H. Abrams, *A Glossary of Literary Terms*, 7th edn (Fort Worth, NY, London: Harcourt Brace College Publishers, 1999), p. 330, defines wit as 'a kind of verbal expression which is brief, deft and intentionally contrived to produce a shock of comic surprise'.

39 For the tradition of love's wars going back to classical elegists, see Helen Gardner's note on 'Love's Warre' in her edition of Donne, *The Elegies and the Songs and Sonnets*, p. 128.

40 Louis B. Salomon, *The Devil Take Her! A Study of the Rebellious Lover in English Poetry* (New York: A.S.Barnes, 1961).

41 Hedley, 'Allegoria', p. 157.

42 Constance Relihan, *Fashioning Authority: The Development of Elizabethan Novelistic Discourse* (Kent, OH and London: Kent State University Press, 1994), pp. 21–2 discusses the relationship between verse and prose in 'Master F.J.' and points out that G.T.'s knowledge gradually far exceeds his original claims.

43 See Pigman's note, p. 580.

44 John Freccero, 'The Fig Tree and the Laurel: Petrarch's Poetics' in *Literary Theory/Renaissance Texts*, ed. Patricia Parker and David Quint (Baltimore and London: John Hopkins University Press, 1986), pp. 20–32 (p. 21).

45 Vickers, 'Diana Described: Scattered Woman and Scattered Rhyme', p. 107.

46 Giuseppe Mazzotta, 'The Canzoniere and the Language of the Self,' *Studies in Philology* 75 (1978): 271–96 (p. 291).

47 Sir Philip Sidney, *The Poems*, ed. William A. Ringler (Oxford: Clarendon Press, 1962). Quotations of Sidney's verse will be from this edition with sonnet and line numbers given in parentheses after quotations.

48 Mazzotta, 'The Canzoniere and the Language of the Self', p. 291, writes of Petrarch's verse, 'the poet persistently attempts to achieve a formal adequation to desire and persistently fails, because desire, in its uninterrupted movement towards totality, exceeds any formal adequation.'

49   Anne Ferry's essay on the sequence, in *The 'Inward' Language*, Ch. 3, is a full and detailed examination of the ways in which the sequence thematizes Sidney's concerns with the problems and failures of language to express what is in the heart. My own analysis sees the problem as less one of expressing 'inward' states than the way in the sense of 'inwardness' is a phenomenon constructed by the language itself.

50   See especially Ferry, *The 'Inward' Language*, Ch. 3.

51   From 'Certayne Notes of Instruction' in Gascoigne, *A Hundreth*, p. 454.

52   Richard B. Young, 'English Petrarke: A Study of Sidney's *Astrophel and Stella*' in *Three Studies in the Renaissance: Sidney, Jonson, and Milton* (New Haven, CO: Yale University Press, 1958), pp. 1–88, long ago pointed out that while Astrophil starts as a rebel to Petrarchan sonnet conventions, his last sonnets show him conforming to the conventions.

53   James M. Osborn, ed., *The Autobiography of Thomas Whythorne* (Oxford: Clarendon Press, 1961), p. 211. See my p. 52 above.

54   Quoted from Michael R.G. Spiller, *The Development of the Sonnet: An Introduction* (London and New York: Routledge, 1992), p. 117.

55   For biographical information, see William A. Ringler, ed., *The Poems of Sir Philip Sidney* (Oxford: Clarendon Press, 1962), pp. 435–47. For a reading of the sequence in terms of its possible coded meaning for a coterie audience, see Arthur F. Marotti, '"Love Is Not Love": Elizabethan Sonnet Sequences and the Social Order', *English Literary History* 49 (1982): 396–428.

56   For Sidney's biography during this period, see Katherine Duncan-Jones, *Sir Philip Sidney: Courtier Poet* (New Haven and London: Yale University Press, 1991), Ch. 10.

57   Mazzotta, 'The Canzoniere and the Language of the Self', p. 291.

58   See Ferry, *The 'Inward' Language*, pp. 135–7. On the plain style and its significance in the sixteenth century, see Richard F. Jones, 'The Moral Sense of Simplicity' in *Studies in Honour of F.W. Shipley*, ed. R.F. Jones, *Washington University Studies, N.S. Language and Literature* 14 (St Louis, MO: 1942), pp. 265–87.

59   Ringler has added the quotation marks which are not there in the manuscripts or early editions. See Ringler, ed., *The Poems of Sir Philip Sidney*, p. lxvii.

60   Some of these readings of *AS*, often mutually incompatible, have been proposed by, for example, Thomas Jr Roche, 'Astrophil and Stella: A Radical Reading' in *Sir Philip Sidney: An Anthology of Modern Criticism*, ed. Dennis Kay (Oxford: Clarendon Press, 1987), pp. 185–226, who advocates a moral reading of the sequence; Marotti, '"Love Is Not Love"', who reads it in terms of criticism of court politics, and Ann Rosalind Jones and Peter Stallybrass, 'The Politics of *Astrophil and Stella*', *Studies in English Literature* 24 (1984): 53–68, who see analogies between an idealized Stella and Elizabeth I.

61   Sidney, *An Apology for Poetry*, p. 125. References to this edition will be given in parentheses in the text in the following discussion.

62   Mazzotta, 'The Canzoniere and the Language of the Self', p. 291.

63   Ringler, ed., *The Poems of Sir Philip Sidney*, textual notes, p. 188.

6   'My name is Will': *Shakespeare's Sonnets*

1   Francis Barker, *The Tremulous Private Body: Essays on Subjection* (London and New York: Methuen, 1984), p. 36.

2   Anne Ferry, *The 'Inward' Language: Sonnets of Wyatt, Sidney, Shakespeare, Donne* (Chicago and London: University of Chicago Press, 1983), p. 4.

3   Joel Fineman, *Shakespeare's Perjured Eye: The Invention of Poetic Subjectivity in the Sonnets* (Berkeley, Los Angeles, London: University of California Press, 1986), pp. 83–4.

4   Arthur F. Marotti, '"Love Is Not Love": Elizabethan Sonnet Sequences and the Social Order', *English Literary History* 49 (1982): 396–428, and my brief discussion p. 149 above. Marotti (pp. 410–13) also has some very suggestive comments on the social embedding of Shakespeare's sequence.

5   For a careful review of evidence about dating, including the suggestion that the 'dark lady' sonnets were written first, see William Shakespeare, *Shakespeare's Sonnets*, ed. Katherine Duncan-Jones (London: Arden Shakespeare, 2001), pp. 1–28. Quotations from the *Sonnets* will be from this edition.

6   Ibid., pp. 8–13 and 34.

7   Janette Dillon, *Shakespeare and the Solitary Man* (London and Basingstoke: Macmillan, 1981), p. 90.

8   Emile Benveniste, *Problems in General Linguistics*, trans. Mary Elizabeth Meek (Coral Gables, Florida: University of Miami Press, 1971), p. 227. See p. 4 above.

9   Kaja Silverman, *The Subject of Semiotics* (New York: Oxford University Press, 1983), p. 45.

10 Shakespeare adapts well known Erasmian arguments for marriage in this group of sonnets, see Katherine M. Wilson, *Shakespeare's Sugared Sonnets* (London and New York: Allen & Unwin, 1974), pp. 146–67.

11 For a discussion of Shakespeare's extensive debts to Sidney, see Ferry, *The 'Inward' Language* Ch. 4.

12 Hyder Edward Rollins, ed., *The Paradise of Dainty Devices (1576–1606)* (Cambridge: Cambridge University Press, 1927), no. 91 (pp. 89–90).

13 Fineman, *Shakespeare's Perjured Eye*, p. 18. The italics are Fineman's own.

14 William Shakespeare, *Shakespeare's Sonnets*, ed. Stephen Booth (New Haven and London: Yale University Press, 1977), p. 491, closely analyses the figures of repetition and juxtaposition that characterize this sonnet.

15 Shakespeare, *Shakespeare's Sonnets*, ed. Duncan-Jones, p. 142.

16 Gordon Williams, *A Dictionary of Sexual Language and Imagery in Shakespearean and Stuart Literature*, 3 vols (London and Atlantic Highlands, NJ: Athlone Press, 1994), II. p. 819 for 'lips' and pp. 918–19 for 'mouth'. On the sexual/legal innuendo of 'sealing' see Donne's 'there where my hand is set my seal shall be' ('To my mistress going to bed').

17 With the exception of sonnet 145 where she says 'I hate ... not you'. This has been interpreted by Andrew Gurr as a play on Anne Hathaway's name. See Shakespeare, *Shakespeare's Sonnets*, ed. Duncan-Jones, p. 406.

18 Eve Kosovsky Sedgwick, *Between Men: English Literature and Male Homosocial Desire* (New York: Columbia University Press, 1985), p. 44, comments that 'contagious self-division seems to be the definition of femininity in the Sonnets'.

19 On the multiple meanings of 'will' in these sonnets, see Shakespeare, *Shakespeare's Sonnets*, ed. Booth, pp. 466–7, and the discussion by Sedgwick, *Between Men*, pp. 38–9.

20 Sedgwick, *Between Men*, p. 37.

21 Shakespeare, *Shakespeare's Sonnets*, ed. Booth, pp. 471, and esp. 164–5, note on 20.12.

22   For example, Robert Burton, *The Anatomy of Melancholy* (London: Chatto & Windus, 1907), p. 99, Pt I. Sec.1, Mem.2, Subs.5.

23   Thomas Wright, *The Passions of the Minde (1601), Anglistica & Americana No. 126* (Hildesheim and New York: Georg Olms, 1973), pp. 301–2.

24   Sedgwick, *Between Men*, p. 39, comments: 'the speaker finds himself unexpectedly entrapped in, not quite an identification, but a confusion of identities with the woman.'

Bibliography

Editions and anthologies

Ascham, Roger, *The Scholemaster (1570)*, edited by Edward Arber. Birmingham: English Reprints, 1870

Aughterson, Kate, ed. *Renaissance Women: Constructions of Femininity in England*. London and New York: Routledge, 1995

Becon, Thomas, *The Early Works*, edited by J. Ayre. Cambridge: Cambridge University Press for The Parker Society, 1843

Bright, Timothy, *A Treatise of Melancholie. Reproduced from the 1586 Edition*, edited by Hardin Craig. New York: Columbia University Press for the Facsimile Text Society, 1940

Bryskett, Lodowick, *Literary Works*, edited by J.H.P. Pafford. England: Gregg International, 1972

Bullinger, Heinrich, *The Christen State of Matrimonye (1541)*, translated by Miles Coverdale. Amsterdam: Theatrum Orbis Terrarum, 1974

Burton, Robert, *The Anatomy of Melancholy*. London: Chatto & Windus, 1907

Castiglione, Baldassare, *The Book of the Courtier*, translated by Sir Thomas Hoby, *Everyman's Library*. London: Dent, 1928

Churchyard, Thomas, *A Discourse of the Queenes Maiesties Entertainment in Suffolk and Norfolk Whereunto Is Adjoyned a Comendation of Sir H. Gilberts Ventrous Journey*. London: Henry Bynneman [1578]

——, *The First Parte of Churchyardes Chippes, Containing Twelue Seuerall Labours*. London: Thomas Marshe, 1575

——, *A Generall Rehearsall of Warres, Wherein Is Fiue Hundred Seuerall Seruices of Land and Sea*. London: Edward White, [1579]

——, *A Light Bondell of Liuely Discourses Called Churchyardes Charge, Presented as a Newe Yeres Gifte to the Right Honourable, the Erle of Surrie*. London: Jhon Kyngston, 1580

Clarke, Danielle, ed. *Isabella Whitney, Mary Sidney and Aemilia Lanyer: Renaissance Women Poets*. Harmondsworth: Penguin Books, 2000

Davies, Sir John, *A Discoverie of the State of Ireland: With the True Causes Why That Kingdom Was Neuer Entirely Subdued*. London: for A. Millar, 1747

Derricke, John, *The Image of Irelande*. London: Ihon Daie, 1581

Desiderata Curiosa Hibernica: A Selection of State Papers, Vol. 1. Dublin: David Hay at the King's Arms, 1772

Donne, John, *The Elegies and the Songs and Sonnets*, edited by Helen Gardener. Oxford: Clarendon Press, 1965

Drayton, Michael, *The Works*, edited by Kathleen Tillotson William Hebel and Bernard H. Newdigate, 5 vols. Oxford: Oxford University Press, 1931–41

Fraser, Russell A., ed. *The Court of Venus*. Durham, NC: Duke University Press, 1955

Gascoigne, George, *The Complete Works*, edited by John W. Cunliffe, 2 vols. Cambridge: Cambridge University Press, 1907–10

——, *A Hundreth Sundrie Flowres*, edited by G.W. Pigman III. Oxford: Clarendon Press, 2000

Gates, Geffrey, *The Defence of the Militarie Profession. Wherein Is Eloquently Shewed the Due Commendation of Martiall Prowesse, and Plainly Prooued How Necessary the Exercise of Armes Is for Our Age*. London: Henry Middleton, 1579

Googe, Barnabe, *Eclogues, Epitaphs, and Sonnets*, edited by Judith M. Kennedy. Toronto, Buffalo, London: University of Toronto Press, 1989

Hall, John, *The Court of Virtue (1565)*, edited by Russell A. Fraser. London: Routledge & Kegan Paul, 1961

Henderson, Katherine Usher and Barbara F. McManus, eds, *Half Humankind, Contexts and Texts of the Controversy About Women in England, 1540–1640*. Urbana and Chicago: University of Illinois Press, 1985

Hoccleve, Thomas, *Thomas Hoccleve's Complaint and Dialogue*, edited by J.A. Burrow. Oxford: Oxford University Press for The Early English Text Society, 1999

Howell, Thomas, *The Poems of Thomas Howell (1568–1581)*, edited by A.B. Grosart. [n.p.]: printed for subscribers, 1879

Hughes, Charles, ed., *Shakespeare's Europe: Unpublished Chapters of Fynes Moryson's Itinerary*. London: Sherratt & Hughes, 1903

I.M., *A Health to the Gentlemanly Profession of Serving-Men (1598)*, edited by A.V. Judges. London: Oxford University Press for the Shakespeare Association, 1931

Jansen, Sharon L. and Kathleen H. Jordan, eds, *The Welles Anthology. Ms Rawlinson C.813. A Critical Edition*. Binghampton, NY: Medieval and Renaissance Texts and Studies, 1991

Jonson, Ben, *The Complete Poems*, edited by George Parfitt. Harmondsworth: Penguin Books, 1975

Klein, Holger M., ed., *English and Scottish Sonnet Sequences of the Renaissance*, 2 vols. Hildesheim, Zurich and New York: Georg Olms, 1984

Martin, Randall, ed., *Women Writers in Renaissance England*. London and New York: Longman, 1997

Muir, Kenneth, 'Unpublished Poems in the Devonshire Ms', *Proceedings of the Leeds Philosophical Society: Literary and Historical Section* 6 pt.4 (1947): 253–82

Nashe, Thomas, *The Unfortunate Traveller and Other Works*, edited by J.B. Steane. Harmondsworth: Penguin, 1972

Orgel, Stephen, ed., *Mythologiae, Nathale Conti (1615 Ed.) and Mythologia, M. Antonio Tritino (1616), The Philosophy of Images*. New York and London: Garland, 1979

Osborn, James M., ed., *The Autobiography of Thomas Whythorne*. Oxford: Clarendon Press, 1961

——, ed., *The Autobiography of Thomas Whythorne (Modern-Spelling Edition)*. Oxford: Oxford University Press, 1962

Panofsky, Richard J., ed., *The Floures of Philosophie (1572) by Hugh Plat and a Sweet Nosgay (1573) and the Copy of a Letter (1567) by Isabella Whitney*. Delmar, NY: Scholars' Facsimiles & Reprints, 1982

Quinn, David Beers and Neil M. Cheshire, eds, *The New Found Land of Stephen Parmenius. The Life and Writings of a Hungarian Poet, Drowned on a Voyage from Newfoundland, 1583*. Toronto: University of Toronto Press, 1972

Quinn, David Beers and Raleigh Ashlin Skelton, eds, *The Principall Navigations, Voiages and Discoveries of the English Nation, by Richard Hakluyt, Imprinted at London, 1589*. Cambridge: published for the Hakluyt Society and the Peabody Museum of Salem by the Cambridge University Press, 1965

Rollins, Hyder Edward, ed., *The Paradise of Dainty Devices (1576–1606).* Cambridge: Cambridge University Press, 1927

——, ed., *Tottel's Miscellany (1557–1587),* 2 vols. Cambridge, MA: Harvard University Press, 1928–9

Sermons or Homilies Appointed to Be Read in Churches in the Time of Queen Elizabeth of Famous Memory. London: For the Prayer Book and Homily Society, 1824

Shakespeare, William, *Shakespeare's Sonnets,* edited by Katherine Duncan-Jones. London: Arden Shakespeare, 2001

——, *Shakespeare's Sonnets,* edited by Stephen Booth. New Haven and London: Yale University Press, 1977

——, *The Sonnets and a Lover's Complaint,* edited by John Kerrigan. Harmondsworth: Penguin Books, 1999

Sidney, Sir Philip, *An Apology for Poetry,* edited by Geoffrey Shepherd. London: Nelson, 1965

——, *The Poems,* edited by William A. Ringler. Oxford: The Clarendon Press, 1962

——, *The Prose Works of Sir Philip Sidney,* edited by Albert Feuillerat, 4 vols. Cambridge: Cambridge University Press, 1962

Spenser, Edmund, *The Shorter Poems,* edited by Richard A. McCabe. Harmondsworth: Penguin, 1999

——, *A View of the State of Ireland. From the First Printed Edition (1633),* edited by Andrew Hadfield and Willy Maley. Oxford: Blackwell, 1997

——, *The Works: A Variorum Edition,* edited by Edwin Greenlaw, Charles Grosvenor Osgood, Frederick Morgan Padelford and Ray Heffer, 11 vols. Baltimore: John Hopkins University Press, 1932–57

——, *The Yale Edition of the Shorter Poems,* edited by William A. Oram and *et al.* New Haven and London: Yale University Press, 1989

Turbervile, George, *Epitaphes, Epigrams, Songs and Sonets (1567) and Epitaphes and Sonnettes (1576),* edited by Richard J. Panofsky. Delmar, NY: Scholars' Facsimiles and Reprints, 1977

Tusser, Thomas, *Five Hundred Points of Good Husbandry,* edited by Geoffrey Grigson. Oxford: Oxford University Press, 1984

V[enner], R[ichard], *Englands Ioy.* ?London, ?1601

Whetstone, George, *The Honorable Reputation of a Souldier.* London: Richard Jones, 1585

——, *The Rocke of Regard, Diuided into Foure Parts (1576),* edited by J. Payne Collier: privately printed, 1870

Wright, Thomas, *The Passions of the Minde (1601), Anglistica & Americana No.126.* Hildesheim and New York: Georg Olms, 1973

Secondary texts

Abrams, M.H., *A Glossary of Literary Terms.* 7th edn. Fort Worth, NY, London: Harcourt Brace, 1999

Aers, David, 'A Whisper in the Ear of Early Modernists; or, Reflections on Literary Critics Writing the "History of the Subject"', in *Culture and History 1350–1600: Essays on English Communities, Identities and Writing,* edited by David Aers, New York and London: Harvester Wheatsheaf, 1992, pp. 177–202

Allman, Eileen Jorge, 'Epithalamion's Bridegroom: Orpheus–Adam–Christ', *Renascence* 32 (1980): 240–7

Anderson, Douglas, '"Vnto My Selfe Alone": Spenser's Plenary Epithalamion', *Spenser Studies* 5 (1985): 149–66

Barker, Francis, *The Tremulous Private Body: Essays on Subjection.* London and New York: Methuen, 1984

Barthes, Roland, 'The Death of the Author', in *Modern Criticism and Theory: A Reader*, edited by David Lodge. London and New York: Longman, 1988, pp. 167–72

Bates, Catherine, *The Rhetoric of Courtship in Elizabethan Language and Literature.* Cambridge: Cambridge University Press, 1992

Bell, Ilona, *Elizabethan Women and the Poetry of Courtship.* Cambridge: Cambridge University Press, 1998

Benveniste, Emile, *Problems in General Linguistics*, translated by Mary Elizabeth Meek. Coral Gables, Florida: University of Miami Press, 1971

Berry, Lloyd E., 'Richard Hakluyt and Turberville's Poems on Russia', *Papers of the Bibliographical Society of America* 61 (1967): 350–1

Berry, Philippa, *Of Chastity and Power: Elizabethan Literature and the Unmarried Queen.* London and New York: Routledge, 1989

Bradshaw, Brendan, 'The Reformation in the Cities: Cork, Limerick and Galway, 1534–1603', in *Settlement and Society in Medieval Ireland. Studies Presented to F.X. Martin, O.S.A.*, edited by John Bradley, Kilkenny: Boethius Press, 1988, pp. 445–76

Brady, Ciaran, 'Spenser's Irish Crisis: Humanism and Experience in the 1590s', *Past and Present* 111 (1986): 17–49

Breitenberg, Mark, *Anxious Masculinity in Early Modern England.* Cambridge: Cambridge University Press, 1996

Brennan, Michael, *Literary Patronage in the English Renaissance: The Pembroke Family.* London, 1988

Burckhardt, Jacob, *The Civilization of the Renaissance.* Oxford: Phaidon Press, 1944

Burke, Peter, 'Representations of the Self from Petrarch to Descartes', in *Rewriting the Self: Histories from the Renaissance to the Present*, edited by Roy Porter, London and New York: Routledge, 1997, pp. 17–28

Burrow, J.A., *The Ages of Man: A Study of Medieval Writing and Thought.* Oxford: Clarendon Press, 1986

——, 'Autobiographical Poetry in the Middle Ages: The Case of Thomas Hoccleve', *Proceedings of the British Academy* 68 (1982): 389–412

——, 'Hoccleve's *Series*: Experience and Books', in *Fifteenth-Century Studies: Recent Essays*, edited by R.F. Yeager, Hamden, Conn.: Archon, 1984, pp. 259–73

Cain, Thomas, *Praise in the Faerie Queene.* Lincoln, NE: University of Nebraska Press, 1978

Campbell, Mary B., *The Witness and the Other World: Exotic European Travel Writing, 400–1600.* Ithaca and London: Cornell University Press, 1988

Canny, Nicholas, 'Edmund Spenser and the Development of an Anglo-Irish Identity', *Yearbook of English Studies* 13 (1983): 1–19

Clarke, Danielle, *The Politics of Early Modern Woman's Writing.* London and New York: Longman, 2001

Coote, Stephen, *A Play of Passion: The Life of Sir Walter Ralegh*. London: Macmillan, 1993

Crane, Mary Thomas, *Framing Authority: Sayings, Self and Society in Sixteenth-Century England*. Princeton: Princeton University Press, 1993

Crewe, Jonathan, *Trials of Authorship: Anterior Forms and Poetic Reconstruction from Wyatt to Shakespeare*. Berkeley, Los Angeles, Oxford: University of California Press, 1990

Delaney, Paul, *British Autobiography in the Seventeenth Century*. London: Routledge & Kegan Paul, 1969

Derrida, Jacques, *Of Grammatology*, translated by Gayatri Chakravorty Spivak. Baltimore and London: John Hopkins University Press, 1976

Dillon, Janette, *Shakespeare and the Solitary Man*. London and Basingstoke: Macmillan, 1981

Dop, Jan Albert, *Eliza's Knights: Soldiers, Poets, and Puritans in the Netherlands, 1572–1586*. Alblasserdam: Remak, 1981

Dove, Mary, *The Perfect Age of Man's Life*. Cambridge: Cambridge University Press, 1986

Duncan-Jones, Katherine, *Sir Philip Sidney: Courtier Poet*. New Haven and London: Yale University Press, 1991

Dunlop, Alexander, 'The Drama of *Amoretti*', *Spenser Studies* 1 (1980): 107–20

——, 'The Unity of Spenser's *Amoretti*', in *Silent Poetry: Essays in Numerological Analysis*, edited by Alastair Fowler, London: Routledge & Kegan Paul, 1970, pp. 153–69

Eisenstein, Elizabeth, *The Printing Press as an Agent of Social Change: Communications and Cultural Transformations in Early-Modern Europe*, 2 vols. Cambridge: Cambridge University Press, 1979

Ferry, Anne, *The 'Inward' Language: Sonnets of Wyatt, Sidney, Shakespeare, Donne*. Chicago and London: University of Chicago Press, 1983

Fineman, Joel, *Shakespeare's Perjured Eye: The Invention of Poetic Subjectivity in the Sonnets*. Berkeley, Los Angeles, London: University of California Press, 1986

Fleming, John V., 'Hoccleve's "Letter of Cupid" and the "Quarrel" over the *Roman De La Rose*', *Medium Aevum* 40 (1971): 21–40

Ford, Alan, *The Protestant Reformation in Ireland, 1590–1641*. Dublin: Four Courts Press, 1997

Foucault, Michel, 'What Is an Author?', in *Modern Criticism and Theory: A Reader*, edited by David Lodge, London and New York: Longman, 1988, pp. 197–210

Freccero, John, 'The Fig Tree and the Laurel: Petrarch's Poetics', in *Literary Theory/Renaissance Texts*, edited by Patricia Parker and David Quint, Baltimore and London: John Hopkins University Press, 1986, pp. 20–32

Fumerton, Patricia, *Cultural Aesthetics: Renaissance Literature and the Practice of Social Ornament*. Chicago and London: Chicago University Press, 1991

Goldberg, Jonathan, *Writing Matter: From the Hands of the English Renaissance*. Stanford, CA: Stanford University Press, 1990

Graham, Elspeth, 'Women's Writing and the Self', in *Women and Literature in Britain, 1500–1700*, edited by Helen Wilcox, Cambridge: Cambridge University Press, 1996, pp. 209–33

Greenblatt, Stephen, *Renaissance Self-Fashioning*. Chicago and London: University of Chicago Press, 1980

Greene, Thomas, 'The Flexibility of the Self in Renaissance Literature', in *The Disciplines of Criticism*, edited by P. Demetz, New Haven: Yale University Press, 1968, pp. 241–64

——, 'Spenser and the Epithalmic Convention', *Comparative Literature* 9 (1957): 215–28

Hadfield, Andrew, *Edmund Spenser's Irish Experience: Wild Fruit and Salvage Soyl.* Oxford: Oxford University Press, 1997

——, *Literature, Travel, and Colonial Writing in the English Renaissance 1545–1625.* Oxford: Clarendon Press, 2001

Hamilton, A.C., ed., *The Spenser Encyclopedia.* Toronto, Buffalo, London: University of Toronto Press and Routledge, 1990

Hankins, John Erskine, *The Life and Works of George Turbervile.* Lawrence, Kansas: University of Kansas, 1940

Hanson, Elizabeth, *Discovering the Subject in Renaissance England.* Cambridge: Cambridge University Press, 1998

Harrier, Richard, 'A Printed Source for "the Devonshire Manuscript"', *Review of English Studies* n.s.11 (1960)

Heale, Elizabeth, 'Songs, Sonnets and Autobiography: Self-Representation in Sixteenth-Century Verse Miscellanies', in *Betraying Our Selves: Forms of Self-Representation in Early Modern English Texts*, edited by Henk Dragstra, Sheila Ottway and Helen Wilcox, Basingstoke: Macmillan Press, 2000, pp. 59–75

——, *Wyatt, Surrey and Early Tudor Poetry.* London: Longman, 1998

Hedley, Jane, 'Allegoria: Gascoigne's Master Trope', *English Literary Renaissance* 11 (1981): 148–64

Helgerson, Richard, *The Elizabethan Prodigals.* Berkeley: University of California Press, 1977

Henley, Pauline, *Spenser in Ireland.* Dublin and Cork: Cork University Press, 1928

Hieatt, A. Kent, *Short Time's Endless Monument.* New York: Columbia University Press, 1960

Highley, Christopher, *Shakespeare, Spenser, and the Crisis in Ireland.* Cambridge: Cambridge University Press, 1997

Houlbrooke, Ralph, *Death, Religion, and the Family in England, 1480–1750.* Oxford: Clarendon Press, 1998

Hutson, Lorna, *The Usurer's Daughter: Male Friendship and Fictions of Women in Sixteenth-Century England.* London: Longman, 1994

Izard, Thomas C., *George Whetstone: Mid-Elizabethan Gentleman of Letters* (1942). New York: AMS Press, 1966

Jack, Sybil M., *Towns in Tudor and Stuart Britain.* Basingstoke: Macmillan, 1996

Jardine, Lisa, 'Encountering Ireland: Gabriel Harvey, Edmund Spenser, and English Colonial Ventures', in *Representing Ireland: Literature and the Origins of Conflict, 1534–1660*, edited by Brendan Bradshaw, Andrew Hadfield and Willy Maley, Cambridge: Cambridge University Press, 1993,

Javitch, Daniel, 'The Impure Motives of Elizabethan Poetry', *Genre* 15 (1982): 225–38

——, *Poetry and Courtliness in Renaissance England.* Princeton: Princeton University Press, 1978

Jones, Ann Rosalind and Peter Stallybrass, 'Dismantling Irena: The Sexualizing of Ireland in Early Modern England', in *Nationalisms & Sexualities*, edited by

Andrew Parker, Mary Russo, Doris Sommer and Patricia Yaeger, New York and London: Routledge, 1992, pp. 157–71

——, 'The Politics of *Astrophil and Stella*', *Studies in English Literature* 24 (1984): 53–68

Jones, Richard F., 'The Moral Sense of Simplicity', in *Studies in Honour of F.W. Shipley*, edited by R.F. Jones, St Louis, MO: Washington University Studies, N.S. Language and Literature 14, 1942, pp. 265–87

Kaske, Carole V., 'Spenser's *Amoretti* and *Epithalamion* of 1595: Structure, Genre, and Numerology', *English Literary Renaissance* 8 (1978): 271–95

Kay, Sarah, *Subjectivity in Troubadour Poetry*. Cambridge: Cambridge University Press, 1990

King, John N., *Spenser's Poetry and the Reformation Tradition*. Princeton: Princeton University Press, 1990

Krevans, Nita, 'Print and the Tudor Poets', in *Reconsidering the Renaissance*, edited by Mario A. Di Cesare, Binghampton, NY: Center for Medieval and Early Renaissance Studies, State University of New York at Binghampton, 1992, pp. 301–13

Levy, F.J., 'Spenser and Court Humanism', in *Spenser's Life and the Subject of Biography*, edited by Judith H. Anderson, Donald Cheney and Davis A. Richardson, Amherst: University of Massachusetts Press, 1996, pp. 65–80

Loewenstein, Joseph, 'Echo's Ring: Orpheus and Spenser's Career', *English Literary Renaissance* 16 (1986): 287–302

Lotspeich, Henry Gibbons, *Classical Mythology in the Poetry of Edmund Spenser*. Princeton: Princeton University Press, 1932

Lupton, Julia Reinhard, 'Home-Making in Ireland: Virgil's Eclogue I and Book VI of *The Faerie Queene*', *Spenser Studies* 8 (1987): 119–45

MacCarthy-Morrogh, Michael, *The Munster Plantation: English Migration to Southern Ireland, 1583–1641*. Oxford: Clarendon Press, 1986

MacLean, Ian, *The Renaissance Notion of Women: A Study in the Fortunes of Scholasticism and Medical Science in European Intellectual Life*. Cambridge: Cambridge University Press, 1980

Maley, Willy, *Salvaging Spenser: Colonialism, Culture and Identity*. Basingstoke: Macmillan, 1997

——, *A Spenser Chronology*. Basingstoke: Macmillan, 1994

Marotti, Arthur F., ' "Love Is Not Love": Elizabethan Sonnet Sequences and the Social Order', *English Literary History* 49 (1982): 396–428

——, *Manuscript, Print, and the English Renaissance Lyric*. Ithaca and London: Cornell University Press, 1995

Marquis, Paul, 'Oppositional Ideologies of Gender in Isabella Whitney's *Copy of a Letter*', *Modern Language Review* 90 (1995): 314–24

Mazzotta, Giuseppe, 'The Canzoniere and the Language of the Self', *Studies in Philology* 75 (1978): 271–96

McCabe, Richard A., 'Edmund Spenser, Poet of Exile', *Proceedings of the British Academy* 80 (1993): 73–103

——, *The Pillars of Eternity: Time and Providence in the Faerie Queene*. Dublin: Irish Academic Press, 1989

McCoy, Richard C., 'Gascoigne's "Poemata Castrata": The Wages of Courtly Success', *Criticism* 27 (1985): 29–55

Miskimin, Alice S., *The Renaissance Chaucer*. New Haven and London: Yale University Press, 1975

Moss, Ann, *Printed Commonplace-Books and the Structuring of Renaissance Thought*. Oxford: Clarendon Press, 1996

Mousley, Andrew, 'Renaissance Selves and Life Writing: The *Autobiography* of Thomas Whythorne', *Forum* 26 (1990): 222–30

Nerlich, Michael, *Ideology of Adventure: Studies in Modern Consciousness, 1100–1750*, translated by Ruth Crowley, 2 vols. Minneapolis: University of Minnesota Press, 1987

Newton, Richard C., 'Making Books from Leaves: Poets Become Editors', in *Print and Culture in the Renaissance*, edited by Gerald P. Tyson and Sylvia S. Wagonheim, Newark: University of Delaware Press, 1986, pp. 246–64

Ong, Walter J., *Rhetoric, Romance, and Technology: Studies in the Interaction of Expression and Culture*. Ithaca and London: Cornell University Press, 1971

Owens, Judith, 'The Poetics of Accommodation in Spenser's *Epithalamion*', *Studies in English Literature* 40 (2000): 41–62

Parker, Patricia, *Literary Fat Ladies: Rhetoric, Gender, Property*. London and New York: Methuen, 1987

Parks, George Bruner, *Richard Hakluyt and the English Voyages*, edited by James A. Williamson. New York: American Geograpical Society, 1928

Paster, Gail Kern, *The Body Embarrassed: Drama and the Disciplines of Shame in Early Modern England*. Ithaca and New York: Cornell University Press, 1993

Patterson, Lee, 'On the Margin: Postmodernism, Ironic History, and Medieval Studies', *Speculum* 65 (1990): 87–108

Plant, Marjorie, *The English Book Trade: An Economic History of the Making and Sale of Books*, 2nd edn. London: Allen & Unwin, 1965

Plomer, Henry R. and Tom Peate Cross, *The Life and Correspondence of Lodowick Bryskett*. Illinois: University of Chicago Press, 1927

Pomeroy, Elizabeth W., *The Elizabethan Miscellanies: Their Development and Conventions*. Berkeley, Los Angeles, London: University of California Press, 1973

Prouty, C.T., *George Gascoigne: Elizabethan Courtier, Soldier, and Poet*. New York: Columbia University Press, 1942

Rambuss, Richard, 'Spenser's Lives, Spenser's Careers', in *Spenser's Life and the Subject of Biography*, edited by Donald Cheney, Judith H. Anderson, Davis A. Richardson, Amherst, MA: University of Massachusetts Press, 1996, pp. 1–17

——, *Spenser's Secret Career*. Cambridge: Cambridge University Press, 1993

Relihan, Constance, *Fashioning Authority: The Development of Elizabethan Novelistic Discourse*. Kent, OH, and London: Kent State University Press, 1994

Roche, Thomas Jr, 'Astrophil and Stella: A Radical Reading', in *Sir Philip Sidney: An Anthology of Modern Criticism*, edited by Dennis Kay, Oxford: Clarendon Press, 1987, pp. 185–226

Rollins, Hyder Edward, 'The Troilus–Cressida Story from Chaucer to Shakespeare', *Publications of the Modern Language Association* 32 (1917): 383–429

Rossky, William, 'Imagination in the English Renaissance: Psychology and Poetic', *Studies in the Renaissance* 5 (1958): 49–73

Salomon, Louis B., *The Devil Take Her! A Study of the Rebellious Lover in English Poetry* (1931). New York: A.S. Barnes, 1961

Saunders, J.W., 'The Stigma of Print: A Note on the Social Bases of Tudor Poetry', *Essays in Criticism* 1 (1951): 139–64

Seaton, Ethel, ' "The Devonshire Manuscript" and its Medieval Fragments', *Review of English Studies* n.s.7 (1956): 55–6

Sedgwick, Eve Kosovsky, *Between Men: English Literature and Male Homosocial Desire*. New York: Columbia University Press, 1985

Sheehan, Anthony, 'Irish Towns in a Period of Change, 1588–1625', in *Natives and Newcomers: Essays in the Making of Irish Colonial Society 1534–1641*, edited by Ciaran Brady and Raymond Gillespie, Dublin: Irish Academic Press, 1986, pp. 93–119

Shore, David R., 'The *Autobiography* of Thomas Whythorne: An Early Elizabethan Context for Poetry', *Renaissance and Reformation* 17 (1981): 72–86

——, 'Whythorne's *Autobiography* and the Genesis of Gascoigne's *Master F.J.*', *Journal of Medieval and Renaissance Studies* 12 (1982): 159–78

Silverman, Kaja, *The Subject of Semiotics*. New York: Oxford University Press, 1983

Spiller, Michael R.G., *The Development of the Sonnet: An Introduction*. London and New York: Routledge, 1992

Sprinker, Michael, 'Fictions of the Self: The End of Autobiography', in *Autobiography: Essays Theoretical and Critical*, edited by James Olney, Princeton: Princeton University Press, 1980, pp. 321–42

Staub, Susan C., ' "A Poet with a Spear": Writing and Sexual Power in the Elizabethan Period', *Renaissance Papers* (1992): 1–15

Tallett, Frank, *War and Society in Early Modern Europe, 1495–1715*. London and New York: Routledge, 1992

Taylor, Charles, *Sources of the Self: The Making of the Modern Identity*. Cambridge: Cambridge University Press, 1989

Trim, David J.B., 'Ideology, Greed and Social Discontent in Early-Modern Europe: Mercenaries and Mutinies in the Rebellious Netherlands 1568–1609', in *Rebellion, Repression, Reinvention: Mutiny in Comparative Contexts*, edited by Jane Hathaway, Westport, CT and London: Praeger, 2001, pp. 47–61

Vickers, Nancy J., 'Diana Described: Scattered Woman and Scattered Rhyme', in *Writing and Sexual Difference*, edited by Elizabeth Abel, Brighton, Sussex: Harvester Press, 1982, pp. 95–109

Wall, Wendy, *The Imprint of Gender: Authorship and Publication in the English Renaissance*. Ithaca and London: Cornell University Press, 1993

Warkentin, Germaine, 'The Meeting of the Muses: Sidney and the Mid-Tudor Poets', in *Sir Philip Sidney and the Interpretation of Renaissance Culture: The Poet in His Time and in Ours*, edited by Gary F. Waller and Michael D. Moore, London and Sydney: Croom Helm, 1984, pp. 17–33

Whigham, Frank, *Ambition and Privilege: The Social Tropes of Elizabethan Courtesy Theory*. Berkeley, Los Angeles, London: University of California Press, 1984

Williams, Gordon, *A Dictionary of Sexual Language and Imagery in Shakespearean and Stuart Literature*, 3 vols. London and Atlantic Highlands, NJ: Athlone Press, 1994

Wilson, Katharine M., *Shakespeare's Sugared Sonnets*. London and New York: Allen & Unwin, 1974

Woodbridge, Linda, *Women and the English Renaissance. Literature and the Nature of Womankind 1540–1620*. Brighton: Harvester, 1984

Young, Richard B., 'English Petrarke: A Study of Sidney's *Astrophel and Stella*', in *Three Studies in the Renaissance: Sidney, Jonson, and Milton*, New Haven, CT: Yale University Press, 1958, pp. 1–88

Index